SPEAK·TRUTH·TO·POWER

COMMANDER
STEVEN HAINES
ROYAL NAVY

Palgrave Studies in Development

Titles include:
Sarah Bracking (*editor*)
CORRUPTION AND DEVELOPMENT
The Anti-Corruption Campaigns

Tanja Schümer
NEW HUMANITARIANISM
Britain and Sierra Leone, 1997–2003

Palgrave Studies in Development
Series Standing Order ISBN 978–0–230–52738–6

You can receive future titles in this series as they are published by placing a standing order. Please contact your bookseller or, in case of difficulty, write to us at the address below with your name and address, the title of the series and the ISBN quoted above.

Customer Services Department, Macmillan Distribution Ltd, Houndmills, Basingstoke, Hampshire RG21 6XS, England

Also by Tanja Schümer

THE WIDER IMPACT OF HUMANITARIAN ASSISTANCE: The Case of Sudan and the Implications for European Union Policy

New Humanitarianism

Britain and Sierra Leone, 1997–2003

Tanja Schümer

palgrave
macmillan

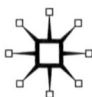

First published 2008 by
PALGRAVE MACMILLAN
Houndmills, Basingstoke, Hampshire RG21 6XS and
175 Fifth Avenue, New York, N.Y. 10010
Companies and representatives throughout the world

PALGRAVE MACMILLAN is the global academic imprint of the Palgrave Macmillan division of St. Martin's Press, LLC and of Palgrave Macmillan Ltd. Macmillan® is a registered trademark in the United States, United Kingdom and other countries. Palgrave is a registered trademark in the European Union and other countries.

ISBN-13: 978–0–230–54517–5 hardback
ISBN-10: 0–230–54517–3 hardback

This book is printed on paper suitable for recycling and made from fully managed and sustained forest sources. Logging, pulping and manufacturing processes are expected to conform to the environmental regulations of the country of origin.

A catalogue record for this book is available from the British Library.

A catalog record for this book is available from the Library of Congress.

10   9   8   7   6   5   4   3   2   1
17   16   15   14   13   12   11   10   09   08

Printed and bound in Great Britain by
Antony Rowe Ltd, Chippenham and Eastbourne

Contents

List of Figures and Tables

Figures

Tables

Acknowledgments

It is a pleasure to thank the people who have been an important part of this project and who have made this work possible.

First thank you to Prof. Mats Berdal, Dr. Joanna Spear and Prof. Christopher Dandeker. Special thanks to Dr. John Mackinlay and Prof. Uli Albrecht, for your encouragement and support in embarking on this project. I am grateful to Geoff Loane for sparking my interest in and passion for this line of work and for introducing me to a world of extremely committed, hard-working people.

Most of all, I am deeply indebted to the many governmental and non-governmental aid workers around the world and in particular in London and Sierra Leone for investing their time answering my manifold questions. Without your support, this study would not have been possible. Given the delicate nature of some aspects of disaster relief and your extremely limited time, I am extremely grateful for your frankness. Thank you to Sierra Leone, for your hospitality. I would like to follow Randolph Kent's example by stating that 'I know all too well that I have risked repeating what for some may be conventional wisdom or, even worse, I may have oversimplified issues . . . With this work I do not mean to belittle the extraordinary commitment and dedication of the vast majority of those interviewed and witnessed in the field and at headquarters level despite the inadequacies of the international system'. And despite the following critical analysis of the British New Humanitarianism, I would like to give credit to the British Government's commitment to Sierra Leone and to the ongoing reform of the international humanitarian system, which is much broader and on which I only touch within the following pages.

Thank you Natalie, Dawda and Ivan, your enthusiasm was infectious and a lot of fun. And finally, a big thank you to Peter and to Monica . . . without you, not only would this adventure possibly never have begun, I would also never have been able to complete it.

Financial support from the following bodies is most gratefully acknowledged: The Friedrich Ebert Stiftung (FES), the Economic and Social Research Council (ESRC), the Deutscher Akademischer Austauschdienst (DAAD), King's College London, the Central

Research Fund/London University. Written copyright permission has been granted from the United Nations Publications Board, Vladimir Bessarabov for the reproduction of maps no. 3902 Rev 5 and no. 3679, and by Panos for the reproduction of the cover photo by Crispin Hughes.

Lastly, thank you to my editor Philippa Grand and to Hazel Woodbridge for believing in this project and making it happen. And finally, please forgive if I have failed to mention you. I certainly have not forgotten the numerous people who have been supportive in this process.

The following analysis is entirely based on my own analysis; the bulk of the manuscript was completed prior to my work for the UK Department for International Development and Oxfam.

Abbreviations

AFRC	Armed Forces Revolutionary Council
APC	All People's Congress
BMATT	British Military Assistance and Training Team
CAD	Children's Aid Direct
CAP	Consolidated Appeal Process
CDF	Civil Defence Force
CHAD	Conflict and Humanitarian Affairs Department
CRP	Community Reintegration Programme (DFID Sierra Leone)
CRS	Catholic Relief Service
DFID	Department for International Development
DPKO	Department of Peacekeeping Operations (UN)
DRC	Democratic Republic of Congo
ECHO	Economic Community Humanitarian Office
ECOWAS	Economic Community of West African States
ECOMOG	Economic Community of West African States Monitoring Group
ERT	Emergency Response Teams (DFID, United Kingdom)
FCO	Foreign and Commonwealth Office (United Kingdom)
GoSL	Government of Sierra Leone
GTZ	Gesellschaft für Technische Zusammenarbeit
HQ	Headquarters
ICRC	International Committee of the Red Cross
IDP	Internally Displaced Person
IFRC	International Federation of the Red Cross and Red Crescent Societies
IHL	International Humanitarian Law
IMATT	International Military Advisory and Training Team
IMC	International Medical Corps
IMF	International Monetary Fund
INGO	International Non-Governmental Organisation
IO	International Organisation

IOM	International Organization for Migration (United Nations)
ISP	Institutional Strategy Papers (DFID, United Kingdom)
MoD	Ministry of Defence (United Kingdom)
MODEP	Ministry of Development (Sierra Leone)
MSF	Médecins sans Frontières
NaCSA	The National Commission for Social Action
NATO	North Atlantic Treaty Organisation
NCDDR	National Committee for Disarmament, Demobilisation and Reintegration
NCRRR	National Commission for Reconstruction, Resettlement and Rehabilitation
NGO	Non-Governmental Organisation
NPFL	National Patriotic Front of Liberia
NPRC	National Provisional Ruling Council
NRC	Norwegian Refugee Council
OCHA	Office of the Coordination of Humanitarian Affairs
ODA	Official Development Assistance
OECD	Organisation for Economic Co-operation and Development
PMC	Private Military Company
PPR	Programme Partnership Agreement (DFID)
PSA	Public Service Agreement (United Kingdom)
RUF	Revolutionary United Front
SCF	Save the Children Fund
SLA	Sierra Leonean Army
SLPP	Sierra Leonean People's Party
UK	United Kingdom
UN	United Nations
UNAMSIL	United Nations Mission in Sierra Leone
UNDP	United Nations Development Programme
UNHCR	United Nations High Commissioner for Refugees
UNOMSIL	United Nations Observer Mission in Sierra Leone
WFP	World Food Programme (United Nations)

Maps

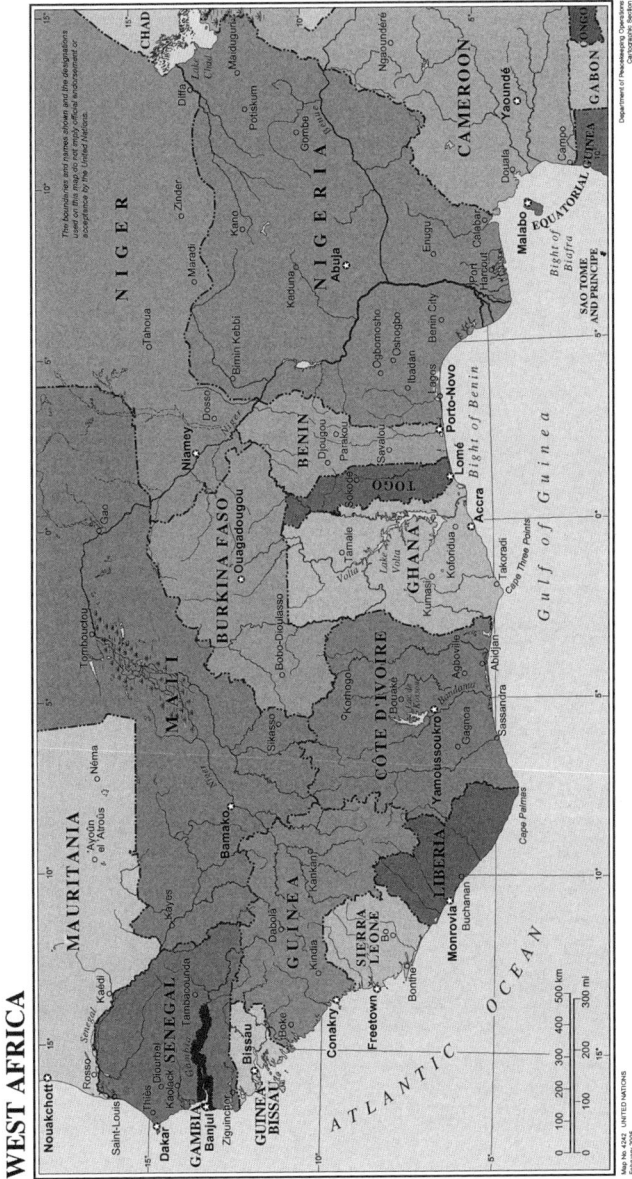

WEST AFRICA

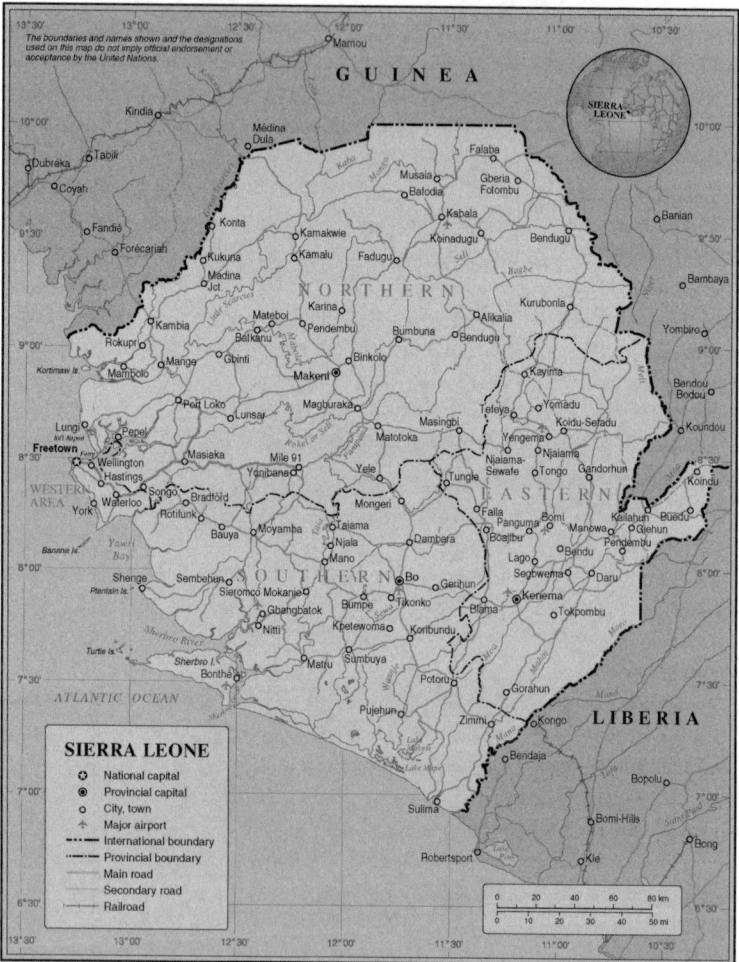

1
The Politics of New Humanitarianism

At the beginning of the twenty-first century, humanitarian emergency assistance has become a complex, dangerous and contested profession. Since the mid-1990s, emergency relief organizations have been criticized for being ineffective in providing sustainable help to those in need. Relief aid has proved insufficient to address the structural causes of armed conflict or bring about sustainable change for the people it was intended to help. This criticism is especially relevant in the light of relief organizations' inadequate performance in measuring the wider and longer-term impact of their actions.

Donors and aid agencies alike have re-evaluated both policy and practice. Britain's New Labour Government has addressed both the alleged shortcomings and the potential role of humanitarian emergency assistance in tackling conflict and human rights abuses, first, by formulating its policy of 'New Humanitarianism', or 'wider relief', and later through its strong support for the reform of the international humanitarian system of the United Nations.

The term 'New Humanitarianism' has been used inconsistently by diverse actors to denote: a number of different practices and objectives. The British variant of New Humanitarianism extends beyond the immediate mandate of traditional humanitarian emergency assistance – to save life. It is intended to address the root causes of conflict, prevent the negative side effects of aid and support human rights. At the same time, humanitarian aid should avoid making the situation worse; for example, by inducing economic dependency or fuelling conflict.[1] It is this definition of the term we refer to for the remainder of this book. New Humanitarianism has also displayed elements of

1

coercion in the use of conditionality as a lever to induce political change within recipient societies. This practice has become known as 'humanitarian conditionality'.

The term 'humanitarian conditionality' denotes those wider pressures or actual policies that have the effect of making humanitarian aid contingent on certain requirements or conditions being met. These might include, for example, that specific parties guarantee a secure environment or respect for human rights, or that the aid itself should contribute to the achievement of social or political aims (such as supporting development or promoting peace).

This book explores the development, contents and rationale of British New Humanitarianism. It also analyses components of its practical application in Sierra Leone by examining the policy's coherent implementation and effectiveness. It does so by tracking the changes in British humanitarian policy from its adoption by the New Labour Government in 1997 up to and including 2003. The case study assesses whether or not New Humanitarianism was developed beyond the overall policymaking level into the formulation of a country strategy for Sierra Leone. Furthermore, it explores whether or not the structure and administration of the implementation process were effective or facilitated policy change.

Our analysis is guided by two key hypotheses. First, at the strategic, senior policymaking level, the British Government formulated New Humanitarianism. Second, the implementation of the policy lacked the degree of administrative control and inter-departmental coordination and support that was needed to achieve significant policy change.

We examine the policy implementation process to identify the main institutional forces that shaped British New Humanitarianism, and to assess the likelihood and depth of policy change. We will show how the differing interests within a given policy coalition can undermine the policy's implementation. This approach offers a framework that helps to explain the transitory and contradictory state of humanitarian emergency policy. Implementation failure is too easily interpreted as policy failure, thereby providing a misleading guide to future policymaking. The practicalities of implementation are all too often not taken into consideration when policies are drafted. 'Policy failure occurs when the policy is fully implemented but fails to achieve what is expected of it',[2] which may reflect flaws in the underlying approach, the assumptions made or exceptional external influences. By the same token, implementation failure occurs if an approach cannot be implemented in practice. This may happen because it proves unacceptable to external actors and stakeholders, but occurs most often when the original policy coalition does not hold. It might also be due to misinterpretations of the policy contents and goals by implementing organizations, or operational differences and contradictory objectives within the implementation coalition.

Argument in brief

The theoretical foundations for, and practical administration of, British New Humanitarianism as developed by the United Kingdom's (UK) Department for International Development (DFID) were not sufficiently explicit and coherent. The policy remained too vague for a possibly innovative approach to be effectively developed into a coherent country strategy, or to win the support of the bureaucracy charged with its implementation. There may have been a vision at the senior policymaking level in the British development administration to bring about a new humanitarian approach; or more specifically one designed to address the root causes of conflict and tackle the inherent contradictions of humanitarian relief. Yet these ambitious plans have not resulted in any substantial policy change at the local level. British New Humanitarianism was never implemented in Sierra Leone as a national country strategy. Attempts to widen the humanitarian mandate, far from representing a coordinated and coherent policy response to contemporary conflict, were both uncoordinated and incoherent.

The implementation process of emergency assistance policy played an important role in explaining both the development of policy and policy efficiency. The fragmented, often contradictory and competitive implementation environment of humanitarian emergency aid policy necessarily made the coherent interpretation of the policy impossible. It obstructed substantial policy change and further complicated its implementation. In practice, British New Humanitarianism was based on a series of poor compromises between a set of transient actor coalitions. While this is a feature of all democratic policymaking, British emergency policy could have been better. In the absence of a clear, long-term political strategy, policy predictability and coordinated implementation, humanitarian emergency relief had comparatively little leverage over local and international policy environments. Without clear principles of mutual accountability and an understanding of the consequences of non-compliance, humanitarian conditionality is bound to fail. Given its very limited development and application, British New Humanitarianism as developed in the late 1990s cannot be deemed to have been constructive. Since 2004, however, British humanitarian emergency policy has changed significantly. The UK is now taking the lead in pushing the reform of the global humanitarian institutions for the benefit of coordinated project identification and implementation, predictable pooled funding and the empowerment of Humanitarian Coordinators (HC).

New Humanitarianism, including humanitarian conditionality, was designed to provide a response to the customary weaknesses of traditional emergency assistance in contemporary armed conflict in two ways. First, it improves the livelihoods of vulnerable populations by addressing not only emergency need, but also medium to longer-term needs for structural change. Second, it exploits the potential of relief aid to ameliorate conflict and support development. However, the roles of humanitarian emergency assistance as part of a broader peace-building framework, and as a tool for political engagement, must be carefully re-evaluated. Furthermore, the structure of policy implementation will require extensive improvements in order to increase policy effectiveness, and the shortcomings of the present approach and practice must not be ignored. Donors, their national constituencies and aid agencies cannot be expected to continue granting emergency assistance that performs inadequately in meeting need or fails to contribute to the forestalling of recurrent crises. If relief involves a capacity for development and peace-building beyond that of saving life, it must be exploited.

Formulating New Humanitarianism: Setting the stage

The end of the Cold War initially brought about a short-lived sense of confidence in the international community in the ability of so-called 'humanitarian military intervention' and humanitarian emergency assistance operations to ameliorate violent conflict. There was widespread hope of reducing violent conflict and human suffering in the long term, and of promoting human rights and democracy.

At the same time, non-governmental humanitarian emergency organizations experienced rapid growth. The funds provided to these organizations increased along with the numbers of actors involved. The institutions also underwent tremendous change in the nature of their engagement in zones of violent conflict. By 2004, 'never have humanitarians been this rich, this powerful or this numerous. Never has humanitarian law been so mainstream in international consciousness'.[3]

Yet, the combination of increased state reliance on non-governmental and commercial actors and donors' subsequent application of rigorous performance and accountability criteria led to the development of new sets of relationships between humanitarian actors and international donor organizations. Some of these may have proved counterproductive. This has also characterized the awkward and harmful integration of international humanitarian assistance and relief organizations into military interventions – as witnessed, for example, in Iraq and Afghanistan. The blurring of roles and responsibilities of intergovernmental organizations, donors, the military and humanitarian agencies aggravated the fragmentation of the aid community. It only emphasized the lack of common principles among the actors involved. Arguably, this merging of relief and security responses has also reduced the security of emergency organizations' personnel and threatened their access to vulnerable populations, by jeopardizing the neutrality of relief organizations (or at least the perception thereof). It has also changed the attitudes of agencies and donors toward the efficient management of the intersection of politics and their own activities in humanitarian emergencies.

Increasingly, humanitarian organizations were used by governments as private service providers and marketed themselves as such. This blurring of emergency assistance, development aid and security – both intentional and inadvertent – prevents us from drawing a clear and consistent analytical distinction between humanitarian emergency assistance and development aid. The breadth of the overall British engagement in Sierra Leone, which affected all aspects of the intervention including emergency assistance programmes, exacerbated *a priori* the difficulty of clearly defining emergency assistance.

By the mid-1990s, the hope for a new world order and multilateralism dissipated following the recurrence of humanitarian disasters, several fraught international peacekeeping missions (in Somalia, Bosnia, Rwanda, Kosovo and, to some extent, Sierra Leone), and the failure of international governments to prevent the genocide in Rwanda. Increasingly, donor governments appeared reluctant either to address international violent conflict assertively outside their immediate spheres of interest or to intervene beyond the provision of humanitarian emergency assistance. This was despite their proclaimed interest in addressing so-called 'soft' security issues such as human rights, poverty and security sector reform. Mark Bradbury and others have suggested that 'there has been an accommodation with the permanence of crisis' and a redefinition of what constitutes an emergency, or what are acceptable levels of suffering.[4] It was hoped that the provision (or suspension) of aid would provide at least limited leverage over the perpetrators of violence and human rights abuses or the potential spoilers of a peace process.

The recurrent nature of many wars and humanitarian emergencies, frequent incidences of diverted emergency aid supplies, and apparent powerlessness of relief agencies to resist or influence belligerent forces resulted in a fear that humanitarian assistance would do more harm than good.[5] Some alleged that relief aid was fuelling conflict, putting people at risk, failing to prevent human rights abuses, causing dependency by undermining local capacities and markets, contributing to the displacement of people, and sustaining war economies.[6] Following the Rwandan genocide, for example, aid organizations were criticized for not speaking out and acting against the perpetrators of violence. They were blamed for not doing enough to protect the victims, and for enabling the perpetrators of genocide to regroup and continue destabilizing the entire region for years to come. This debate on the possible negative impact of relief aid highlighted a policy discrepancy between relief's primary objective of securing emergency assistance for those in need, its capacity to provide them with protection and its potential constructive role in promoting political change.

Many donors and some relief organizations responded to the perceived failure of traditional humanitarian assistance within armed conflict in five main ways:

First, they subordinated the principles of a right to humanitarian assistance, neutrality and impartiality (or unconditional relief aid) to the wider interests of peace-building and development in conflict.

Indeed, some aid organizations abandoned these principles entirely in order to support the victims of abuse.

Second, they suspended humanitarian assistance in the face of rights abuses and in support of political change. David Bryer and Edmund Cairns, for example, question whether in some cases 'the abuse of aid outweighs its benefits' and disproportionately puts people at risk.[7] Mickael Barfod of the European Community Humanitarian Office (ECHO) has argued that in some cases the limited or negative net benefit of relief aid requires a reassessment of whether to continue the relief operations.[8] Arguably, ECHO has suspended its operations on these grounds in several cases as, for example, in Afghanistan (in protest at the Taliban's treatment of women), without adopting it as a policy principle.

Third, donors have held humanitarian agencies accountable for recipients' protection, including their physical protection. Measures taken to achieve this include speaking out against the perpetrators of violence or the abusers of human rights. Speaking out in support of recipients' rights (and thereby potentially jeopardizing the principles of neutrality) risks cutting off humanitarian access from those in need by offending local authorities and/or belligerents. Numerous examples of the extremely complex role of humanitarian advocacy and protection can be witnessed in Sudan, where relief agencies (and, to a lesser degree, foreign government agencies) advocating the rights of the civilian population have come under increasing pressure from belligerent forces, including the Sudanese Government. This is impacting on the effectiveness of their assistance and has at times jeopardized access to vulnerable population groups, just as much as not speaking out has limited their engagement and effectively muzzled them, both politically and operationally.

Fourth, some donors have limited their funding for non-earmarked humanitarian emergency assistance in an attempt to raise the efficiency of, and their control over, relief operations. Others have prioritized a small group of large relief organizations and at times agreed upon partnership agreements.

Fifth, donors and relief organizations have advocated a deepening and broadening of the humanitarian mandate as an instrument in support of wider political objectives. In some instances, this has included the implicit or explicit use of relief to secure leverage over combatants and political leaders.

Making the granting of relief aid subject to political conditions led to widespread criticism within the international aid community.[9] Humanitarian conditionality was criticized for punishing vulnerable populations for something over which they have little control (namely, the actions of their leaders). Critics argued that humanitarian emergency assistance organizations should not be held responsible for undertaking actions that exceeded their capacity and essential mandate, and that were critically dependent on other actors, especially governments.

As a consequence, between 1994 and 2003, humanitarian organizations and academics agonized over the future role of humanitarian emergency assistance. Could and should humanitarian assistance provide protection to a vulnerable population (and, if so, which kind of protection)? Could humanitarian organizations work effectively alongside a military intervention? By 1997, a rift had developed in humanitarian policy and practice: There was no longer a united framework for humanitarian emergency assistance but rather a cacophony of diverse and – at times – contradictory approaches. Some humanitarian organizations focused on ensuring the survival of vulnerable individuals. Others adopted a more political stance, speaking out against human rights abuses and the diversion of aid, in an attempt to affect the political environment in support of lasting change and the ultimate protection of a vulnerable population rather than of vulnerable individuals. In the late 1990s and early 2000s, the British Government tended towards the latter approach. In formulating New Humanitarianism, it attempted to alter British emergency aid politics accordingly. At the time of writing (April 2007), it is playing a key role within the ongoing reform of the international humanitarian system, which focuses on strengthening the predictability, reliability and speed of humanitarian response as well as agency coordination and assessment of needs.

In 1997, just after the election of the New Labour Government, as DFID was formulating its New Humanitarianism and the Foreign and Commonwealth Office (FCO) was developing an 'ethical dimension' to British foreign policy, Britain committed itself to the restoration of democracy in one of its former colonies: Sierra Leone. On May 29 of the same year, a military coup had overthrown the elected President, Tejan Kabbah, which immersed Sierra Leone in a devastating civil war. The nature of the war and the subsequent international foreign policy response severely challenged international aid operations and had a significant impact on the psyche of many aid organizations and their personnel.

In the autumn of 1997, DFID suspended its humanitarian emergency assistance to Sierra Leone in order to pressure the rebels to reinstate the ousted President. DFID initially defended this action by arguing that it was concerned for the safety of the relief workers. This explanation was misleading, however, since the British Government continued to support relief efforts by the European Union and some other European humanitarian organizations. Also, as soon as President Kabbah was reinstated through an exceptional display of international political and military force by the UK, the United Nations and a regional peacekeeping operation, it resumed its relief aid to Sierra Leone. This was despite the continuing high levels of insecurity. The allegation that DFID had subordinated humanitarian emergency assistance policy to political objectives and conditions was subsequently the subject of critical discussion by the International Development Committee of the British Parliament.[10] It also caused unease and criticism in European aid circles.

Once President Kabbah was returned to power, the UK embarked on an ambitious and unique recovery programme. For a short time, it integrated humanitarian emergency assistance within a broad peace-building and recovery strategy. Sierra Leone became a test case for the UK's New Humanitarianism and engagement in so-called complex political emergencies. The British strategy in Sierra Leone was to become instrumental in shaping future international aid relations. Trends that were first noted in Sierra Leone – such as the privatization and the militarization of emergency assistance – were later observed in humanitarian emergency operations in Afghanistan and Iraq.

The nature of the beast: Organizational behaviour

British New Humanitarianism is a weak compromise of a highly disjointed and transient policy implementation coalition. It is further distorted during its implementation phase. Humanitarian emergency assistance policy is no more than a compromise between various donor departments, between donor departments and implementing agents, and between all of these and international actors. To complicate matters further, these often act in response to external influences or events. Powerful institutional imperatives subvert assertive policy change, by prolonging inappropriate aid projects, promoting destructive organizational and individual behaviour and increasing competition. On the other hand, organizational rules and standard operating procedures can also assure an element of policy stability.

If New Humanitarianism originated in the rational behaviour of a policy bureaucracy working towards agreed general objectives and according to a given set of preferences and rules, then it should be possible to analyse and predict policy in terms of its ability to attain a set objective. In such a case, policy failure will be caused by faults in policy design. This, however, cannot account for a number of features of New Humanitarianism in Sierra Leone.

First, there has been a high degree of divergence between the humanitarian policy implemented locally and the strategy proclaimed at the senior policymaking level within the British Government.

Second, policymakers have been unable to define long-term strategic policy objectives concisely.

Third, there has been an inability to acknowledge failure and reluctance on the part of organizations to 'learn' and to alter their processes.

In this section we first identify those characteristics of the international aid environment and the relationships between its diverse and transient members that explain the policy implementation process and its impact on policy results. In the following section we will develop our methodology, which is informed by theoretical models of organizational behaviour and its effect on policy contents and impact. These include system theory approaches, in particular several approaches in the field of bureaucratic politics, the organizational process model, advocacy-coalition and principal–agent theory. Our methodology is also informed by cognitive approaches, which focus on the origins and motivations of individual behaviour within a group or organizational setting, and management theory, which includes aspects of the above developed within the corporate world. This methodology will be used in later chapters to analyse British New Humanitarianism and its application to Sierra Leone.

None of the above theories has previously been applied substantially to the field of humanitarian emergency assistance, although a handful of case studies have employed principal–agent or cognitive science approaches.[11] Few have been tested regarding international policy implementation and most studies have focused on a limited implementation environment (in particular US foreign policy). All system theory approaches assume and discuss the fragmentation, contradiction and ambiguity of organizational behaviour. Each provides a model to analyse an organization's action process and organizational constraints. The focus of analysis shifts from the kind of action that was taken to 'the processes, motives, interests, sources of power [and weaknesses] of the various policymaking and implementing participants'.[12] According to these models, policy and its implementation are outcomes of (1) organizational policy preferences as outlined in an organization's mandate, (2) a bargaining process of decision makers, or (3) an organization's routine behaviour.[13]

Analysis of the implementation environment in which humanitarian emergency assistance policy takes place in terms of bureaucratic politics tends to be a mechanical exercise. Given the high degree of fragmentation and inconsistency, and the large number of independent variables, it certainly leads towards conclusions that are highly critical. Nevertheless, a bureaucratic politics approach can provide a holistic and definitive method for analysing international humanitarian emergency policy. By evaluating the worst-case policy implementation scenario within a changing policy environment, this approach addresses the sources rather than the symptoms of policy change or failure.

By examining the policy implementation process, we will identify the relevant institutional and societal forces that shaped British New Humanitarianism, assess the likelihood and depth of sustained policy change, and show how the differing interests within the implementation coalition may curtail a policy of wider relief from the outset. This approach offers a framework that can explain the transitory and contradictory state of humanitarian emergency policy and the contradiction between policy inputs and outputs. Focusing on the local and international implementation environments highlights the contradictory pressures on implementing organizations, which are aiming to meet different demands from different actors and act on behalf of a distant clientele rather than national or organizational interest alone.

In order to bureaucratize (break humanitarian policy into small action steps and assign responsibility for executing it to a range of departments) and therefore simplify the implementation of relief, the delivery of humanitarian emergency assistance 'has been broken down into tasks done by specialists hired and trained to do each action efficiently and effectively'.[14] Within such an environment, characterized by routine processes, policy implementation tends to become the policy.[15] As donors and implementing agents are accountable to distant stakeholders and overarching or secondary principles and interests, and have diverse organizational needs, they are likely to pursue different objectives. Donors' policies must remain consistent with national domestic and foreign policy. Implementing agents are responsible to local stakeholders, their own local representatives and other implementing agents. They are therefore relatively independent from broader policy constraints. This leads to a contradiction between upward accountability (to the public, policymaker or donor) and downward accountability (to the implementing agent or recipient). It also demonstrates the need to pursue 'positive' action to benefit a constituency and the difficulty of undertaking action geared towards an opposition.

In theory, the implementation of aid policy is left in the charge of aid agencies. In practice, however, their actions are directed towards the achievement of agreed outcomes. Most often this is on the basis of contractual agreements with donor organizations. It is also restricted by their own organizational capacity, so they have only limited room for manoeuvre. Adherence to standard operating procedures and obedience to overarching organizational goals and the decision-maker's directive tend to be stronger for organizations that have relatively hierarchical structures, closed systems and a less flexible ethos, and for those that are less subject to external behaviour/events. Yet,

> An agent's fulfilment of a principal's directives cannot be taken for granted, and donor-principals face the problems of hidden action and information. Because contractor-agents often have de facto control over a project's resources, they will try and guide the project so that it promotes their own goals, which may or may not be identical to those of the donor.[16]

In conclusion, policy implementation is far from straightforward. It is subject to diverse influences from multiple actors. In order to provide an adequate assessment of British New Humanitarianism and its application to Sierra Leone, and to differentiate between policy success or failure and more systemic implementation success or failure, the subsequent study must be based on a set of clear guiding questions or indicators. We now discuss those characteristics of the international humanitarian emergency assistance environment that challenge the implementation of a wider relief policy. The objective is to identify the minimum standards of successful policy implementation that we will use in our case study of British-led relief programmes in Sierra Leone.

Challenges to the implementation of New Humanitarianism

Multitude and diversity of actors

Because of the empowerment of international NGOs in the 1980s and 1990s in terms of their political weight, available resources and access, the world has seen an exponential increase in both their sheer numbers and the skills they provide. This development has been encouraged by many donors' preferential treatment of their own national agencies. This has led many organizations to open multiple international franchises, which have been eager in turn to increase their organizational independence. This leads to an even greater cacophony of objectives, mandates and funding requests. Acting both jointly and independently, international relief organizations can mobilize significant resources and public support. As a result, they are capable of both compartmentalizing responsibility and sharing resources. This increases the international non-governmental sector's overall strength and level of responsibility in international politics and humanitarian emergency assistance.

The rise in the number of relief organizations has also led to a number of adverse consequences.

First, increased inter-agency competitiveness has had negative effects for some organizations' access to resources and coordination. As one humanitarian aid worker in Sierra Leone has put it 'emergency assistance has become a cut-throat business as NGOs become their own operations and cannot abstract from their individual institutional needs any more'. To complicate cooperation further, many humanitarian NGOs working in Sierra Leone and many other emergencies like Sudan believe that cooperation (in particular with parties to the conflict including the UN, UK and USA) is counterproductive, since it threatens the fragile perception of their neutrality, impartiality and independence.

Second, there have been reductions in levels of funding for some organizations, leading to increased programme instability and the pursuit of short-term, micro objectives. This has also enticed humanitarian organizations to plan programmes 'on the cheap', in order to undercut their 'competitors'.

Third, there has been an increase in confusion at the operational level, reflecting both a lack of coordination and a multiplicity of objectives and mandates, some of which may be mutually exclusive or may involve unnecessary duplication of effort. 'The presence of multiple contractors also increases recipients' [and donors] ability to play contractors and donors off against each other'.[17]

Finally, the multiplicity of agencies may have contributed towards donor fatigue.

Marketization, organizational insecurity and fiscal uncertainty

The proliferation of organizations and the resulting increased competitiveness among them has also generated the development of a competitive market among relief organizations. Donor attempts to raise managerial effectiveness through competitive bidding, stringent accountability criteria (often on the basis of result-oriented contracts) and reluctance to finance core (e.g., administrative) costs have had similar effects.[18] Alexander Cooley and James Ron suggest that the marketization of many IO [international organisations] and INGO [international non-governmental organisations] activities generates incentives that produce dysfunctional outcomes:

> Contractors incur significant start-up costs to service a new contract – [undertaking project appraisals,] hiring staff, renting offices, and leasing new equipment – and can recoup their expenses only by securing additional contracts.... INGOs are under constant pressure to renew, extend, or win new contracts, regardless of the project's overall utility.[19]

This trend exemplifies the donor – agent power asymmetry: humanitarian organizations are rarely capable of resisting donor pressure to fit into broader donor objectives. In most cases, implementing agents have only limited information on broader donor objectives, strategies or requirements. Increased accountability in terms of measurable outcomes is certainly necessary for donors and implementing agents alike, but it is also counterproductive in several respects.

First, it further increases competitiveness and reduces cooperation among implementing agents.

Second, there is increased opportunism, which may involve succumbing to broader donor objectives and even withholding information about the ineffectiveness of some projects in order to ensure the organization's stability. Implementing agents are also highly sensitive in their reactions to criticism. This also leads organizations to imitate donor- and market-oriented organizations' structures and behaviour, in order to increase their predictability and hence their competitiveness.[20] This reduces the particular contribution they can provide as non-profit driven, morally motivated entities.

Third, the withholding of information (e.g., on the misuse of aid) may empower uncooperative local stakeholders. This creates new relationships and incentives between transnational and local actors and reduces implementing agents' operational leverage.

Fourth, there is an increased likelihood that bureaucratic organizations will 'shirk' responsibility and, as Richard Waterman and Kenneth Meier suggest, 'produce outputs at a higher than needed cost, or [. . .] produce a level of outputs that is lower than desired'.[21]

Fifth, implementing agents are more likely to pursue larger projects and generate economies of scale in order to maximize income. Aid organizations are therefore prone to expansion and diversification, which compel them to underestimate programme expenditure and reduce costs by neglecting efforts that go beyond essential donor requirements. These might include stakeholder involvement and capacity building.

Sixth, there is an increased need for implementing agencies to invest in maintaining their own visibility.

Finally, organizations are less likely to undertake comprehensive prior project and needs appraisals or impact assessments that go beyond measuring the immediate project output (e.g., the amount of food delivered or the number of patients seen).

Some organizations, in particular those with easy access to private funding, have been able to resist marketization or some of its negative effects, but they remain under significant pressure to cooperate with in-country needs assessments and project prioritization mechanisms, and to comply with donor reporting and financial accountability requirements.

Lack of policy stability, contradictory donor and implementing agent objectives

As previously discussed, donors and implementing agents possess diverse rationales and *modi operandi*, pursue different objectives on behalf of different and changing clients, and operate within highly unlike environments. They also work according to different time lines. Given the comparatively short-lived and changing political landscape and frequent personnel rotations, donors tend to be less capable and less willing to take on long-term visions and commitments. Given their even greater fragmentation and dependency on coalition building, they tend to react conservatively to change. Donor bureaucracies are also more likely to search for standard operating procedures, 'one-size-fits-all' solutions, in order to ease policy decision-making and to reduce staff capacity requirements and costs. Both principals and agents are highly subject to external shocks such as global or national political transformations (like the end of the Cold War or an electoral defeat), or negative experiences in other operational theatres.

Diversity in objectives and rationales might increase the need to compromise and adopt a range of different approaches. As such, it serves as a mechanism of policy checks and balances. Conversely, it leads to essentially vague mandates and objectives. Policy vagueness is often vital to preserve a coalition. More importantly, it causes misunderstandings, confusion, antagonism, fear of losing control and secrecy. Both individual donor departments and implementing agents must choose which principle to follow and compromise between various objectives. This further undermines effective policy implementation, coordination and programme sustainability.

Lack of control and performance-based contracts

Given the complexity of the implementation environment, the multitude of implementing agents, the broad range of donor engagements in conflict environments and multiple accountabilities, control over policy implementation is inevitably weak. This is exacerbated by the remoteness of many operational theatres from policymaking headquarters, which reduces donors' access to reliable information on local conditions and programme performance. As a result, donors are less able and less inclined to intervene directly and effectively in matters of programme implementation.

While grants are frequently tied to a recipient organization's programme proposal and agreed results, the project-specific implementation is at a recipient organization's discretion. Once funding has been granted, DFID has little control over project implementation: donor organizations lack the capacity to monitor field-based project implementation closely, especially in areas that are difficult to access. Donors are also generally interested in entering into aid partnerships. Like most other bureaucracies, DFID is under pressure to spend allocated programme funds that cannot in general be rolled over into the next financial year. Once resources have been allocated, the organization depends upon their speedy and complete disbursement in order to justify future financial allocations. This is only plausible if previous budgets have been spent or even overspent within the allocated funding year. DFID's success in policy execution (or profit) is measured in terms of the amount spent on development projects and emergencies. This increases DFID's willingness to relinquish control over programme implementation and monitoring and to continue projects irrespective of their utility. It also reduces the likelihood that DFID will demand the return of funds an account of an agent's failure to meet performance-based targets.

Donors' inability and unwillingness to control or closely guide programme implementation threatens to reduce policy coherence. It, therefore, also weakens the leverage of both donors and implementing agents. Most of all, it further limits effective programme evaluation, learning from experience and the identification of best practice.

In order to strengthen project and programme accountability, as well as control over policy implementation, many donors, including DFID, have tightened their conditions for greater project evaluation in accordance with prior contractual agreements. Often, such evaluations consist of client self-assessments on the basis of result-oriented indicators identified in cooperation with (or by) DFID. In addition, DFID and implementing agents, in particular multilateral organizations and large humanitarian organizations, conclude so-called Programme Partnership Agreements (PPAs) or Institutional

Strategy Papers (ISPs). Originally, ISPs were designed and driven by DFID's Conflict and Humanitarian Affairs Department (CHAD) and in particular its former director, Mukesh Kapila. They have since been extended across other departments and supported by both the administration and implementing agents. Such framework or partnership agreements have increased the predictability and transparency of policy and funding. Nevertheless, at the time of writing, few strategy papers specifically focus on humanitarian relief (or those that do exist are classified), other than country strategy papers.[22] Also, Mukesh Kapila's conflict-sensitive programming methodology has not taken hold throughout DFID (although conflict analysis is increasingly tied to funding applications submitted to DFID). On the contrary, the bureaucracy has in large parts rejected such change. Such PPAs and ISPs commit DFID to medium-term funding. Both partners agree upon areas of engagement, common objectives, rules of engagement and the accountability conditions an implementing agent must fulfil. With mandates and organizational objectives often at odds with one another, some donors (e.g., DFID) are also now 'taking a more "result-based management" approach to the funding of both development and emergency aid programmes'.[23] Results-based or output-based programming shifts the focus of evaluations to the outcome of programmes, rather than the input of resources. In theory, it is also meant to look at their wider impact, above and beyond the project level.

The introduction of strict monitoring and evaluation criteria allows public bureaucracies like DFID to strengthen control over the formulation and implementation of humanitarian emergency programmes. It is also intended to give the impression of facilitating public accountability and policy success. PPAs or ISPs represent a means of providing greater agency upward accountability and donor control. Arguably, such agreements also provide implementing agents with greater (financial) stability.

Agency field staff are rarely fully aware of the contents of such agreements, however, and this justifies the assumption that such agreements do not control the behaviour of implementing agents. Furthermore, such agreements, when combined with increased earmarking and monitoring, may 'discourage agencies from engaging in high-risk or expenditure activities, and actions that do not have easily quantifiable outputs'.[24] As such, they stifle flexible programming according to needs and local conditions. If agreed objectives cannot be met, or do not fulfil local requirements, agents are nevertheless compelled either to implement programmes according to the contract or to shirk responsibility for the failure of quality- and impact-based evaluations. Furthermore, performance-based evaluations offer very limited meaningful information on the broader and longer-term impact of humanitarian emergency assistance programmes. International humanitarian emergency organizations threaten to become public service contractors, with measurable output benchmarks and limited long-term planning and ethical *raisons d'être*. The establishment of such partnership agreements and DFID's increasing tendency to work primarily with large international organizations threaten to transform the humanitarian NGOs into an oligopoly of quasi-privatized aid agencies, rather than a balanced and flexible base of humanitarian actors.

Information asymmetry

Given their divergent organizational cultures, resource bases, levels of operation and degrees of proximity to political and programme decision-makers, donors and implementing agents (at the headquarters and field levels) have access to rather different levels and types of information. This is especially true in remote locations, where contractors acquire specialized information that is typically not available to donors. Donors, on the other hand, have much greater oversight over each programme as a whole and better information on regional and global developments that might impact on local project implementation. Agents and donors can both utilize their access to specialized information and filter it selectively to increase their leverage. Joanna Spear suggests that 'information is power and is often reluctantly given in a bureaucracy'.[25] A lack of information is not necessarily a disadvantage, however, and it may even be an asset to the extent that it reduces complexity and therefore facilitates policy and project implementation.

Overall, a lack of information, transparency and clarity are likely to cause misunderstandings and secrecy. They may also lead to programme implementation and decision-making based on anecdotes and rumours. This is particularly probable in tense and rapidly changing environments involving a multitude of actors, such as complex humanitarian emergencies. A lack of transparency is also

likely to lead to a greater degree of personal initiative in inter-
preting and implementing policy. At the operational level, organizational interaction revolves around personal, often informal and
ad hoc relationships. It is frequently through personal contacts that
project technicalities or bottlenecks are resolved and, for instance,
donor objectives are interpreted. Such informal contacts allow
for cooperation, flexibility and a degree of information sharing.
On the other hand, such informal contact may further increase
confusion and decrease sustainability, since they limit institutional
memory.

*Field-based moral judgments and reconciling material needs with
normative motivation*

'When an organization's survival depends on making strategic
choices in a market environment characterized by uncertainty, its
interests will be shaped, often unintentionally, by material incentives.' This is irrespective of whether or not such choices correspond with an organization's normative rationale.[26] This highlights
a potential tension between the morally based rationale of both the
relief organization and its staff on the one hand and its organizational ability and needs on the other. This increases the probability
of vaguely specified mandates. At an individual level, such vague
mandates require field personnel to make decisions on the basis of
their personal beliefs or emotions, which might well lead to decisions
or actions that go beyond the organization's objectives. This causes
stress and confusion in environments that are often highly volatile or
extremely dangerous. The closer the staff are to those in need, the less
likely they are to comprehend or defend organizational or material
requirements. As a result, many relief workers are especially subject
to burnout, fear and prejudice. They are also more likely than most
employees to oppose change. This tendency is reinforced by field
staff's distance from policy decision-making and their perception of
their own disempowerment. The greater an organizational bureaucracy, the less each individual feels that he or she is able to make
a difference. Field-based decision-making further reduces the coherence and coordination policy implementation, which may trigger a
multiplicity of divergent actions. On the other hand, the resultant
response might respond more closely to the immediate humanitarian need.

Legitimacy and credibility

Emergency aid conditionality represents the bluntest policy tool available under New Humanitarianism in terms of its potential impact. It threatens the withholding of the assets required to sustain a life-threatened community in an attempt to secure a future good, which can never be guaranteed. Humanitarian conditionality based on recipients' adherence to political conditions replaces need as the basis for humanitarian assistance. It is likely to cause suffering. The greater the negative impact on both local power structures and on those in need, the greater the likelihood that agents of emergency assistance, both donors and humanitarian agencies, will be regarded as enemies. Humanitarian conditionality becomes even more questionable if its proponents promote policy objectives to which they themselves frequently fail to adhere. It is assumed that humanitarian conditionality and wider relief can only be credible and effective if based on local ownership and paralleled by an active foreign policy on the part of donors that safeguards human lives and entails a commitment to rebuilding recipient societies. Local ownership also raises the likelihood of sustainability and reduces the risk of paternalism.

Indicators for successful implementation of wider relief

The above analysis enables us to identify a set of minimum conditions under which the implementation of a wider humanitarian emergency assistance is likely to prove successful. These indicators, which will guide our case study, include the following:

1. Clear and consistent objectives
2. Agency and donor credibility and adequate empirical and theoretical reasoning for policy contents
3. Transparency, predictability and long-term policy stability
4. Support of a committed and well-qualified implementation bureaucracy and support from implementing agents
5. Control and clear rules of implementation
6. Coordination and coherence
7. Ownership and proportionality of impact
8. Monitoring and evaluation
9. Flexibility.

Some of these criteria entail inherent contradictions that may well not be easily overcome within an international democratic policy environment. Successful implementation requires both clear mandates and a high level of control throughout all project stages. At the same time, it demands both flexibility in implementation (to take account of local conditions and requirements) and vagueness (to ensure the support of a wider policy coalition). Flexible policy implementation on the basis of transparent policy guidelines without contradicting either principle is more easily achieved at the local level than at the tactical level. Flexible implementation is likely to reduce coordination and coherence, however, as policy is shaped according to local criteria rather than general overarching standards. Most of all, a potential contradiction remains between the rights of the individual and those of the collective.

These minimum standards guide the subsequent analysis of British New Humanitarianism in Chapter 2 and of the British engagement in Sierra Leone in Chapters 4 and 5. In the next section we shall discuss the methodology we use to assess the implementation of British policy, and to evaluate the effectiveness of New Humanitarianism.

Project implementation: A methodology

Our model was developed following a comprehensive analysis of the existing primary and secondary literature on the debates that have essentially influenced the still limited discourse on New Humanitarianism and humanitarian conditionality. The analytical material specifically devoted to wider humanitarian emergency assistance and humanitarian conditionality remains very limited and virtually no empirical data are available on its implementation and impact.

The data that were available are characterized by a ubiquitous lack of record keeping and inconsistent usage of jargon and definitions. Decision-making at both project and programme levels has very often been personalized, that is, decisions have been made informally on the basis of personal relationships. Often they have not been recorded. This was clearly perceptible, for example, with regard to financial records and decision-making processes, which were muddled and lacked transparency. The analytical secondary data that could be obtained were not generated specifically for the purpose of this study. They may have been recorded using incompatible methodologies (and this has been made worse by the persistent lack of differentiation between humanitarian emergency assistance and development aid) and/or heavily influenced by anecdotal evidence and bias. Because of the complexity and the highly emotional nature of the operational environment, the contentious issues at stake and the distrust amongst organizations with very different operating procedures and objectives, there is a general lack of transparency and information sharing. This gives rise to rumours, predispositions and even distortion of information. However, a consistent effort has been made to overcome these difficulties.

These primary and secondary sources were complemented by extensive semi-structured interviews with key informants in the major bilateral and multilateral aid agencies and donor organizations. Most interviews were conducted in Freetown, the Sierra Leone capital, and in London in May/June 2002 and 2003. A conscious effort was made to interview staff at different levels within organizational hierarchies, and to interview all 53 INGOs engaged in Sierra Leone at the time. Interview partners included:

- DFID personnel (both at headquarters and field representation level) and selected operational consultants, primarily people involved in both the policymaking and implementation stages (including humanitarian assistance, financial and personnel matters, governance, conflict prevention, human rights and security sector reform);
- Members of the UK Cabinet Office responsible for humanitarian affairs, and selected Members of Parliament;
- UK Ministry of Defence (MoD) personnel seconded to the Sierra Leone Government, and in the framework of the International Military Assistance and Training Team (IMATT);
- UK personnel responsible for Sierra Leone and inter-departmental coordination within the Foreign and Commonwealth Office (FCO) and the Ministry of Defence (MoD);
- Key ministries in the Government of Sierra Leone (GoSL) and personnel directly involved in humanitarian issues (Armed Forces, the National Committee for Disarmament, Demobilisation and Reintegration (NCDDR), and the National Commission for Social

Action (NaCSA) (formerly known as the National Commission for Reconstruction, Resettlement and Rehabilitation (NCRRR));
- Selected United Nations agency personnel directly involved in humanitarian issues (United Nations Children's Fund (UNICEF), World Food Programme (WFP), Office for the Coordination of Humanitarian Affairs (OCHA), International Organization for Migration (IOM) and selected key personnel of the United Nations Mission in Sierra Leone (UNAMSIL), with a focus on those involved in the reintegration of former combatants and civil–military relations;
- European Union and EC Humanitarian Office (ECHO) personnel.

Outline

Chapter 1 introduces the main objectives of this book and traces the evolution of the British New Humanitarianism. It also identifies an analytical approach and methodology based on implementation theory and organizational theory that guides the following analysis.

Chapters 2–4 identify and evaluate a wider British emergency assistance policy at the strategic level and its adaptation to a country strategy in Sierra Leone. Chapter 2 assesses the extent to which British New Humanitarianism has constituted a definite policy. It also discusses the debates and concepts that have influenced the UK Government in rationalizing, designing and executing New Humanitarianism, and comments on the various policy departments' competing interests. Chapter 3 analyses the political and humanitarian history of Sierra Leone so far as they relate to our objectives. It introduces the relevant actors, their rationale and the international and national humanitarian and political parameters in which they operated. Chapter 4 explores British policy in Sierra Leone and the role of humanitarian emergency assistance within the full scope of the British engagement. On this basis, it is possible to draw conclusions on the extent of British policy change towards a more critical and more integrated humanitarian emergency policy, as well as the divergence between national policy and country strategy.

Chapter 5 evaluates the effectiveness of implementing British New Humanitarianism in Sierra Leone. It does so on the basis of a comparative analysis of the actions and approaches of a broad range of international humanitarian emergency assistance organizations in

Sierra Leone. All of these organizations have, or have had, contractual agreements with the British Government, or specifically with DFID. Their actions were therefore an important aspect of British policy implementation in Sierra Leone.

Chapter 5 draws conclusions and evaluates the implementation of British emergency assistance policy and the British policy engagement in Sierra Leone. It identifies causes of the divergence between policy and its execution in Sierra Leone. In conclusion, it offers recommendations that may contribute towards the creation of more effective future policy and practice.

2
DFID and New Humanitarianism

Introduction

Since its election victory in 1997, the British Labour Government has been influential in addressing both the shortcomings of humanitarian emergency assistance and its potential capacity to further political change. The Government has done this by integrating humanitarian emergency assistance within a policy of conflict management and development – both in theory and in some areas of engagement. More recently, the British Government has become a key advocate of reform of the UN-led international relief system.

The new British Government institutionalized its commitment to international development, poverty reduction and multilateral engagement by creating an independent and greatly strengthened development ministry: the Department for International Development (DFID). Despite a number of earlier attempts by successive governments to create an independent development agency, the new department's predecessor, the Overseas Development Administration (ODA), had remained a functional wing of the Foreign and Commonwealth Office (FCO). The new department's political head, Clare Short, was given a seat in the Cabinet and set out to develop an assertive DFID policy independent of the control of the FCO.

In June 1998, DFID published the principles of 'New Humanitarianism'. It vowed to make humanitarian emergency assistance more efficient and accountable. In rationalizing its policy, DFID drew – albeit incoherently – on discourses that were already prevalent in the aid community, in particular: (1) Do No Harm (the assumption that humanitarian emergency assistance may be harmful but can also do good in supporting conflict prevention), (2) the existence of a continuum from relief to development and (3) the identification of poverty and greed as the primary causes of violent conflict.[1]

In May 2000, the UK intervened in Sierra Leone in response to widespread violence. The military forces' initial objective was to evacuate British nationals, but their mandate was subsequently extended to include support for international peacekeeping troops. Since then, the UK has invested heavily in restoring democracy in Sierra Leone and the ongoing rebuilding of state institutions. The UK's unique, wide-ranging, costly and – relative to its other engagements in Africa – disproportionate intervention became a test case for New Humanitarianism.

However, until 2004, no clear and consistent humanitarian emergency assistance policy was either developed or implemented. New Humanitarianism never amounted to more than a set of general and inconsistently applied principles, and it failed to win the support of the implementation bureaucracy and the wider aid community. DFID had dropped its assertive public campaign in defence of New Humanitarianism by late 1998. This left a policy vacuum that further undermined programme management. Humanitarian emergency assistance policy was outsourced, predominantly on a bilateral basis, to humanitarian organizations. Policy was implemented in response to local needs and capacity and in reaction to key international political events and national foreign policy objectives, and not on the basis of a coherent and innovative policy.

In this chapter we define the main concepts of British New Humanitarianism, its rationale, justification and subsequent alteration. This analysis forms the background for the chapters that follow, which explore DFID's attempts to flesh out and implement a wider humanitarian policy in Sierra Leone.

This chapter has three main objectives: First, we characterize the British policy of New Humanitarianism, and assess whether it constituted a concrete humanitarian strategy. Second, we evaluate the acceptability of a policy of wider relief across the various government departments, in order to assess the likelihood of its effective and standardized implementation. Finally, we assess the rationale, thoroughness and stability of such a wider relief policy.

We begin by reviewing DFID's ascendancy following New Labour's electoral victory in 1997. We then appraise the shift towards a broader interpretation of humanitarian mandates and the introduction of conditionality into humanitarian emergency assistance. We then go on to discuss New Humanitarianism's rationale and justification, its transparency and stability, and the level of administrative collaboration and control it entails. Our analysis is therefore facilitated by the minimum standards for successful policy design and implementation defined in the previous chapter, in particular minimum standards 1–5.

Background: From ODA to DFID

In 1997, the international political arena seemed favourable to New Labour's reform programme: other (Social) Democratic governments had been, or were about to be, elected in other European countries and the United States. The clear election victory on 1 May gave the new British Government a mandate for change and provided it with the political leeway to implement it. 'New Labour' and its political platform of the 'Third Way' attempted to integrate mainstream political thinking across ministerial and party lines. The then Foreign Secretary, Robin Cook, identified four core areas of foreign policy engagement: (1) the promotion and safeguarding of democracy and human rights, (2) the promotion of free trade and the British economy, (3) the eradication of poverty and (4) the fight against the proliferation of arms and the support for security sector reform.[2] He maintained that the Government should 'deliver a long-term strategy, not just manage crisis intervention'. He also promoted cooperation across ministerial areas of responsibility to implement these overarching policy goals. This policy approach was labelled 'joined-up government'. Two years later, in April 1999, and in response to the war in Kosovo, the Prime Minister further spelled out Britain's 'ethical foreign policy' in what is now called the 'Blair Doctrine'. He argued that globalization – in its economic, political and security aspects – compelled Britain to engage in an active multilateral foreign policy, and that strong states had an ethical responsibility and a national interest in promoting and securing adherence to universal human rights, democracy and the eradication of global poverty.[3] These two themes (an 'ethical dimension to foreign policy' and 'joined-up government') pervaded Labour politics and led to the promotion of a much more interventionist foreign policy. The government was driven by the desires both to 'do good' (by addressing ethical, rights-focused issues) and to 'look good'. These political aims had a direct impact on the use of humanitarian emergency assistance policy to achieve foreign policy objectives, despite their inconsistent execution and general vagueness.

However, the new government did not define the agenda of its foreign policy with sufficient clarity to overcome the inherent contradictions between this new 'ethical dimension' and other national objectives, in particular the promotion of British trade and employment. It was also rather selective about the UK's international engagement on ethical grounds, confining its interventions to cases where it was in the national interest for other reasons and where there was a strong likelihood of success.[4] The extent to which the Blair Doctrine included elements of human rights, because of their inherent value or because they were 'classic' components in the construction of a 'just' case in favour of international military action in Kosovo is therefore open to question. This policy vagueness and selective implementation therefore undermined the emergence of a coherently implemented and morally driven form of New Humanitarianism.

Between 1997 and 2003, DFID in effect replaced the Foreign Office in the UK's dealings with certain less strategic areas. It was able to do this because of its greater capacity (in comparison to other departments) to implement and manage projects and programmes, its substantial financial base and its relative operational flexibility. Independence allowed DFID

> to establish direct contacts with parts of government previously denied it. Policy briefs in relation to specialized humanitarian agencies... were being formulated directly by DFID, and copied to – not drafted by – the UN department of the FCO. DFID's new autonomy gave it the ability to establish direct contacts with key international political bodies.[5]

DFID now became involved in questions of trade and security in developing countries, which had not traditionally been fields open to the UK's development administration. In 1998/99, Clare Short personally and assertively called for military intervention in Kosovo on the basis of moral considerations, thereby supporting the Prime Minister who had already taken a keen personal interest in Kosovo.

According to DFID personnel, it was Clare Short and her immediate advisers who pushed the limits of her own and the department's independence, political influence and area of responsibility. It was the Secretary of State herself who set broad policy objectives and got involved in major programme and project decisions. She also secured greatly increased financial allocations. DFID's support for poverty reduction and, to some extent debt relief, was to foster its good relations with the Treasury and Britain's finance minister, Gordon Brown. Even before the establishment of DFID, Clare Short had become a driving force behind Labour's assertive poverty-reduction agenda. There were repeated clashes with other departments, and the relationship between DFID and the FCO in particular became strained as the new department attempted to define and assert its role among the UK's political institutions. Personality clashes between the departments' political heads and within DFID itself did not improve this relationship.

The creation of an independent and greatly strengthened development ministry led to a re-evaluation of its programmes. In November 1997, for the first time in 22 years, the UK Government set out its development policy in a White Paper: *Eliminating World Poverty: A Challenge for the 21st Century.*[6] The White Paper and subsequent policy statements by senior political figures explicitly called for a coherent, rights-based approach to development cooperation, humanitarian relief and conflict management. A second White Paper followed in December 2000: *Eliminating World Poverty: Making Globalisation Work for the Poor.*[7] Neither of the White Papers, nor the government's declarations in support of the UN Millennium Development Goals, the 2002 'International Development Act' or the new 2002 DFID Public Service Agreement (PSA) went into any detail regarding humanitarian emergency assistance policy, but all of them impacted upon it indirectly. At no point did DFID explicitly and publicly set out its approach to humanitarian emergency assistance in unambiguous terms beyond the list of principles with which Clare Short had characterized the New Humanitarianism. In order to analyse British humanitarian relief we have, therefore, had to infer the underlying policy from the public speeches of key personnel, from development aid-related sources such as the documents on development cited above, and from DFID's actions. The agenda that emerged displays a clear focus on the objectives of democratization and development within the context of humanitarian emergency assistance.

Towards a 'Rights and Conflict-Based New Humanitarianism'

Under the leadership of Clare Short's predecessor, the Minister of Overseas Development Baroness Chalker, the ODA was already developing an institutional orientation with a greater emphasis on conflict awareness within humanitarian emergency programmes. Its objective was to develop a humanitarian emergency policy that was better suited to support conflict prevention. ODA, and later DFID, thereby joined in the prevailing international intellectual and political movement towards a more holistic approach to conflict, development and emergencies; this political development was picked up by many other European Governments and the US Administration.[8]

In recognition of DFID's greater awareness of conflict issues, its Emergency Aid Department (EMAD), the 'Disaster Relief Initiative' and 'Emergency Logistics Teams' were reorganized into its 'Conflict and Humanitarian Affairs Department' (CHAD) in 1998. CHAD has since been responsible for rapid onset humanitarian emergency programmes and projects, project implementation within conflict and emergency-related policy development. 'The co-location of conflict policy and humanitarian policy meant that CHAD was able to influence not only the provision of relief, but also the shape of the UK's political response to conflict', acting as the de facto desks for several major emergencies.[9] After the Sierra Leone elections in 2002, and as other emergencies such as the Balkans assumed a higher profile and greater urgency, DFID's geographical department took over responsibility for the British engagement in Sierra Leone. CHAD then assumed responsibility for operations in the Balkans.

Public statements, the two White Papers on development and other official DFID publications all committed the Government to an ethical code of conduct for humanitarian operations. This code was meant to be consistent with the White Papers' concepts of poverty elimination, good governance and universal human rights. According to both White Papers, development aid policy was designed to promote strategies to reduce poverty and prevent and resolve conflict;

humanitarian emergency assistance policies should complement it.[10] The concept of 'joined-up government' was to have an impact on humanitarian assistance policy as it deepened the merging of humanitarian emergency policy with development and security policies. This inevitably transformed the policy of conditionality into one of humanitarian emergency relief. Strategic concepts such as *coherence* and *co-ordination* and working in *partnership* with friendly recipient societies that are committed to international liberal principles, including human rights and/or areas in which British engagement promises to make a difference, have since also been applied to humanitarian emergency assistance.

The concept of working in partnership with friendly states introduced an aspect of selectivity into humanitarian emergency relief (with regard to both implementing partners and areas of engagement). This unequal approach to emergencies was not specific to the UK and is characteristic of international emergency assistance. It has resulted in the underfunding of certain crises (as, e.g., in the Democratic Republic of Congo). Newly developed mechanisms are addressing this as part of the continued effort to reform the international emergency assistance system, which the UK Government and, in particular, the current Secretary for Development, Hilary Benn, vigorously support. One such mechanism is the 'Central Emergency Response Fund' of the United Nations, established in 2006.

DFID defines its humanitarian assistance objectives as: 'to save lives and relieve suffering while also helping to protect and rebuild livelihoods and communities, and reduce vulnerability to future crises'. Since the development of New Humanitarianism, DFID has recognized 'the obligation to provide humanitarian relief in a principled and accountable manner, while at the same time addressing the underlying causes of crises'.[11] Instead of responding to needs alone, in theory DFID also attempts to influence conflicts: it identifies and addresses the 'root causes' of conflict and integrates humanitarian emergency assistance into approaches to bring about lasting peace.[12] In April 1998, Clare Short stated that humanitarian principles

> imply equal – and crucially, coherently linked – attention to the causes and consequences of humanitarian crises caused by conflict . . . This new, rights-based humanitarianism . . . is about defending, advocating and securing enjoyment of human rights

which have been recognized by the global community but which have been transgressed or neglected in a crisis.[13]

Prior to this, in March 1998, the Parliamentary Under-Secretary to the DFID, George Foulkes, had pronounced:

> It may be uncomfortable for some to move on from a 'needs-based humanitarianism' to a 'rights based humanitarianism'. . . A more active humanitarianism requires taking sides with the oppressed and against the oppressor . . . Humanitarian relief is more and more expected to take a developmental approach. Even more than this, humanitarian assistance is now expected to contribute to conflict resolution and peace-building. This implies the application of conditionality.[14]

In mid-1998, DFID launched its *Principles for a 'New Humanitarianism'*,[15] which read as follows:

- We will seek always to uphold international humanitarian and human rights laws and conventions.
- We will seek to promote a more universal approach in addressing humanitarian needs wherever they arise. People in need – wherever they are – should have equal status and rights to assistance.
- Our humanitarian policy will seek to work with other efforts aimed at tackling the underlying causes of a crisis and building peace and stability.
- We will seek to work with other committed members of the international community and, in particular, seek collaboration across the North/South divide to secure better international systems and mechanisms for timely joined humanitarian action.
- We will agree 'ground rules' that prevent diversion of humanitarian goods and collusion with unconstitutional armed groups.
- We will be impartial: our help will seek to relieve the suffering of non-combatants without discrimination on political or other grounds with priority given to the most urgent cases of distress.
- We will seek the best possible assessment of needs, and a clear framework of standards and accountability from those who work to deliver our assistance.

- We will encourage the participation of people and communities affected by crises to help them find durable solutions which respect their rights and dignity.
- We will, where possible, seek to rebuild livelihoods and communities, and build capacity to reduce vulnerability to future crises.
- We recognize that humanitarian intervention in conflict situations often poses genuine moral dilemmas. We will base our decisions on explicit analyses of the choices open to us and the ethical considerations involved and communicate our conclusions openly to our partners.[16]

This list of principles and, in particular, policy statements by Clare Short and other senior DFID personnel clearly indicate that senior policymakers within the British Government no longer regarded humanitarian emergency assistance as the automatic response. Rather, such assistance would have to complement objectives broader than the survival of a vulnerable population. New Humanitarianism was meant to ground DFID programmes on working principles sufficiently explicit to translate the White Paper – so far as it relates to humanitarian assistance – into policy and programming and place it within a coherent development framework. DFID had begun to implement its New Humanitarian emergency strategy in selected operational theatres. Sierra Leone was to become a test case for the UK's New Humanitarianism and its application in contemporary conflict.

The British intervention in Sierra Leone was not brought about solely by the development bureaucracy's intent to reform its humanitarian policy and the desire to promote values and be seen to look good. On the contrary, the initial British intervention and the subsequent broader country strategy were triggered by and originated in a combination of domestic and international demands and objectives.

The immediate triggers of the British military engagement were that British troops had been taken hostage and that allegations about the 'arms to Africa' affair had been published.[17] It was suggested that the UK Government had played a role in, and knew of, the breaking of the UN arms embargo on Sierra Leone. Once British soldiers were on the ground in Freetown, 'mission creep' compelled them to assume more and more responsibility. Years of atrocious violence in the former British colony had not led to any broader UK engagement, but the negative legacy of the Rwandan genocide, which the international community had done nothing to prevent, contributed to the British Government's willingness to become engaged. Furthermore, a failure to engage in Sierra Leone, while investing heavily in the Balkans, would have led to accusations of hypocrisy from developing countries. The so-called 'CNN effect' could have influenced public perceptions and led to a public outcry. Long-established personal ties with the former colony, the existence of a relatively large group of Sierra Leonean exiles in Britain, and a historical sense of responsibility and possibly guilt most certainly contributed to the UK's decision. Another factor that might have raised ministerial interest and that was repeatedly mentioned in interviews undertaken in Sierra Leone was the fact that Tony Blair's father had once been a lecturer at the university in Freetown, and the Prime Minister had spent some time in Sierra Leone as a child.

The British policies on New Humanitarianism and in Sierra Leone were being developed just as the New Labour Government and DFID were asserting themselves. This might well have led the department's leaders to use Sierra Leone to maximize its influence over foreign policy issues, in particular in developing regions. Sierra Leone, a small and seemingly 'manageable' country, became a test case for Labour's New Humanitarianism and a new development aid policy that concentrated on security sector reform as an essential aspect of good governance and, eventually, poverty reduction. It became an experiment in increasing the coherence of British policy response across political departments and ministries to issues that were deemed a threat to international peace and security. Despite widespread electoral irregularities, the toppled President Ahmad Tejan Kabbah had been democratically elected. Many foreign governments, including that of the United Kingdom, had strongly supported these elections. Sierra Leone's strategic position, its relatively rich endowment of primary resources (diamonds and other minerals, oil and lumber) and its critical position within a subregion with a history of violent conflict certainly all contributed further to the UK's willingness to become engaged.

Last but not least, the UK saw an opportunity to assert its position within global power politics, particularly vis-à-vis Europe and within the United Nations. Once the UN had committed its greatest-ever peacekeeping mission to Africa, United Nations Mission in Sierra Leone (UNAMSIL), and the UK had engaged militarily, the latter's creditability was on the line. UNAMSIL's success has now become ever more important to the UN, given its continued difficulties in preserving its leading role in international conflict in the context of the US-led wars in Iraq and Afghanistan. If the UN and the UK are unable to ensure success in a comparatively small country such as Sierra Leone, how can they hope to take on other, much greater, international tasks?

While the UK Government called for a 'rights-based' humanitarianism, it failed to establish clear political guidelines on how to deal with the potential abuse of humanitarian principles or human rights, other than by withdrawing from projects altogether. Nor did it guarantee any lasting political support for human rights. British New Humanitarianism never amounted to an explicit, transparent and rigorously supported humanitarian emergency assistance policy. At no point was it implemented beyond some localized areas of engagement. Moreover, despite the intervention by the UK and the UN and several years of relative peace, Sierra Leone remains inherently unstable.

British New Humanitarianism lacked clear and consistent objectives and mandates. In consequence, it also lacked clear rules, regulations and administrative structures that were designed to optimize the achievement of the organization's goals; that is, it lacked control. This further undermined its strength. The policy's general vagueness had important consequences for the implementation of humanitarian emergency operations and for DFID's relationship with implementing partner organizations. Without any clear rules of behaviour, field agencies were left to assess the local situation, evaluate project impact, and make a moral choice of how to respond. While doing this they were expected, ideally, to promote broader, countrywide political objectives beyond those of delivering emergency assistance. Field personnel have neither the time nor the capacity, professionally and financially, to do this. Nor would it be in their interest.

Ultimately, this is a question of defining what is good and bad, appropriate and inappropriate . . . Emergency implies the presence of war, and thus inherently requires evaluating enemies and making moral judgments. It also implies defining what is acceptable and not acceptable in the conduct of war, who is a combatant and who is a refugee... [Such] judgment introduces strong elements of emotion and irrationality. Rules, clear objectives and mandates, are necessary in order to enable the field worker to act quickly and reliably and according to a strategy beyond local project implementation.[18]

Leaving such moral decisions to field agencies and in particular staff might improve implementation to the extent that it takes better account of local information (including needs assessment), ownership and coordination, and therefore promote efficiency and downward accountability. For the most part, however, it diminishes accountability and coordination, as vital implementation decisions – with possible far-reaching and long-term effects – are left to agencies with very limited national or regional overview (and that are largely unaccountable to the British public). There is already a disconnect between policymaking and implementation, and between headquarters and field agents. The broadening of humanitarian mandates is likely to exacerbate this effect and lead to even greater controversy.

DFID's public defence of New Humanitarianism and the government's assertive rhetoric concerning the benefits of a wider approach to humanitarian emergencies have been weakened almost since the first publication of its principles in June 1998. While elements of New Humanitarianism, including the application of conditionality, could be identified in several operational theatres, the original rights-based approach has been dropped, at least in public. No common institution-wide interpretation and application of New Humanitarianism was achieved. Rights-based humanitarianism was not applied throughout the DFID bureaucracy, and it was also belittled or criticized. Moreover, the stated principles of DFID's New Humanitarianism lacked the assertive rights-based language of earlier public statements by the Parliamentary Under-Secretary of State George Foulkes in March 1998, the Permanent Secretary John Vereker in June 1998, and the Secretary of State Clare Short in April 1998.[19] This indicates that DFID was already attempting – as early as mid-1998 – to backtrack from its earlier ambitions to reshape British emergency assistance policy and intervene selectively in countries or issues of strategic interest. The national and international public indignation concerning aspects of DFID's 1997/98 humanitarian emergency assistance policy in Sierra Leone, or the lack thereof, may have contributed to this.

The perception of a broadening of humanitarian emergency assistance to incorporate broader political objectives and the alleged application of political conditionality in certain operational theatres had led to criticism from some humanitarian implementing organizations and other, mostly European, development ministries. For example, the UK Parliament's Select Committee on International Development had discussed DFID's application of political conditionality in Sierra Leone in late 1997/98 but had restricted itself to some general criticism.

Nevertheless, in 2000, DFID publicly reiterated its theoretical commitment to a rights-based development approach – empowering poor people – and called for a coherent approach across institutional boundaries.[20] In practice, the department increasingly concentrated on standardizing the delivery of humanitarian emergency relief and strengthening its technical efficiency. In so doing, the British Government placed stricter accountability requirements on implementing agents and chose to cooperate selectively with those organizations that supported its new humanitarian and political objectives. Rather than entering and maintaining an active and impartial dialogue with non-governmental humanitarian emergency assistance service providers, the department selectively supported (and still supports) large, established and mostly international or multilateral agencies (like the International Red Cross or Oxfam) to the detriment of smaller and, in particular, local NGOs. Arguably, an agency's failure to meet DFID's accountability or security requirements could be used as a reason to suspend aid operations or withdraw DFID funding altogether. It is possible to conceal political conditionality behind stricter accountability requirements. Such an allegation has been made by implementing partner organizations – in particular with regard to DFID funding for humanitarian organizations working in Sierra Leone – although Clare Short has emphatically denied this.[21] Furthermore, DFID gradually moved away from a project-based focus on conflict and rights issues to broader developmental and political goals such as the reform of the security sector and the global system of emergency assistance, and support for good governance in selected areas of engagement.

In the next section we analyse British New Humanitarianism's fulfilment of minimum standards 2–4. We first discuss the rationalization and justification of British New Humanitarianism, that is, its empirical and theoretical foundations (standard 2). We assume that New Humanitarianism was founded on contested theoretical assumptions which threatened to undermine its effectiveness within violent conflict. We then examine the level of support for the policy, from both the implementation bureaucracy within the British Government and implementing agents at the headquarter level (standard 4). Finally, we weigh up the overall stability and predictability of New Humanitarianism (standard 3).

Fulfilling minimum standards of implementation

Policy rationale and justification

British New Humanitarianism is premised on three primary assumptions.

First, violent conflict represents an aberration from a country's progression towards development and democratic governance. It is caused by poverty and the greed of a minority. Just as war is triggered by poverty, so violent conflict causes poverty. As a consequence, democratization and development assistance help to overcome violent conflict. We discuss this in relation to the root causes of conflict in Sierra Leone in the next chapter.

Second, humanitarian emergency assistance can do just as much harm to vulnerable population groups as it can do good in supporting them. Relief can provide a net benefit, however, if it is employed in support of conflict management and human rights. Third, there exists a natural continuum from relief to development. We discuss the second and third assumptions in greater detail in the remainder of this section.

The UK is not alone in following these assumptions. On the contrary, they express the beliefs that underpin policies that have also been formulated in part by the World Bank, the United Nations and the European Union (specifically the EC Humanitarian Office – ECHO). However, these assumptions cannot be generalized across conflicts or emergencies, and they have distorted the design and implementation of the UK Government's humanitarian emergency assistance policy in Sierra Leone. In particular, they have led it to apply inappropriate blueprints to complex humanitarian emergencies.

Do No Harm

The British Government assumes that humanitarian assistance may do harm to those it seeks to help to the extent that it leads to economic dependency, fuels (violent) conflict and justifies predatory government. DFID has maintained, for example, that 'the uncritical or unregulated provision of humanitarian assistance can create long-term dependency and, during conflicts, can even perpetuate crises by inadvertently supporting warring groups and fuelling war economies'.[22] It can also 'discourage self-reliance and the pursuit of solutions for underlying problems'.[23] 'It is possible that humanitarian assistance becomes the key element in a resource-starved environment and therefore subject to predatory behaviour'.[24] Given this risk that aid will do harm, DFID has assumed that it can also do good if employed to the benefit of wider political objectives such as reconciliation, and the support of good governance and human rights. DFID has assumed that tackling both conflict and humanitarian crises requires an explicit link to be made between the objectives of assistance and conflict management.[25] This approach is influenced by Mary B. Anderson's work, 'Do No Harm: How Aid Can Support Peace – or War (1999)'.[26] The doctrine of 'Do No Harm' has influenced many aid agencies in the formulation of conflict-sensitive or conflict impact assessment mechanisms and the strengthening of their protection strategies. It has helped to foster the merging of development, relief and peace-building and, inadvertently, humanitarian conditionality.

While humanitarian emergency assistance most definitely has some bearing on conflict, neither assumption, that emergency assistance projects do harm or good, is based on sufficient empirical evidence. On the contrary, we still lack the data that would be required to reach any broader conclusions on how to redesign humanitarian emergency assistance projects to make them more conflict- and rights-sensitive and enable them to promote conflict resolution or prevention and human rights effectively. The negative impact of applying New Humanitarianism, which might reduce the immediate availability of relief to a vulnerable population, may quite possibly outweigh its benefit.

Despite this critique, it must be recalled that both academics and practitioners have been calling for quite some time for better-informed and more critical policies on both development and emergency aid. Humanitarian emergency aid operations would benefit from more politically informed and longer-term impact analysis. This is not currently available as operations are increasingly selected on the basis of political opportunism and cost efficiency.

Continuum thinking

Underlying the Government's attempt to integrate humanitarian emergency assistance, development aid and peace-building is its belief in the natural progression from relief to development and the benefits to be derived from development even during conflict: the so-called 'relief-to-development continuum'. By adopting capacity building and risk reduction approaches during conflict, dependency on relief can be avoided and the root causes of conflict and vulnerability addressed. Furthermore, adopting a developmental approach in the design and implementation of relief strategies is thought to maximize their contribution towards sustainable development and peace-building. Such continuum thinking has now led to the merging, in both theory and practice, of security, development and humanitarian emergency assistance.[27] In essence, this means that emergency assistance is subordinated to a general and possibly short-term developmental approach. In the last few years, many policymakers have withdrawn from active political engagement or unconditional emergency assistance in favour of a developmental emergency assistance. Consequently, they have taken on responsibility for vulnerable populations. Are donors prepared to reconstruct war-torn societies in areas outside their immediate spheres of interest and far removed from local constituencies?

Despite its own line of reasoning that very modest and short-term humanitarian assistance (relative to the amounts spent on development aid and trade) *can* fuel conflict, DFID encourages humanitarian organizations to incorporate development approaches into their operational planning.[28] This policy is premised on the assumptions that humanitarian and developmental operational requirements are complementary, that development during war is possible and does not exacerbate conflict, and that new, post-war state institutions can utilize and build upon the assets and infrastructure provided as part of the earlier emergency assistance package. This has five important implications:

First, humanitarian emergency assistance takes on an important function within an integrated policy response to contemporary conflict and human suffering.

Second, emergency assistance alone is not a sufficient response to reduce human suffering and a vulnerable population has no inherent right to emergency assistance. It may be more responsible to withhold emergency assistance in order to prevent a potential negative impact, that is, to think of the long-term public good rather than the survival of particular individuals. This introduces an element of selectivity in the granting of humanitarian assistance. Humanitarian emergency assistance is not to be provided as a basic right, but rather granted selectively on the basis of vague criteria with a view to a possible future benefit. Such an approach requires a case-by-case analysis of the impact of humanitarian aid interventions and an assessment of their chances of sustainable success. It may have been this reading of Anderson's 'Do No Harm' approach that led the British Government to suspend humanitarian aid operations in Sierra Leone in 1998, following the overthrow of the elected president.

Third, it is politically plausible to work with governmental partners that are interested in, and capable of, working towards peace and good governance for the benefit of sustainable development. In an inverted logic, it is also plausible to refuse cooperation with regimes and/or agencies that are critical of UK political objectives or in areas where progress is unlikely, even in cases of severe need for international humanitarian assistance.

Fourth, in order to prevent recipients from becoming dependent on aid, emergency assistance must be small-scale and short-term with a clear exit strategy. Emergency assistance must pave the way for longer-term development and economic and political independence, if it is to benefit both conflict management and sustainable development.

Fifth, emergency aid appropriations and structures can be utilized for longer-term provision of public services. Not only is it appropriate to work closely with local governmental structures, but the latter are also capable of providing the necessary political guidance. This assumes that medium- to long-term developmental assistance and effective development can be sustained without substantial domestic political agenda setting.

Needless to say, many of these implications remain controversial. As noted above, continuum thinking is premised on the understanding of violent conflict as a temporary crisis and an obstacle to sustainable development and, ultimately, democratization. The continuum model and the concept of development in conflict conceive of a progression from crisis through rehabilitation and development. It is assumed that the adoption of capacity-building approaches during conflict enables relief dependency to be avoided, the root causes of conflict and concerns regarding sustainable development and peace-building to be addressed simultaneously, and emergency assets to be utilized for longer-term development. This is despite their short-term, rudimentary, externally maintained and designed and essentially unsustainable nature. This assumption is, however, incorrect.

Development aid, humanitarian relief and conflict management are based on distinct belief systems and working processes, which do not necessarily correspond but require diverse levels of local administrative capacity. Joanna Macrae demonstrates that problems of legitimacy and administration in transitional states '[confine] the forms of aid to those that are least likely to meet developmental goals'.[29] Development assistance is premised on the assumptions that a benign government exists and has both the capacity and the will to set the political parameters and maintain the administrative structures for the provision of public services. This argument is discussed in much greater detail in the framework of an analysis of governance and its impact on and interaction with emergency assistance in Sierra Leone in Chapters 4 and 5. Development also warrants a certain degree of security – a rather fickle concept within a wartime or postwar environment. Only local authorities, or local factions, can guarantee security and, relying on their support, implicitly legitimize their actions. This was pointed out by DFID itself when it refused to continue British-funded humanitarian emergency assistance operations in Sierra Leone.[30] Very rarely – and Sierra Leone is a possible exception – has the UK Government been prepared to invest sufficient force to provide such a security guarantee.

By merging its approaches to humanitarian emergency assistance, development and security on the basis of continuum thinking, the concept of conditionality is implicitly transformed into one of humanitarian emergency relief. Also, by placing stricter guidelines on humanitarian operations and/or becoming more directly involved in operational decision-making, DFID threatens 'the impartiality and independence of humanitarian organisations and humanitarian action may be compromised'.[31] This, as much as donor selectivity, gives local authorities (or factions) a power of veto: project survival depends on their continued consent. During a war, it is difficult to ensure the continued local ownership of development projects or guarantee that development projects meet local needs. Without a longer-term donor commitment, which cannot be guaranteed in a conflict situation, development projects are not sustainable.

DFID nevertheless remains a strong supporter of the concepts of a relief-to-development continuum and development in conflict. These assumptions underlie the UK Government's attempt to integrate humanitarian emergency assistance, development aid and peace-building policies to develop a coherent and coordinated approach to contemporary conflict. The continuum concept and its inherent contradictions have contributed towards vague and possibly weak policy principles, generating overambitious strategies and policy guidelines. This has clearly been the case with DFID's New Humanitarianism and its application in Sierra Leone.

Joined-up government or bureaucratic competition

> The 'maker' of government policy is not one calculating decision-maker, but rather a conglomerate of large organisations and political actors who differ substantially about what their government should do on any particular issue and who compete in attempting to affect both governmental decisions and the actions of their government.[32]

DFID, one of the world's largest donor organizations, works in cooperation with a great variety of agents to implement its New Humanitarianism. These include multilateral donors and international organizations (e.g., the United Nations and its agencies, the World Bank and the European Union), other national governments, and national and international non-governmental humanitarian organizations. DFID's in-house operational capacity is limited.

With the ongoing expansion of DFID's in-country field offices, and through the employment of external consultants and in particular the Conflict and Humanitarian Affairs Department's Operations Team (CHAD OT), it has created its own, albeit limited, implementation capacity. Nevertheless, DFID still implements its humanitarian programmes or projects almost exclusively by funding other organizations.

Following the election in 2002, 53 international NGOs were registered in Sierra Leone. The UK has cooperated with many of them. The number of local NGOs was considerably higher, though they were much less significant in terms of mandate, size, expertise and sustainability. These were complemented by a plethora of multilateral organizations, donor agencies, private service providers, consultancies and private military companies.

The broadening of the relief agenda has also led to a broadening of the group of actors involved in its implementation. Together, they form a highly heterogeneous, yet largely mutually dependent, changing and competitive implementation environment, which is characterized by mutual distrust and a lack of coordination and information. DFID itself, or those responsible for designing British humanitarian emergency assistance, is made up of many individuals, often on secondment from a range of other units and departments. It is after all just one cog in the overall UK Government machine. Figure 2.1 tries to capture the nature of this policy implementation environment.

This international relief network implements New Humanitarianism on behalf of a distant donor organization and local stakeholders. Many agents function both as implementers and as donors to other implementing agents. All pursue their own objectives and work on the basis of their distinct *modi operandi*. This further complicates common agenda setting and donor–agent relationships.

> The diverse set of actors that has potential relief roles displays little structural interdependence, nor does it share a common boundary, other than the fact that each component may on occasion contribute to the relief process... This network is devoid of any institutional framework, lacks coherent goals, reflects few patterned relationships, yet points to a variety of transnational and functional linkages that have emerged probably more out of informal contacts than formal institutional arrangements.[33]

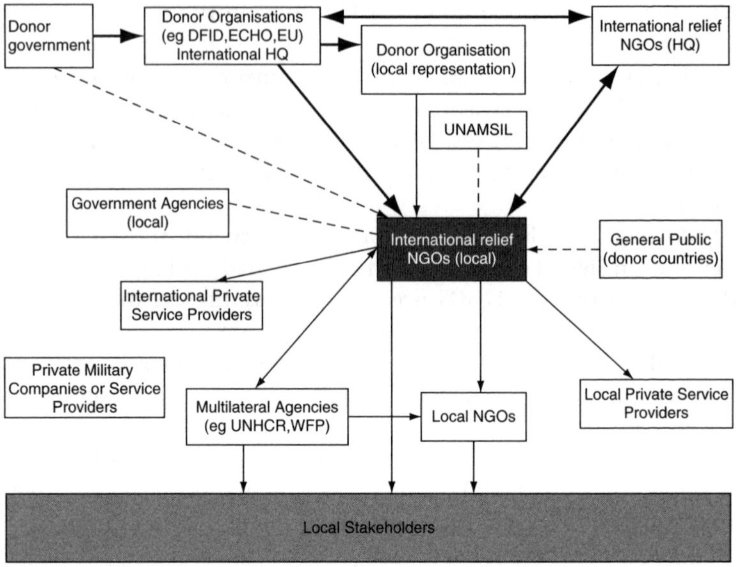

Figure 2.1 Implementation environment wider relief, Sierra Leone

Greatly expanded in personnel, budget and political influence relative to its predecessor, the ODA, DFID became and continues to be a source of institutional envy and competition.[34] The drive of key DFID personnel, in particular the former Secretary of State, Clare Short, and CHAD's former Director, Mukesh Kapila, clearly played a substantial role in supporting both the enthusiasm and ambitiousness of policy development and implementation. It is only rarely, however, that charismatic leaders alone achieve substantial policy change. A policy compromise must be driven by an implementation coalition that has an interest in driving the policy process forward, and this was not forthcoming in the case of New Humanitarianism.

Bureaucratic tension and competition were not limited to inter-departmental relations. Given the complex structure of sometimes overlapping departments and different working styles within DFID, cooperation between its various units was not always forthcoming. This was aggravated by high staff turnover. Because it had responsibility for rapidly developing emergencies, CHAD's working style differed sharply from the rest of DFID. The sometimes difficult relationships between CHAD, the senior advisors and the desks (and between DFID and other ministries) are crucial to any understanding of why DFID's New Humanitarianism was never rigorously defended and implemented. This effect was over and above that of New Humanitarianism's being subject to broader national interests and affected by both international and local events. The administration never fully succeeded in reaching a policy consensus, and inter-departmental rivalry only exacerbated the resulting inconsistency and competitiveness.

Indicative of this competitive policy environment and of attempts to increase control over policy design and implementation were the publication of the 2002 audit report of humanitarian emergency assistance, the July 2002 Public Service Agreement (PSA) and the Service Delivery Agreement (SDA). These departmental Public Service Agreements (PSAs) established a set of objectives and targets that each department is working towards over the period 2001–04. The implication is that departmental budgets will be linked increasingly to how well each department performs in relation to its PSA. The PSA reflects DFID's overall approach as set out in the 1997 and 2000 White Papers on International Development and, in particular, their focus on the International Development Targets. The [new] Service Delivery Agreement (SDA) focuses on the processes DFID supports to ensure that the targets in the Public Service Agreement are met. Neither agreement specifically mentions humanitarian emergency assistance. [35] The audit report stated:

> The division of responsibility between geographical and CHAD, however, has often not been formalised, with CHAD's role being decided in many instances on a case-by-case basis. A degree of flexibility in DFID's organisational response will always be needed but this ad-hoc approach creates a risk that humanitarian assistance will not be provided in a timely manner whilst roles are clarified.[36]

The report comments at length on a lack of formalized evaluations, impact assessments and common indicators across all emergency operations.[37] It also calls for a greater integration of DFID emergency responses into longer-term development and criticizes a general lack of transparency and communication in DFID's relationship with implementing agents.

Ever since 2002, DFID, and in particular those units responsible for humanitarian emergency assistance, have undergone a fundamental restructuring process. Mukesh Kapila has been replaced. Clare Short, who had assertively fought to promote a development agenda throughout government, resigned in opposition to the conduct of the 2003 war in Iraq and the handling of the reconstruction phase. In terms of influence over key international operations and policy development, DFID has lost some of its power within the British Government. CHAD's areas of responsibility and capacity, including its control over external consultants, have been reduced. CHAD has since lost some of its influence to DFID's geographical desks.

It is yet to be seen whether the department's internal restructuring represents a further streamlining of a conflict- and rights-based approach across all DFID units. Conflict and humanitarian advisors are now in place within all the geographical departments and several field offices. In theory, DFID's proximity to implementing agents and the area of operations should increase its capacity to control and evaluate policy implementation in Sierra Leone and elsewhere. This should strengthen accountability and project efficiency and, in the long run, lead to better-informed and better-coordinated policy implementation. It may also lead to a further politicization of emergency aid. In reality, DFID abroad, in particular its humanitarian unit, is usually overstretched. It is focused on internal management processes and highly dependent on orders from London-based decision-makers, who act in accordance with much broader political requirements. As of mid-2004, DFID has retracted to implementing humanitarian emergency assistance in an ad hoc and compartmental fashion rather than on a strategic basis.

Predictability and long-term policy stability

Departmental financial allocations in the UK are debated and allocated every 3 years when the government undertakes a Comprehensive Spending Review. In the last two Comprehensive Spending Reviews, DFID has managed to secure budgets that were significantly higher than originally envisaged. DFID benefited both financially and politically from Clare Short and Gordon Brown's common objectives on poverty reduction and Clare Short's support of Gordon Brown's strategy of debt relief.

An innovative feature of the UK Government's policy of 'joined-up government' has been the so-called 'Conflict Prevention Fund for Sub-Saharan Africa' managed by DFID (and the 'Global Conflict Prevention Fund' managed by the FCO). Both provide integrated budgets for the FCO, DFID and MoD on issues broadly in the realm of conflict prevention. DFID has disproportionately benefited from these pools.[38]

All these factors suggest the potential for a strong and independent DFID to achieve long-term policy stability. Yet, given the multitude of implementing agents, competing and contradictory objectives and the department's exposure to national and international policy developments, DFID humanitarian emergency policy is neither predictable nor stable; it is quite the contrary.

It has been argued that policy represents a compromise between a multitude of diverse actors, which must be continuously renegotiated and reconfirmed. Larger political objectives and programmes are subject to inter-departmental debate, coalition building and compromise, both politically and financially. DFID is compelled to coordinate with the Cabinet Office and other UK departments, in particular the FCO, the DTI and MoD, in order to safeguard the British national interest and general strategic policy objectives. Furthermore, policymaking and implementation are greatly influenced by public opinion and the media. DFID's humanitarian interventions are usually made in reaction to heightened public interest and increased reporting in the media; they are therefore inherently instable.

Examples of DFID's lack of influence over policymaking included Clare Short's inability to prevent the UK's sale of a hi-tech military air surveillance system to Tanzania, military equipment to Indonesia and Zimbabwe or, in general, the use of the 'Conflict Prevention Fund' to buy military equipment. This was despite her vigorous attempts to block such sales and to strengthen arms exports licence controls in order to safeguard human rights and a rights-based development policy. When confronting the DTI, the MoD and the Prime Minister over arms sales and export licences, or other trade issues, DFID has lost out time and again.

Conclusions

A new approach to development, humanitarian relief and security is required if Britain is fully to exploit their accumulated benefits. Policy coherence, coordinated implementation and accountability must undoubtedly be strengthened. There is no 'blueprint' for operations to end violent conflict and provide humanitarian emergency assistance. A 'rights- and conflict-based' humanitarian approach will necessitate a long-term political and economic commitment that extends well beyond the ending of violent conflict and the pursuit of possibly short-term strategic interests.

Our analysis of New Labour's New Humanitarianism has shown that it defies many of the minimum standards for successful policy implementation defined in Chapter 1. A consistent implementation of DFID's New Humanitarianism is at best problematic. This does not in itself preclude the successful implementation of policy aspects on the project level; nor does it call into question the underlying policy vision (the potential role of humanitarian emergency assistance in support of human rights and conflict prevention or resolution), which is yet to be implemented.

New Humanitarianism was based on disputed assumptions and suffered from contradictory and often vague political objectives. The theoretical underpinnings of DFID's humanitarian emergency assistance policy were contested. The policy lacked the support of implementing agents and clients. DFID applied political conditionality to humanitarian relief in conflict situations in an inconsistent and ad hoc way rather than in a strategically focused manner. A fragmented, competitive, critical and at times obstructive implementation bureaucracy undermined a coherent, headquarters-driven policy and its implementation. Bureaucratic rivalries both within DFID and between it and other departments inhibited institutional and policy reform. Inter-departmental confrontation, suspicion and rivalry undermined joined-up agenda setting and longer-term planning. The case study that follows shows that DFID-funded humanitarian implementing partners proved unable to exert significant influence over DFID's agenda setting. Nor were they adequately informed about DFID's broader and longer-term policy objectives.

DFID's humanitarian assistance policy and implementation lacked stability and predictability because of its dependency on wider domestic and international political development, fluctuating policy objectives and constituencies. It is, however, a sign of responsible policymaking when particular policy areas, such as emergency policies, depend upon the consent of a larger policy constituency and the wider national interest.[39] Policy vagueness can be interpreted as an attempt both to reconcile differences and to enable compromise.

Alternatively, it may be seen as a conscious or unconscious effort to shirk responsibility and accountability. It is a mechanism of checks and balances to the benefit of the majority of traditional policy responses. As such it can also stifle innovation and change.

Because of the large number of actors involved, the design, implementation and evaluation of DFID policy have suffered from unclear lines of responsibility, rules of implementation, lack of control, accountability and policy appraisal. They have been further undermined by the distance of those in overall charge of DFID humanitarian emergency policy from the areas of its implementation, and the difficulty in assigning responsibility for success and failure. The immediate clients, the recipients of humanitarian emergency aid, were highly vulnerable. Those targeted by wider policy objectives within the political and military establishment were not. They had the means to evade the conditions attached to emergency aid. The impact of a wider humanitarian emergency assistance policy, therefore, threatened to be disproportionate.

Ambiguity allowed for flexibility in the implementation of humanitarian programmes, but it also reduced coherence and coordination – two essential aspects the government had set out to improve. The absence of clear policy objectives and longer-term donor commitments put extra pressure on implementing agents, who were forced to make moral decisions in the midst of crises.

> DFID's humanitarian policy . . . lacks clear principles for action and resource allocation and creates "room for maneuver" for both politicians and bureaucrats to do what may be appropriate, opportune or convenient . . . [The policy] can justify both large-scale humanitarian operations as well as the possible withholding of relief.[40]

Policymakers and implementing agents at the strategic and tactical levels – and at different locations – are subject to widely differing political pressures and often pursue widely differing objectives. They are stuck between the need for efficiency and the institutional requirement to perpetuate operations – and therefore influence future funding. The policy responses that result are necessarily vague and tend to shift in accordance with both domestic and external shocks.

Some of DFID's difficulties in implementing a coherent humanitarian policy have been due to the policy inconsistencies inherent in its basic approach; others are clearly based on structural institutional weaknesses within DFID itself and within the wider humanitarian emergency assistance implementation network. Some of these inconsistencies, together with a general lack of control, coordination and common agenda setting, may well be aspects of bureaucratic policy implementation that cannot be overcome, given the complexity and diversity of humanitarian emergencies, international conflict and their implementation environments.

We suggest that the UK Government never intended to standardize New Humanitarianism beyond the establishment of some general overarching policy objectives to be applied in selected areas of engagement. The early enthusiasm for a rights-based approach, conflict management rhetoric and assertive advocacy was clearly driven by a minority within DFID's, and especially CHAD's, senior policymaking leadership. It has since been dropped in favour of a less public, more selective, and bilateral approach to the implementation of humanitarian emergency assistance policy. It has also been surpassed by the UK's strong support for the reform of the international humanitarian system. It might be argued that the British Government has responded to and taken on board criticism within the aid community in response to its initially conflict-oriented emergency assistance policy. DFID must be commended for its substantial efforts to obtain expert advice on how to improve its operations and develop effective response mechanisms.

As a public service provider, DFID is itself under increased public scrutiny and obliged to ensure both efficiency and accountability. Given DFID's policy inconsistencies and the UK Government's structural inability to speak with one voice or to follow one overarching agenda, New Humanitarianism is expected to remain a weak compromise. Despite its inconsistent record of implementation, New Humanitarianism has had a strong impact on donor–agent relations and the future of humanitarian relief in complex emergencies. Furthermore, an analysis of the implementation of British humanitarian policy (even if it shows multiple inconsistencies) provides valuable insights concerning the limitations to the coherent execution of public policy.

The degree of the UK Government's current privatization and militarization campaign (i.e., the assumption that military forces can play a central role within complex emergencies and post-conflict reconstruction) and its continuing attempt to integrate the management of emergency assistance, development and military conflict threaten to have an equally important impact on future emergency operations. They will determine the relationship between the UK Government as a donor and civil society organizations as implementing service providers.

In its second and third term, New Labour faced growing criticism from both the British electorate and its former European allies for its unequivocal support for the US Republican administration and its bellicose posturing in the so-called 'War on Terror'. If the development aid and humanitarian emergency assistance bureaucracies are to improve the efficiency of New Humanitarianism, the presently vague 'ethical dimension' of Britain's foreign policy will need to be replaced with clearer guidelines for content and implementation. At the very least, this will require an agreed definition of what constitutes humanitarian emergency assistance; agreed interpretations of humanitarian principles, rules of implementation, and responsibility for action; and clear allocation of individual accountability. This will be essential in order to strengthen the support from a hitherto reluctant UK bureaucracy and its implementing partner organizations. If humanitarian emergency assistance is to play a role within peace-building, it must do so on the basis of clear objectives and a long-term political commitment to particular areas of operation. Steps to improve effectiveness must also include the adoption of quality impact analysis and the introduction of more transparent procedures for communication with implementing agents.

3
Agents of War and the Causes of Violent Conflict

Introduction

In 1991 a small group of fighters crossed into Sierra Leone from Liberia, thus triggering a protracted war that was to last until 2002. The Revolutionary United Front (RUF), led by a former army sergeant Foday Sankoh, was thrown together from a mixture of Sierra Leonean political exiles, disgruntled youth, economic refugees in Liberia, mercenaries and – in its later stages – deserters from the Sierra Leonean army. Ever since the mid-1960s, Sierra Leone had suffered from coups and counter-coups, autocratic government and economic mismanagement. During 1991–2002 it endured horrific violence, changing administrations and a further economic decline. The war was fuelled and sustained by a vibrant regional war economy, which remains largely intact today. In an economic and political power struggle, rebels, soldiers, mercenaries, politicians, national and international companies, and local and international governments all benefited from the chaos: they maximized profit and influence by gaining access to, or controlling, the extraction and trade of Sierra Leone's abundant resources, in particular diamonds. Successive weak administrations were incapable of effectively managing the state and its resources, guaranteeing security, or breaking with personal and national patronage networks.[1]

Since the mid-1990s, the country has seen years of peace talks, international intervention and reconstruction initiatives, and their subsequent failures. The United Nations and the United Kingdom

invested extensively in the restoration of the 1996 elected government of President Ahmad Tejan Kabbah and the rebuilding of state
institutions. The UK's unique, wide-ranging, and disproportionate
commitment became a test case both for New Humanitarianism and
for an integrated approach to violent conflict, complex political emergencies and an ethically informed foreign policy.

The conflict has cost Sierra Leone dearly. Out of a population of
some 4.5 million, between 75,000 and 200,000 were killed, two-
thirds of the population (including 1.8 million children) were internally displaced, thousands were kidnapped, wounded or deliberately
mutilated, and an estimated 500,000 fled to neighbouring countries. Large parts of the country's infrastructure were destroyed, the
resettlement and reintegration processes were slow, and people still
live in deplorable conditions today. The conflict further undermined
the government's already acute lack of capacity to govern effectively. It also debilitated humanitarian, development and governance
programmes. By 2004, Sierra Leone had one of the world's youngest
populations, with more than half the country's population aged
under 15. Unemployment and under-employment have grown at
alarming rates, with the majority of Sierra Leoneans employed in the
informal sector. There is a significant brain drain, as the majority
of the educated population work for aid agencies or have left the
country altogether. For many years and despite large-scale international assistance, Sierra Leone has remained at the bottom of the
United Nations Human Development Index, and locked in a vicious
cycle of destruction (Table 3.1). Even as the current 'negative peace'
consolidates (i.e., the absence of violence), the underlying causes and
triggers of instability are far from removed.

In this chapter we analyse the war in Sierra Leone, its root causes,
its impact on humanitarian emergency assistance and peace-building
programmes, and vice versa. First, we provide a brief account of the
background to the war and highlight those historical events that
are important to an analysis of New Humanitarianism. Secondly,
we draw out the key features of the war that impacted upon (or
were affected by) the external aid intervention. These include the
role of the military, external military intervention, the breakdown
of representative government and the phenomena of violence, aid
dependency and a regional war economy. This enables us to assess
the UK Government's understanding of the causes of conflict in

Table 3.1   Human development indicators, Sierra Leone

HDI rank out of 175	Life expectancy at birth	Under-5 mortality rate (per 1000 live births)	GDP per capita (PPP US$)	Adult literacy (% age 15 and above)	Population without sustainable access to an improved water source	Population below income poverty line (%) under 2$
175	34.5	316	470	36.0	43	74.5

Sources: UNDP, *Human Development Report 2003* and Jane's, *Sentinel: Security Assessment West Africa*[2]

Sierra Leone. An appreciation of the complexity of the war and the environment within Sierra Leone is essential to any understanding of the difficulties entailed in delivering aid. This enables us to assess the appropriateness of the aid intervention, in particular the utility of emergency assistance as a tool within the peace process in Sierra Leone. An understanding of the war in Sierra Leone also facilitates an appraisal of the viability of the objectives of New Humanitarianism.

An abridged history of the 1991–2002 war in Sierra Leone

When the war began in 1991, the Sierra Leonean rebel movement counted a few hundred poorly trained and poorly equipped soldiers. Some had fought for Charles Taylor's National Patriotic Front of Liberia (NPFL) against the government of Samuel Doe. Unemployed youth, disgruntled military and mercenaries subsequently joined or cooperated with them. Others, in particular children, were press-ganged or kidnapped into service. Through a combination of initiation rituals (often involving atrocious violence including the rape or murder of family members or friends), drugs, material and psychological rewards, the spreading of fear and an assertive education programme, the RUF leadership ensured the fighters' obedience and loyalty.

In April 1992, a junior officer within the Sierra Leonean Army (SLA), Valentine Strasser, overthrew the Government of President Momoh. The military coup had begun as a protest by junior officers against poor conditions at the front. The apparent ease of the upheaval had a lasting impact on the public perception of government authority and military efficiency, or the lack thereof. By drawing the armed forces into the new government, Strasser subsequently established the National Provisional Ruling Council (NPRC), which initially received widespread public support. Between 1991 and 1995, the SLA was expanded from 5000 to 14,000 soldiers, largely through the recruitment of poorly educated youths from the city streets, including children as young as 12.

The forming of the NPRC administration was the first major setback for the rebels, who until then had roamed the rural areas of Sierra Leone relatively freely. A second, more lasting setback was the formation of civil militias. This was in response to the RUF's advances and an increasingly destructive campaign by renegade Sierra Leonean soldiers. These SLA soldiers, who were rebelling against years of mismanagement and poor conditions of service, became known as soldier-rebels, or *sobels* (soldiers by day, rebels by night). Some cooperated unofficially with the rebels in exploiting the rural population, trading arms and avoiding outright confrontations. Civil militias received much public and, later on, international support.

In 1994, one of the militias, the Kamajors, repelled an attack on Bo by rebels and rogue elements of the SLA. This had lasting effects on the morale of both rebels and civilians, and on the army's relationship with the civilian population. It also increased the perception that the central government was not only unable but also unwilling to protect its citizens. Subsequently (and with the support of mercenaries and the British Government), the Kamajors were reorganized into the Civilian Defence Force (CDF) under the leadership of Hinga Norman and drawn into the government. However, they were never fully under government control and they always had an antagonistic relationship with the military. Eventually, the civil militias also became entangled in the conflict, in particular as illegal and exploitative trade flourished and they came to wield significant power. Their status as irregular fighters remained unclear and continued to cause problems throughout the eventual process of national disarmament, demobilization and reintegration.

When the NPRC became entrapped in the same web of corruption as previous governments and lost some of its popular backing and internal cohesion, the RUF was able to reconfigure. The rebels engaged in a brutal campaign of terror that targeted civilians and the diamond-rich south-east of the country. During late 1994/early

1995, as the RUF made advances on the capital, Strasser found himself increasingly dependent on foreign troops. In order to hang on to his crumbling regime and support the counter-insurgency efforts (many of them against his own officers), he engaged the Gurkha Security Group (based in the Channel Islands), a private military company (PMC). Later on, he engaged other PMCs, including Executive Outcomes (from South Africa) and Sandline International (from the UK). This practice was also adopted by a number of subsequent governments.

Shortly before a general election in 1996, Brigadier General Julius Maada-Bio overthrew Strasser. Following intense international political pressure, the election was held on 15 March 1996. Amidst large-scale controversy, involving allegations of fraud and violence, Ahmad Tejan Kabbah of the Sierra Leonean People's Party (SLPP) was elected President with 59.9 per cent of the vote. In November of the same year, the government and the RUF signed the *Abidjan Peace Agreement*. However, it soon became clear that the Kabbah Government was unable to assert control over rural areas, and had only survived with the help of the peacekeeping troops of the Nigerian-led Economic Community of West African States (ECOWAS) – which had been deployed to Sierra Leone in 1993 – and foreign mercenaries. The peacekeepers had been drawn from the Economic Community of West Africa Monitoring Group (ECOMOG), which had previously been fighting Charles Taylor's incursion in Liberia. The regime's support from its own armed forces – which were now heavily infiltrated by the RUF – was at best delicate. The Government's relationship with the armed forces was fraught with rumours, misinformation, resentment and fear.

In May 1997, a junior officer, Johnny Paul Koroma, ousted President Kabbah. Koroma was to win an almost cult-like following within and beyond the Sierra Leonean armed forces, which lasted until his alleged death in June 2003. Koroma suspended the constitution, abolished political parties and established the Armed Forces Revolutionary Council (AFRC). In the following days, soldiers, rebels and irregular forces ransacked the capital. In June 1997, the AFRC invited its former enemies, the RUF, to join the government.

On 13 February 1998, Nigerian-led ECOMOG peacekeepers, backed by logistics and intelligence support from a UK-based PMC (Sandline International) and civil militias, stormed Freetown. They toppled the

AFRC/RUF junta, whose leadership fled into the country. ECOMOG subsequently returned President Kabbah to power. In June 1998, the UN Security Council established the United Nations Observer Mission in Sierra Leone (UNOMSIL), whose objectives were to monitor and advise efforts to disarm combatants, restructure Sierra Leone's security forces, and support the West African peacekeepers.

Less than a year later, in January 1999, a mixture of RUF rebels, rogue elements of the SLA and irregulars launched an assault on Freetown, seizing parts of the city and unleashing a rain of terror. By the time the Nigerian peacekeepers managed to retake control of the capital, at least 5000–6000 people had been killed, many neighbourhoods had been destroyed and thousands of people had been abducted. In the following days, Nigerian peacekeepers were witnessed taking ruthless revenge. As of today, the country remains traumatized by atrocities committed by all sides during the war. The unarmed UNOMSIL staff were subsequently withdrawn.

In July 1999, the government and the RUF signed another accord, the *Lomé Peace Agreement*, which controversially included a clause that provided a blanket amnesty for atrocities committed during the war. This accord provided for the establishment of a unity government that included members of the RUF and former AFRC junta. The leader of the RUF, Foday Sankoh, was appointed the country's Minister for Mineral Resources – the very commodity that had sustained the rebellion and the war all along.

On 22 October 1999, the United Nations Security Council established another, much expanded and strengthened UN peacekeeping mission. The United Nations Mission in Sierra Leone (UNAMSIL) became the largest and most comprehensive UN peacekeeping mission in Africa at the time, deploying around 17,500 troops and civilian personnel throughout Sierra Leone at its peak. The mission was intricately involved in all aspects of the rebuilding of the Sierra Leonean state. In May 2000, before it had become fully operational and taken over from ECOMOG, the rebels startled the world by abducting 500 UN peacekeepers. The peacekeepers were subsequently released, but the efficiency of UNAMSIL had been put into doubt. The collapse of the Lomé Accord brought about a marked increase in the numbers of human rights abuses by government forces, civil militias and rebels alike.

Also in May 2000, the British Government sent 800 paratroopers and military advisers to Freetown with the objective of securing the airport and evacuating British nationals. The war, and more particularly the British engagement in Sierra Leone, changed fundamentally in August of that year, when one of the rebel splinter groups (the *West Side Boys*) took 11 British soldiers hostage. The latter were subsequently rescued and, in the words of one British soldier, British troops hunted down the remaining rebels.[2] This incident contributed enormously to the British military's invincible, no-nonsense reputation in the country, and this forms the basis of the respect (and apprehension) with which Sierra Leoneans still view the British military today. The British troops' apparent comparative ease in rescuing these hostages contributed to the British Government's decision to prolong their stay and extend their mandate to include support for the beleaguered UN and ECOMOG troops.[3] The United Kingdom became intricately involved in the war and the subsequent rebuilding of Sierra Leone (both militarily and politically). In the same month, pro-government forces arrested Foday Sankoh, who remained in prison until his death in July 2003. He was never prosecuted for war crimes.

On 11 November 2000, the RUF and the government signed the *Abuja Ceasefire Agreement*. Skirmishes continued throughout 2001, however, despite the gradual deployment of UN peacekeeping troops into rebel-held territory. The war was officially declared over in January 2002. In the elections of May 2002, President Kabbah won a landslide victory and was reconfirmed as President. The RUF suffered a devastating electoral defeat; receiving just 1.7 per cent of the vote; the myth of the rebels' popularity within civil society was broken. Almost immediately, many rebels vanished across the Guinean and Liberian borders and many of them took up arms in the Liberian civil war that was to heat up in the coming months. Some were killed in revenge attacks.

It was not only the intervention by the United Kingdom and the increased strength of the UN presence that led to a scaling down of the war. David Keen, for instance, has argued that the much greater degree of respect, and to some extent trust, that the new UN leadership (and British Government officials) showed to the RUF in 2000/01 as an important party in the peace process played an important role. Both UN and UK officials also made it clear that they would never accept a military solution, which may have convinced some rebels to engage more seriously with the peace brokers.[4] Most importantly, as the conflicts in Guinea and Liberia heated up, the rebels were increasingly denied access to their external bases and trading routes, and they lost the financial and military backing of one of their key foreign supporters, President Charles Taylor of Liberia.

Despite the consolidation of peace, Sierra Leone and its immediate neighbours, Guinea and Liberia, remain inherently instable. The international donor community and the people of Sierra Leone have become frustrated with stagnating process of reform and recovery.

> Since the elections there have been at least five minor coup attempts. This is a powerful signal for continued unrest. Much depends on whether or not new opportunities can be created for the people and how the region is stabilized. As much depends on whether the army will produce another charismatic leader.[5]

Root causes of conflict

DFID assumes that poverty and underdevelopment, the greed of a minority and the lack of basic human rights – including political rights – are the main causes and triggers of civil strife and violence.[6] In a reverse logic, violent conflict either deepens or causes poverty. DFID maintains that 'poverty can only be eradicated through the resolution of violent conflict' and vice versa[7] and believes that violent conflict, while indicative of a structural deficiency, is an aberration of a historical movement towards sustainable development and liberal democracy. War, despite its inherent transformative function, is understood as a destructive force. Poverty reduction measures are therefore regarded an essential component of conflict prevention and peace-building efforts, just as peace-building supports poverty reduction.

This logic alone does not explain the conflict in Sierra Leone. Nor did it easily lead to the development of a useful framework for peace and reconciliation. The UK's understanding of the war in Sierra Leone did, however, guide its engagement in that country. It also had important consequences for its humanitarian and peace-building intervention. We now discuss DFID's understanding of the causes of conflict and the key features of the war of which it took insufficient account or which strongly impacted upon the UK's intervention.

This analysis provides an important background for our subsequent assessment of the UK's country strategy for Sierra Leone and the implementation of New Humanitarianism.

DFID: The causes of conflict and Sierra Leone

DFID public documents reveal a number of assumptions regarding the causes of conflict. First, violent conflict takes place within weak states. The weakening or 'collapse is rarely sudden, but arises out of a long degenerative process that is characterized by predatory governments operating through coercion, corruption and personality politics to secure political power and control of resources'.[8] Greedy elites and predatory regimes abuse political authority to benefit from violent conflict. They benefit both economically and politically from so-called 'war economies' and political chaos, and are therefore likely to block conflict resolution efforts.

Secondly, contemporary violent conflict in developing countries

> rarely has a defined front line, and fighting is frequently opportunistic rather than strategic. Warfare is low tech, self funded and often small arms are the main weapons. Such wars are not costly and can easily be sustained without external support (in particular in countries wealthy of natural resources). Factions will seek to involve, exploit and control a significant proportion of the civilian population in order to sustain the conflict.[9]

Civilians are the main victims of such wars. Reform of the security sector and restrictions on the spread of small arms and light weapons are essential components of conflict resolution and hence of development policy. The UK Government assumes that 'the development agenda and the security agenda are inseparable'.[10] DFID intends to integrate conflict reduction objectives into all aspects of development policy, including humanitarian emergency relief.[11]

Thirdly, economic and political inequalities between population groups and rising levels of deprivation aggravate existing grievances. Leaders often manipulate perceptions so that such contemporary inequalities become conflated with historic prejudices, hatreds and lack of identity, thus strengthening their supporters' motivation to engage in violent conflict.

Fourthly, capacity building, including institution building, and support for human rights represent primary approaches to overcoming a temporary crisis of governance and strengthen development.[12]

All these symptoms of conflict were detectable in the case of Sierra Leone. However, the two assumptions that poverty is a root cause of conflict and vice versa (and that violent conflict is therefore temporary) and that it is a minority's greed rather than a majority's grievance that causes contemporary violent conflict (and that war is therefore destructive) remain in dispute. These assumptions entail an inherent contradiction[13] and certainly cannot be applied across a wide range of contemporary conflicts. If greed is indeed a cause of conflict, then poverty alleviation and capacity building programmes will not reduce it; rather, they will enable competing factions to maximize their extraction of resources, including aid resources. Similarly, humanitarian emergency assistance in support of conflict resolution may even provoke conflict if those benefiting from chaos attempt to disrupt local empowerment. If grievance rather than greed is an essential cause of violent conflict, then conflict reduction or containment measures may prevent necessary and potentially beneficial political or socio-economic change. Nor are conflict or violence always irrational or illegitimate. The assumption that underdevelopment and poverty cause violent conflict is not a new one. On the contrary, it has shaped development thinking and practice for at least several decades. It is doubtful, however, that it suffices as an explanation of contemporary conflict or, more importantly, an approach to overcoming it.

A potentially violent political and economic transformation may well form part of a long-term process as societies adjust to the pressures and limits of modern economies and/or democratization. The reshaping of a country's governance structures and the prolonging of its war economy may well serve the interests of a large part of its population, since they open up alternative means of resource accumulation. In the longer term, war may lead to the creation of new governance structures that are different from Western-style democracy and externally imposed structures of accountability.

Most conflicts are the result of a combination of parallel, overlapping and competing causes. The immediate trigger of the war in Sierra Leone was the 1991 invasion from Liberia, but its root causes lie much deeper. The war's background, duration and distinctive nature were characterized by a complex web of factors that often reinforced and moderated one another. Primary causes of conflict in Sierra Leone included the following.[14]

- First, there was a breakdown of representative governance, neglect of the countryside and marginalized groups, widespread corruption, a collapse of infrastructure and high levels of unemployment.
- Secondly, the entrenchment of national and regional war economies benefited the country's elite, local and international entrepreneurs and those with access to weapons.
- Thirdly, international and regional intervention and expansionism as well as regional instability all played significant roles. The involvement of Liberia (and to a lesser degree Nigeria, Ivory Coast, Guinea and Libya) was certainly an essential and destabilizing feature of the war. It not only allowed the RUF to strike and retreat across the border but also supplied a stream of regional mercenaries with recent experience of war. It also provided rebels (and soldiers) with arms, facilitated cross-border smuggling that financed the war effort and destabilized the region through endless refugee flows. The spread of small arms and light weapons throughout and beyond the region continues to haunt the African continent. Conversely, ECOWAS peacekeeping troops (mostly Nigerian) were crucial in preventing a rebel takeover of Freetown and in restoring the previous democratically elected government. ECOWAS, UNAMSIL and several foreign governments provided the platform and foundation for the present peace agreement and restructuring effort.
- Fourthly, the country had a psychology and history of violence. The militarization of society led to collaboration between rebels and the army and, as a consequence, the rise of civil militias.

Without this cooperation between various forces and society groups, the war in Sierra Leone would have been far less dramatic and much shorter. There was (and still is) a considerable group of actors that thrived on chaos and opposed or actively destabilized efforts aimed at bringing the conflict to a peaceful and sustainable end. The destruction of the infrastructure and countryside and of other, non-war-related, sources of income, together with their responsibility for large-scale war crimes, discouraged perpetrators from giving up their chosen path of criminality.

In contrast with the popular interpretations of contemporary conflict in Africa, the war in Sierra Leone was not for the most part fought along so-called ethnic lines. Only during, and in the period after, the May 2002 elections did ethnicity (in terms of genealogy and religion) begin to feature in national and particularly party politics. On polling day, for example, rumours spread throughout the northern and south-eastern provinces that voters were being disenfranchised and displaced on the basis of their cultural background. President Kabbah has been blamed for promoting the interests of the Mendes.

In the next section we discuss the key features of the war in Sierra Leone that impacted on the external aid intervention and vice versa. Our objective is to develop the essential background for our subsequent assessment of the appropriateness of New Humanitarianism, or of aid, as a means of furthering the peace process in Sierra Leone.

Governance and aid dependency

The root causes of the recent conflict in Sierra Leone lie in decades of unrepresentative government and the marginalization of the majority of the population, widespread corruption and the collapse of the public infrastructure, which gave rise to a flourishing shadow economy. The state's ability to function was further undermined by international structural adjustment efforts that – with the objective of curbing corruption and public spending – weakened the state bureaucracy and prevented leaders from providing basic public services.[15] Ever since independence, international development aid and generous international credits had sustained the State's survival. International humanitarian emergency assistance had substituted for a crumbling public welfare system. Together, they added to Sierra Leone's total dependency on foreign assistance, as aid became (and continues to be) the backbone of this fragile West African state. As such, international aid fulfilled an essential containment function, both before and during the war. Some have argued that it contributed to the prolonging of the war – even though without it, thousands of people would have been denied humanitarian assistance with extremely harmful consequences, and the emerging peace process might well have collapsed.

Two of the primary causes of the war were the imminent disintegration of a patrimonial social structure and the collapse of the country's once-praised education system. Both pitched large sections of society, in particular the youth, against an ever-weakening state and provided fertile ground for rebellion. Popular discontent at the mismanagement and undemocratic character of the Sierra Leonean state are widely regarded as root causes of the war.

The social fabric of Sierra Leone and the present Government are still crippled by a tradition of client-based rule, personal entitlement and aid dependency. A study commissioned by DFID states that even by 2004:

> The organisational, technical, strategic and advocacy capacity of civil society is weak... There is limited horizontal accountability or transparency between Freetown based organisations and the rural poor... Civil society organisations... exist in a historical and political climate which perpetuates their weakness. Sierra Leoneans therefore have little experience of being citizens with universal rights. In general, they distrust the State, government, the judiciary and elected representatives.[16]

David Keen and others stress, however, that:

> [t]he war has not simply seen the collapse of a system, but the creation of new systems – systems of profit, power, protection and even affection. Despite a catalogue of massacres and mutilations... not only did the majority of Sierra Leoneans reject the rebels and their atrocities; many have also been able to develop a new kind of political awareness in the context of mass displacement.[17]

During the war, Sierra Leone saw several rudimentary alternative systems of governance, some of which drew on traditional systems of identification, representation and justice, such as traditional leaders (Chiefs and Paramount Chiefs) and so-called secret societies (in particular the Bondo, Sande or Poro Societies). The temporarily established youth councils also provided a new form of authority, and one that may merit further study before external agencies commit further support to the rebuilding of the former traditional state system, which contributed to the outbreak of the war. Ongoing reconstruction and state-building efforts must take care not to recreate the pre-war political and economic system, or focus on the security needs of the state alone. Doing so would fail to address the longer-term root causes of the conflict. Patrimonialism, governance and their interaction with the provision of humanitarian emergency assistance are the subject of a more in-depth analysis in Chapter 4.

War economy

The conflict enabled an intricate web of actors to reap economic and political benefits from a vigorous regional war economy. These included politicians, Sierra Leonean elites, soldiers (including rebels, mercenaries and private military companies), local and international traders, regional and international governments and other profiteers. As the survival of these profiteers depended on the continuation of chaos, they had (and still have) little interest in supporting an end to the war and a consolidation of the peace process. The porous Sierra Leonean borders allowed these groups to launder the proceeds from the extraction of valuable minerals, in particular diamonds, and the theft of international aid. These illegal activities enabled them to finance the war. As a highly sought-after resource in a resource-starved environment, humanitarian emergency assistance and its providers became a cause of competition and distrust and a target throughout the conflict. Because of the large quantities of alluvial diamond deposits, diamond mining in Sierra Leone is comparatively simple. Given the ease with which diamonds can be concealed, smuggling and illegal mining are difficult to control. The Sierra Leonean Government estimates that it has lost tens of millions of US dollars per year in taxation revenues from diamond mining, as a result of illegal mining and cross-border smuggling.

As a possible explanation for contemporary conflict and the role of war economies within it, the greed and grievance debate (in particular the writings of Paul Collier) has had a crucial impact on the UK Government's understanding of – and policy approach to – war and development.[18] It has at times led to the application of tighter donor development conditionality and the restriction of humanitarian emergency assistance during or immediately following periods of violent conflict. However, this model largely ignores the impact of a globalized international economy on local markets. It also fails to explain the causes of greed-driven behaviour and focuses on its symptoms instead. It does not analyse whether alternative peaceful behavioural choices and opportunities for future development existed.

With regard to the political and military conflict in Sierra Leone, and the phenomena of war economies and warlordism, analytical models on transformation, war economies and global governance are more satisfactory. Humanitarian organizations and the exploitation of their assets form essential parts of this process of global governance. The current debates on the relationship between contemporary conflict and humanitarian assistance and on humanitarian conditionality are witness to this.

Militarization: The SLA, sobels and private military companies

David Keen explains that 'the military success of a few hundred rebels and the massive destruction they inflicted on Sierra Leone was possible in large part because a range of other groups [in particular the army and political and traditional leaders] found it convenient to lend support to the rebellion for purposes of their own'.[19] The military, for example, consisted of large numbers of irregulars, including children who had been recruited very rapidly. It never amounted to a professional army that could effectively maintain a stable political environment. Furthermore, neither the rebels nor the army was ever in full control of their mercenary elements.

The SLA unintentionally assisted the consolidation of the RUF when it executed suspected rebels at an early stage of the conflict. Fighters that had been recruited or press-ganged from the rural population were now less likely to return to their home communities for fear of retribution. President Kabbah permanently damaged his government's relationship with the SLA when he downgraded the armed forces and had 24 soldiers executed on 19 October 1998 for their role in the coup of 25 May 1997, thus engendering the army's fury and distrust. The fragile relationship between the government and the military became apparent after the 2002 elections, when it became known that large sections of the military (80 per cent of the 50 per cent who voted on the special voting day for the armed forces) had voted for the incumbent Johnny Paul Koroma, despite his reputation as a war criminal and coup leader. The SLA's role in the war and its present restructuring has had an important impact on the public's relationship with the armed forces, international donors and aid agencies.

A significant factor in limiting the rebels' military effectiveness was the military involvement of a series of mercenary groups, such as the Gurkha Security Group in 1994/95, the Executive Outcomes in 1995/96 and Sandline International. 'Under President Kabbah and with the facilitation of officials from the UK's Foreign and Common-wealth Office (FCO), Executive Outcomes supported the government in reorganising civil vigilante groups into a militarily remarkably successful national militia force.'[20] The mercenaries were rewarded for their services with lucrative diamond and other mining concessions. When evidence emerged that Executive Outcomes personnel were involved in illegal diamond trading and that the company received an exorbitant monthly fee to maintain fewer than 100 personnel, public sentiment turned against them. The formal withdrawal of the mercenaries from Sierra Leone was one condition within the peace agreement signed in January 1997 between the government and the RUF.

In October 1997, Sandline International, a UK-based mercenary and logistics company that was affiliated with Executive Outcomes, supplied President Kabbah's allies with 'logistical support', including rifles – thereby breaking the UN arms embargo. After the story was published in a British newspaper the company claimed to have acted with the knowledge of the FCO and in particular the British High Commissioner in Sierra Leone, Peter Penfold. Subsequently, the war in Sierra Leone, Sandline's involvement, its breaking of the UN's arms embargo and the FCO's knowledge thereof were all discussed in the British Parliament and in particular by its Select Committee on Foreign Affairs. Peter Penfold was compelled to take early retirement.[21] In a confidential interview, an FCO staff member maintained:

The Sandline affair drew the UK in, so did the rebel hostage taking of UK troops. The UK felt obliged to take a stand and 'do something'. Extreme human suffering hadn't sufficed. The Sand-line affair and hostage taking finally raised personal interest at ministerial level. It was important that the UK was welcomed in by the democratically elected government, a government it had positive relations with. The rearming of Kabbah was a breach of the embargo, but the embargo was not logical.[22]

One outcome of the Sandline affair was the publication of a Green Paper outlining legislative options for the control of private military companies that operate out of the United Kingdom. Private military and logistics companies nevertheless continue to play a significant and increasing role not only in the politics and technicalities of West African recovery, but also in British and US foreign policy. This was witnessed, for example, in the international intervention in Afghanistan and Iraq. Increasingly, PMCs and international military forces have taken over responsibility both for the delivery of humanitarian emergency assistance on behalf of donor governments and also for the protection of humanitarian aid organizations' personnel. This has had negative consequences for the public perception of aid agencies as neutral service providers.

Violence

The war in Sierra Leone became notorious for the recruitment and kidnapping of children into both the SLA and the RUF, and for atrocious violence against deserters, suspected collaborators and the civilian population. Political economists and anthropologists, in particular David Keen and Paul Richards, have taken pains to analyse the rationality of both RUF and SLA violence.[23] This analysis was not reflected within British (aid) policy on Sierra Leone. Keen and Richards both maintain that violence and terror against civilians are highly strategic elements of war. The horrific accounts of fleeing aid workers who flooded into the capital and across the border inflated the perception of the RUF's manpower, military success and brutality.

Violence has become accepted as a means of achieving economic and political change. The psychological rationales for threatening or committing violence against others are thought to include the following: the quest for identity and a sense of belonging to a group; a sense of self-worth gained by demanding respect from others; the gaining of pleasure and satisfaction by a display of power; resentment against an oppressor and perceived betrayal. Such motivations may also include fear, shame and guilt but also excitement, not to mention revenge for colleagues who have been killed in the fighting and an inability to accept defeat (which would mean that colleagues had died for nothing). Such rational explanations of the war's violence may be persuasive, but they do not conclusively explain why human beings turned to indiscriminate violence, to the destruction of the countryside and eventually of themselves, when they could have pursued better targeted violence against enemies, oppressors or those with access to resources, or indeed other, more profitable and peaceful actions. Up to 2004, the British intervention did not suffi- ciently address the long-term social and psychological effects of this violent history, which continues to undermine the country's recon- struction and development.

External intervention and regional instability

From the very beginning of the war, the intervention of external actors and the political and economic interaction of local actors with the wider region were of primary importance. They were critical in both prolonging the war and in bringing it to an end. International aid appropriations and loans had long bolstered the fragile Sierra Leonean economy. They had also ensured the survival of the polit- ical regime. Initially, the insurgency was masterminded and manned from Liberia. Later on, the rebels used neighbouring states as loca- tions for some of their bases and to escape a head-on confrontation with the Sierra Leonean army. The West African region also provided the rebels with new recruits with experience of war and readily avail- able arms. The movement of refugees throughout West Africa added to the region's instability and the war's complexity. The fighting in Sierra Leone, on the other hand, provided regional powers with the justification and background for their own hegemonic object- ives. As soon as neighbouring states such as Nigeria, Guinea, and international actors such as Libya, Israel, the UK and the US became involved, the war had mutated from a localized civil uprising into a significant war that destabilized the region as a whole.

The Economic Community of West African States (ECOWAS) has been involved in the war in Sierra Leone since 1993, when the regional hegemon Nigeria sent troops to support President Strasser against the RUF rebels. With support from the Nigerian peacekeepers, the government managed to win back significant territory from the RUF. ECOMOG troops were also crucial in retaking the capital, Free- town, and reinstating President Kabbah in 1998, and in halting the rebel takeover in January 2000. Ever since, most Sierra Leoneans have viewed the Nigerian peacekeepers with mixed feelings. They are grateful for the role they played in protecting the civilian population and bringing the war to an end, but they also view the occupying troops with trepidation and resentment, given their ruthless revenge attack following the rebels' storming of Freetown.

Internationally, the coup against the democratically elected government of President Kabbah in 1997 was officially shunned. In July 1997, the Commonwealth suspended Sierra Leone. Then, on 8 October 1997 (after close involvement by the British Government), the UN Security Council passed Resolution 1132, which imposed sanctions on the Sierra Leonean regime and authorized ECOWAS to implement them. ECOMOG troops, mainly from Nigeria, were subsequently deployed to guard the Sierra Leonean border. In practice, the embargo applied to supplies of arms and petroleum products, but it also meant that only limited humanitarian assistance could reach the beleaguered capital; most supplies were stopped by the ECOMOG peacekeepers on the Sierra Leonean border.

> Agencies were short of supplies, due to what they perceived as the quite deliberate policy of President Kabbah, ECOWAS, Ambassador Okelo, the UN Humanitarian Coordinator and the UK Ambassador to use their influence to hold up relief supplies at the border. . . The deposed Kabbah regime and their supporters launched vicious verbal attacks on 'junta NGOs', the term they gave to NGOs maintaining headquarters in Freetown. This caused a deep loss of mutual trust that endured long after the end of this period.[24]

From October 1999 until 2004, a United Nations peacekeeping operation, UNAMSIL, was authorized to establish and uphold stability in the country and to rebuild the fragile Sierra Leonean state. The comprehensive UN and UK involvement provided the foundation for both the present (albeit negative) stability and the rebuilding of the country. UNAMSIL, ECOMOG and the aid community have all contributed to the distortion of local markets, and all have been implicated in the recurring scandals and allegations of sexual abuse.

Conclusion

The legitimacy of the state in Sierra Leone and the success of the ongoing recovery programmes remain unclear. Large parts of the country continue to require comprehensive basic humanitarian assistance. The structures of public services in Sierra Leone continue to lack political agenda setting and basic infrastructure, and there has been little progress in terms of community empowerment or the creation of employment opportunities. Despite the continuing high level of need, humanitarian emergency assistance is being phased out in favour of longer-term development programmes, although these currently remain rather vaguely defined. UNAMSIL and many aid organizations have withdrawn or are likely to do so soon. On 31 March 2004, the UN Security Council unanimously voted to 'scale down the size of the peacekeeping force to a residual presence'. This was despite its analysis of the peace in Sierra Leone and the West African region as a whole remaining fragile, and its assumption that the Government of Sierra Leone (GoSL) was unable to guarantee security. This had a severely destabilizing effect on the fragile Sierra Leonean economy and state of governance. In the medium term, much depends on the regional peace process, in particular the future of Liberia, Côte d'Ivoire and Guinea.

In this chapter we have presented the political and historical background to the war in Sierra Leone and discussed its root causes. In the process, we introduced the key national and international actors and discussed their role and interests within the war, its eventual resolution and the present peace. Our objective was to indicate the complexity of the war and the environment in which the British aid intervention took place, which is important to the analysis of the appropriateness of the aid effort that follows. This is essential to the identification of reasons for the difficulties encountered during the intervention (or for the continuation of the conflict). We have shown that aid became a key resource in a resource-starved environment. While it played an essential role in temporarily containing the violence and kick-starting the peace process, aid alone was not sufficient to buy stability and peace. The provision of aid was not sufficient to address the root causes of the war and the temporary imposition of aid conditionality was (and remains) ineffective in holding Sierra Leonean leaders accountable and preventing the potential resurgence of the war.

We also discussed several primary causes of the war, in particular the state of governance and Sierra Leone's dependency on the influx of external assistance (for both security and aid). We discussed the popular legitimacy of various governments and local leaders and the role played by a vibrant regional war economy throughout the conflict. Cross-border resource extraction enabled rival factions to finance the war, and much of the Sierra Leonean population continues to have a high personal stake in upholding these paralegal (economic) structures and quite possibly in instability and weak governance. It also remains doubtful whether the current restructuring programmes can successfully create alternative sources of employment and resource accumulation. We also discussed the roles of the military and paramilitary forces (including foreign PMCs). Rogue elements of the SLA played a significant destructive role throughout the war, and the relationship between the armed forces and the government remains strained. Despite the UK Government's extensive efforts to reform the SLA, its role remains a potential cause for concern. The UN's encompassing recovery programme provided the framework for targeted donor assistance and the rebuilding of Sierra Leone.

British Government analysis of the root causes of war in complex emergencies has not been consistent. The British Government has cherry-picked apparently relevant approaches from academic debates on the causes of conflict but disregarded inconsistencies. It is inappropriate either to generalize the causes of conflict globally or to draw from this example equally generic approaches to international intervention. Instead, effective policy should be based on individual country conflict assessments.

Last but not least, we discussed the often-cited phenomena of violence and brutality as a defining feature of the war. Large parts of the Sierra Leonean population have been traumatized, some of them as perpetrators of violence. Not only does this make national reconciliation, reintegration and recovery tremendously difficult, but it also puts the ongoing peace process at risk. Too many people are falling through the safety net of ongoing recovery programmes, and there are simply too few remaining alternative employment opportunities. Formerly marginalized groups remain marginalized and are only slowly beginning to play a political role. The absence of representative government was a primary cause of the war. Once again this has become a focus of public discontent, now fuelled by the memory of more than 10 years of civil war.

Chapter 4 evaluates the British humanitarian engagement in Sierra Leone in greater detail, focusing on its interaction with local governance structures (and the extent of local ownership) and with international aid providers. This enables us to compare New Humanitarianism as formulated at the policy level in London and as applied in Sierra Leone. In other words, we assess the coherence of New Humanitarianism as a consistent British humanitarian emergency strategy. Together, Chapters 2–4 facilitate an assessment of the British (aid) intervention and in particular the effectiveness of emergency assistance.

4
Pax Britannica: New Humanitarianism in Sierra Leone

Introduction

In the previous chapter we analysed the complex nature of the war in Sierra Leone and discussed the roles of external actors and aid in fuelling or mitigating the war. Our aim was to investigate the context in which British aid was granted and to discuss its appropriateness to the case of Sierra Leone. In this chapter we discuss the application of New Humanitarianism to Sierra Leone between 1997 and 2003. We first introduce the contents and scope of the British relief intervention. We also discuss broader aspects of the British intervention to the extent they impacted upon emergency assistance. We then explore the current governance structures in Sierra Leone and their impact on, and relationship with, humanitarian emergency aid. In particular, we evaluate the level of ownership and control exercised by the Government of Sierra Leone (GoSL). We conclude the chapter with a discussion of the significance of humanitarian emergency assistance operations within the overall British engagement in Sierra Leone. Our primary objective in this chapter is to establish the extent to which the British engagement in Sierra Leone drew on and promoted the concept of New Humanitarianism, as a contribution to our overall assessment of the policy's coherence. We also assess the feasibility and effectiveness of emergency assistance in promoting conflict management and development.

A British Marshall Plan for Sierra Leone

Between 1998 and 2003, the UK's aid commitments to Sierra Leone totalled £40 million per year on average. This figure does not include the UK's own military expenditure, logistics support (including arms, etc.) and training for the Sierra Leonean armed forces, or indeed its contributions to UN peacekeeping operations, which would make it significantly higher.[1] Following the Abuja Ceasefire Agreement in November 2000, the UK embarked on a comprehensive and (relative to its other commitments in Africa) disproportionate peace-building and development programme. The majority of the budget for Sierra Leone was drawn from the interdepartmental Africa Conflict Prevention Fund. 'As a result of the scale of its investment in Sierra Leone, the UK's ability to finance conflict prevention and reduction work in other parts of Africa has been reduced'.[2] However, relative to its engagement in some other regions, in particular the Middle East, the British financial commitment in Sierra Leone remained comparatively small.[3]

The British intervention in Sierra Leone emphasized the restoration of peace and security as prerequisites for reconciliation, good governance and development. The British humanitarian relief programme spanned all three phases of emergency relief in parallel: emergency, rehabilitation and post-conflict rehabilitation (development).[4] Traditional emergency assistance accounted for only a fraction of the overall British engagement in Sierra Leone in financial terms, particularly in relation to the military engagement.[5] Yet even the rudimentary stabilization of war-torn communities through the influx of urgently required basic commodities and capital proved essential to the continuation of the peace process. Following an initial focus on humanitarian emergency relief, the UK concentrated on the reform of the security sector and a broad community reintegration and capacity building programme. The latter, situated between developmental humanitarian emergency assistance, development assistance and peace-building programmes, was an expression of the merging of relief and development and demonstrated the UK Government's belief in the continuum concept. The UK Government played a central role in retraining and rearming the Sierra Leonean army. Within that framework, it exported large quantities of so-called 'small arms and light weapons' to a country that was regarded as highly unstable at the time.[6]

Given its sheer breadth, the UK intervention is unique inasmuch as it attempted holistically – and in many cases almost unilaterally – to address all aspects of post-war peace-building and reconstruction.

It is an example of an interdepartmental, joined-up though not trouble-free endeavour. Despite the fact that sustainable change in Sierra Leone is not forthcoming, the UK should be complimented for making such a uniquely generous and comprehensive commitment. The British intervention and longer-term political and financial commitment to the rebuilding of Sierra Leone were crucial in stopping the fighting and in initiating and maintaining international donor interest. Between 1997 and 2004, the UK supported (or led) programmes in Sierra Leone in several areas.

First, in security, the UK initially supported the UN-led process of disarmament, demobilisation and reintegration (DDR) but later withdrew from it. Instead, it established a British-run community reintegration programme and invested in a similar programme run by the German Agency for Technical Cooperation. The UK Government has also supported the restructuring and training of the Sierra Leone armed forces, provided budgetary and logistic support for selected ministries, re-established and trained the police force (in parallel with a partly overlapping UN programme since 2003), and played a role in the creation of a politically neutral intelligence service (again in cooperation with the UN).

Secondly, the UK has supported improved governance. It provided budgetary and personnel support for the establishment and maintenance of an anti-corruption commission. DFID seconded its staff to various Sierra Leonean ministries to build the capacity of the civil administration to provide public services and manage community-based programmes. It supported the re-establishment of district and local authorities (through Paramount Chiefdoms, decentralization and infrastructure rebuilding programmes). It also provided technical and logistic assistance to the National Election Commission in its conduct of the national and district electoral process in 2002 and 2004.

Thirdly, the UK has supported humanitarian and development programmes. Measures taken included assistance in humanitarian emergency assistance and rehabilitation, and support for the Community Reintegration Programme (CRP), civil society capacity building, and the rebuilding of the country's infrastructure.

Finally, the UK has played a key role in re-establishing the judicial system, including rebuilding of the basic judicial infrastructure, and it has also provided limited support for the Truth and Reconciliation Commission and the Special Court.[7]

We were unable to differentiate clearly between humanitarian emergency assistance and development aid in our examination of British-sponsored aid programmes in Sierra Leone. There were three reasons for this – over and above the *a priori* difficulty of providing a clear definition of emergency assistance. First, a lengthy transition period from humanitarian emergency assistance to development led to a blurring of the line between the different types of aid intervention. This was exacerbated by the attempts of most donors to establish their own bilateral relationships with the GoSL (while maintaining quasi-independent humanitarian assistance programmes) and to implement livelihood and developmental relief programmes. Secondly, the weakness of national and local governance structures obliged the British Government and the humanitarian agencies charged with implementing its policies to maintain control over social service programmes or establish parallel, quasi-privatized health and social welfare systems. Thirdly, the breadth and assertiveness of the overall British engagement (in particular its military presence and its role as an actor within the recent war) had an important impact on aid interventions, both in reality and in public perception. The co-option of New Humanitarianism into British foreign policy formed its very essence, just as the wider British intervention in Sierra Leone rested on the UK's commitment to a broad programme of emergency assistance and state building. For this reason, we focus in this chapter on an assessment of the UK's humanitarian emergency assistance policy in Sierra Leone, while also introducing other aspects of the British intervention that directly impacted upon or grew out of the initial relief intervention.

Emergency assistance

Following the coup against President Kabbah in June 1997, DFID suspended the direct funding of all British NGO-supplied humanitarian emergency assistance to Sierra Leone. It did not suspend its contribution to ECHO, which continued to work in the country. ECHO's budget, though, fell to 3.7 million Ecus (European Currency Units) for 1997, and 6.5 million in 1998, representing the two smallest ECHO budgets of the period 1993–2002. The resumption of British emergency assistance was made conditional upon the restoration of the elected government.[8] Initially, DFID cited the risk to aid workers as its primary reason for suspending its emergency assistance. Subsequently, 'DFID claimed that the provision of relief and negotiations for humanitarian access would legitimize the illegal regime'. Later on, DFID claimed that 'NGOs were unable to prevent the diversion and looting of humanitarian supplies'.[9] Later that summer, DFID played down agencies' warnings of an impending crisis, blaming aid agencies for abusing the situation in order to maximize organizational gain. However, Sierra Leone experienced serious shortfalls in emergency assistance throughout the 1990s.

Successive Sierra Leonean governments as well as donors had colluded in tolerating the misappropriation of relief supplies and the failure to make adequate assessments of humanitarian need was never challenged.[10] 'During the period of May 1997 to March 1998, the volume of funding available for humanitarian activities fell sharply'.[11] The UK Parliamentary Select Committee for International Development subsequently discussed this suspension and the allegation that DFID had withheld humanitarian emergency assistance from Sierra Leone in order to pressure the rebels to reinstate the ousted Sierra Leonean Government. Although the case was later dropped, and no further action was taken regarding the suspension of relief and apparent application of political conditionality to the granting of humanitarian aid, the Select Committee criticized the UK Government for its humanitarian emergency assistance policy in 1997/98.[12] Despite continued widespread insecurity, the UK resumed and increased its humanitarian programme in March 1998 following President Kabbah's return to power. In so doing, it acted against its own previous line of reasoning that no effective humanitarian emergency assistance was deliverable in the presence of violence and instability. The provision of emergency assistance in these years proved extremely difficult, and deeply traumatic for many emergency staff.

> January 1999 saw the consequences of the politicisation of humanitarian action that had been encouraged and indeed driven by senior figures in the Government of Sierra Leone, donors and the UN figures in Conakry. After the RUF had entered Freetown in January 1999, several NGO and ICRC staff were verbally and physically abused by ECOMOG soldiers, and accused of helping the rebels to enter the capital. The Government of Sierra Leone publicly repeated this allegation.[13]

Prior to the signing of the 2001 peace agreement and the 2002 elections, few new humanitarian aid agencies had entered Sierra Leone. Several had suspended their operations during the war. Many NGOs had reorientated their existing programmes to reflect the changing levels of security and donor interest. This led to a concentration of aid agencies in the south and west of the country. 'Access was the major constraint on humanitarian assistance, due to insecurity. The situation throughout the country was made more complicated by poor discipline in the army. There were regular reports of the diversion of aid supplies in rebel-held areas'.[14] Prior to the 2002 election and the deployment of UNAMSIL's troops throughout the country, most humanitarian NGOs followed UNAMSIL as it entered rebel-controlled areas.

Apart from the military intervention, the greater part of the British engagement throughout these years and in the immediate post-conflict phase was administered through humanitarian emergency assistance personnel and budget lines. The bureaucratic structures and processes of humanitarian emergency assistance agencies provided a greater degree of flexibility and donor independence than more developmental structures could have done. Humanitarian funds were more flexible and could be dispersed comparatively rapidly and with minimal bureaucratic oversight. Also, they could be reallocated more easily from one project line to the next. At the same time, they lacked predictability, and many agencies were reluctant to cooperate closely with the GoSL. The GoSL's lack of authority over rural areas and the high degree of insecurity severely challenged the delivery of aid, and it also restricted GoSL agenda setting and undermined developmental relief approaches.

Following the cessation of violence and the 2002 elections, both the GoSL and the donor community were eager to strengthen the fragile peace by ensuring immediate improvements in security and the provision of social services. They were also eager to minimize their financial responsibility for humanitarian programmes, broaden the donor base and the range of available funding mechanisms, hold the GoSL to prior agreements and make it more accountable for good governance. This was despite the perception that Sierra Leone still required substantial levels of primary assistance on account of the widespread destruction of its basic infrastructure. It was also despite a continuing lack of absorptive capacity, a substantial brain drain affecting all parts of the country and the inability of the GoSL to implement public policy effectively. Since the government's publication of the 2002/2003 National Recovery Strategy and Poverty Reduction Strategy Paper (PRSP), implementing agents have been held responsible for meeting the government's recovery benchmarks. Already in mid-2003, there was a shortage of emergency funding, and development aid allocations were slow to materialize. While more international NGOs than ever were present in Sierra Leone, the overall level of funding was considerably lower than it was previously.

In February 2003, the Governments of the United Kingdom and Sierra Leone committed themselves to a 10-year partnership development programme. Between 2003 and 2005, the agreement committed the UK to maintaining its extraordinary support for the stability and rebuilding of Sierra Leone. Until 2005, the UK was obliged to provide at least £120 million in development assistance, of which £40 million was dedicated to humanitarian assistance and civil society development programmes.[15] In return, the GoSL must display real progress in terms of governance and regional development; progress that was to fulfil a wide range of mutually agreed benchmarks that were to be evaluated annually. The two countries' close bilateral relationship and the assertiveness of the British engagement provided the UK Government with a substantial degree of political and programmatic freedom, but it has also increased its own financial and political burden. Other international donors avoided providing significant support for the GoSL. By 2004, the UK Government depended politically on progress in Sierra Leone and the continuation and strengthening of the peace process. This reality and the perception thereof contributed to the UK's loss of leverage over the GoSL's progress in implementing significant reform. The United Kingdom had committed itself to rebuilding the country and supporting the Kabbah Government. As such, both politically and rhetorically, it had accepted (and promoted) Kabbah's legitimacy and sovereignty. Ian Stuart, the DFID's First Secretary in Sierra Leone until 2004, suggested that it had been hoped that the Memorandum of Understanding concluded between the UK and the GoSL would increase the UK's ability to hold the GoSL accountable.[16] He also suggested, however, that it would be difficult, if not impossible, for the UK to withdraw in case of non-compliance.[17] Furthermore, the former

British High Commissioner, Alan Jones, argued that a British withdrawal, or the threat thereof, would have a serious impact on the donor community and operations in Sierra Leone in general, leading to a mass withdrawal. This might well lead to a resurgence of violence.

Throughout the war and the immediate post-war period, DFID's humanitarian priorities lay in the provision of basic services (in particular primary health services and shelter). Subsequently, DFID encouraged humanitarian agencies to integrate rights and rural empowerment strategies within their humanitarian aid programmes, such as CARE's rights-based approach and the 2003 rural capacity building programme developed in cooperation with Action Aid. Yet, despite New Humanitarianism's rights-based language, in Sierra Leone DFID merely latched on to such rights and capacity building programmes, rather than driving them forward.

In a confidential interview, a senior British Government official stated that, in principle, humanitarian emergency assistance in Sierra Leone was not burdened with political conditions as long as it did not jeopardize other wider peace-building and recovery objectives.[18] The integration of humanitarian emergency assistance programmes with wider political objectives was hampered by the UK Government's decision not to make public a clear and transparent policy on Sierra Leone. Up to 2005, DFID did not publish a humanitarian strategy paper on Sierra Leone. DFID does not generally produce strategy papers for countries that are primarily regarded as recipients of humanitarian assistance, so by 2005 there was no single public comprehensive document articulating DFID's aims, objectives and strategy in this field.[19]

As already discussed in Chapter 2, British New Humanitarianism, in particular its ten principles and the integration of humanitarian emergency assistance into peace-building objectives, was developed as the crisis in Sierra Leone was unfolding. The British response must be seen as a test case for future policy development. The 'vagueness of the UK policy response . . . [both with regard to the principles of New Humanitarianism and the unfolding policy in Sierra Leone] . . . must be understood in the shifting context and lessons of Sierra Leone'.[20] 'The policy experiment in Sierra Leone illustrates that human rights concerns may override "purely" humanitarian concerns and lead to a situation where the provision of relief becomes conditional upon "good government" [previously reserved for development aid]'.[21]

However, this test case also showed that as of 2004, the UK Government lacked the appropriate mechanisms to integrate humanitarian emergency assistance effectively into wider political strategies or to implement and uphold conditionality. In the case of British humanitarian emergency assistance to Sierra Leone between 1997 and 2003, the UK Government placed wider policy conditions on humanitarian assistance, albeit inconsistently and arguably reluctantly.

New Humanitarianism and the mechanism of humanitarian conditionality were meant to contribute to improving the livelihood of the population, by addressing not only emergency needs but also a medium to longer-term structural need for change. The previous suspension of humanitarian assistance must be interpreted as an effort to implement humanitarian political conditionality: democratic reform was set as a condition for the restoration of humanitarian emergency assistance. It was relatively quickly withdrawn. Instead, the British Government selectively chose relief programmes that were consistent with its overall foreign policy programme, while also outsourcing developmental relief projects to a tightly controlled private service contractor.

In summary, the humanitarian emergency programme represented only a fraction of Britain's overall engagement in Sierra Leone, and it was subject to political objectives from the outset. Later on, implementing partners were encouraged to integrate rights and governance features within their humanitarian strategy. Overall humanitarian assistance remained reactive.

Reintegration, reconciliation and reconstruction

The UK has supported two large-scale reconciliation and reconstruction programmes: its own Community Reintegration Project (CRP), outsourced to a private service provider, Agrisystems, and the ReACT programme operated by the Deutsche Gesellschaft für Technische Zusammenarbeit (GTZ). 'Both of these provide[d] community reintegration activities in the form of job opportunities and short term skill training and education, with ex-combatants working alongside other war-affected people.'[22] Both were essential components of the immediate peace dividend; they were intended to encourage combatants to give up their weapons and reintegrate into society, and to encourage society to accept them. Following widespread criticism regarding the UK's focus on security sector reform and the limits of CRP, in 2003 DFID commissioned research on civil society and community governance in Sierra Leone. This followed two primary approaches to local capacity building and rights issues. The first favoured prioritizing the reform of national governance structures. The second emphasized the need to strengthen civil society at the local level and enable communities to hold national political structures accountable. Until 2004, DFID was not willing to become engaged at the micro level and address political accountability issues. Instead, it addressed macro issues (such as the establishment of judicial structures, the building of court houses, etc.).[23] The British approach changed in 2004 as DFID became more involved in community-based social programmes and additional funds became available following the 2003 ratification of the UK/Sierra Leone Memorandum of Understanding.

In order to pour much-needed resources into local communities, CRP focused on initiating projects rather than monitoring their positive, accountable and sustainable impact. It maximized output with minimal organizational spending. Many of the projects have since been terminated, indicating a lack of local ownership and sustainability. According to other international humanitarian/development organizations, by 2003 CRP proved highly inflexible in operating beyond its own narrow project lines. It would neither cooperate with other humanitarian and development organizations nor adopt longer-term participatory approaches. Nor did it address any gender, rights or capacity building issues in a meaningful way.[24] Under strong pressure to spend its budget (to justify continued financial appropriations and fulfil output conditions) and rather removed from the policymaking authorities (despite strict DFID reporting requirements), CRP was both required and tempted to set strategic objectives, and to develop and amend policy as it went along, rather than acting in accordance with a clear, medium-term strategic concept.[25] The donor-imposed restructuring processes in Sierra Leone had encouraged the creation or extension of private monopolies. Given the limited local capacity to execute and administer projects, and in order to speed up project implementation, CRP repeatedly financed identical local and international private companies. Many of these were administered from Freetown or even from abroad, with little community participation.[26] In another confidential interview with DFID personnel in London, it was argued that within the next policy appraisal planning and assessment will be taken much more seriously and expectations are likely to be much greater. Possibly, this implies a much stricter future relationship between the UK and the GoSL.[27]

Because of its cooperation with traditional local authorities and local strongmen, CRP was criticized for sustaining local patronage networks and for reinforcing private monopolies. CRP was also criticized for promoting local competition and thus encouraging conflict by injecting resources into a resource-starved environment with few accountability checks and balances. Despite the approach's obvious shortcomings and the continued lack of governmental capacity to administer programmes at the district or community level, the programme played an important role in kick-starting local development programmes and upholding the peace. The World Bank and multilateral donors have maintained a similar approach to community development.

In contents and approach, developmental humanitarian emergency assistance and community development projects were similar. Both were primary aspects of the British wider relief policy.

Security and Security Sector Reform

Ever since the 1996 elections and, in particular, since the signing of the Lomé Agreement in 1999, the UK has been incrementally and extensively involved in restructuring the security sector in Sierra Leone. Ever since independence, and especially throughout the recent decade of war, the Sierra Leonean army and civil militias have been at the core of the political and military conflict. The Sierra Leone Security Sector Reform Programme (SILSEP) is one of the most comprehensive donor-driven security sector restructuring efforts. The programme assists the GoSL in improving the governance of the military and intelligence services, strengthening civilian oversight and control, and improving the armed forces' effectiveness. The security sector reform programme in Sierra Leone has six main objectives.

First, it is necessary to strengthen the supremacy of civilian control over the armed forces. This involves instituting changes to the law and a restructuring of the civil and defence administrations. Secondly, the Sierra Leonean military must be transformed into a reliable and

efficient army that effectively upholds security and does not constitute a threat to the civilian government. This involves facilitating
change both within the army as an institution and also in individual personnel's approach to, and perception of, their duties and
rights. Thirdly, the various military and militia groups and previous
recruitment clusters are to be integrated into one unified, effective
Sierra Leonean army with broadly similar levels of training. Fourthly,
the overall size and structure of the armed forces are to be reduced.
Fifthly, standards of discipline and training are to be improved
and poorly qualified soldiers or potentially troublesome personnel
removed. Finally, accountability to civilian authorities and transparency – with regard to human resources (including promotions),
planning, management and budgeting – are to be increased.

The Sierra Leone Army (SLA) has undergone a retraining and
restructuring programme operated by the International Military
Advisory Training Team (IMATT).[28] The overall programme was
an example of a joined-up government by DFID (with a primary
focus on the support and restructuring of the Sierra Leonean armed
forces and the police), the MoD (giving advice on defence management and assuming responsibility for training and equipment)
and the FCO. DFID also provided support for a 3-year Commonwealth Community Safety and Security Project, which focused on
community policing as an essential aspect of security sector reform
(and in parallel to ongoing UNAMSIL-led efforts to support the
police services). The British-led effort followed the GoSL/UN-led
Disarmament, Demobilisation and Reintegration Programme (DDR),
which began in 1998.

The British security sector reform programme was deeply embedded
within the UK's overall engagement in, and approach to, Sierra Leone:
the conduct and progress of each programme directly affected the
others. The British Government assumes that inefficient, repressive or
corrupt security structures threaten the stability and independence of
governments and undermine peace processes, and that security and
stability are 'an essential condition for sustainable development'[29] and
an important area of interest and engagement for DFID.[30] In following
these assumptions, the UK Government is not alone. Throughout
the late 1990s, security sector reform has become an important
element of Northern (Western-European or North-American)
peace-building, development aid and good governance policies.[31]

By 2004, there were perceptible improvements in the effectiveness and behaviour of the armed forces. The SLA has never been better trained or equipped than it is today. Up to January 2004, there had been no bloodletting of the armed forces following the restoration of the elected government on the scale that had been seen on similar occasions in the past. It is only after the withdrawal of UNAMSIL and the UK-led IMATT, however, that it will be possible to judge the success or failure of the security sector restructuring process. If the definition of success in this case is simply the absence of failure, then early indications of progress achieved are nevertheless problematic. What remains uncertain is whether the restructuring and retraining have been merely cosmetic (in which case the UK may simply have trained the perpetrators of a future coup), or whether lasting change really has been achieved. There are many reasons to suggest that the recent changes may be seriously threatened, if not reversed, once the foreign troops are withdrawn, unless there is a substantial improvement of the economy and a strengthening of the civil administration.

From the very beginning, the programme has been plagued by problems and inconsistencies. The SILSEP leadership was obliged to compromise with the previous military leadership in order to secure the continued support of the GoSL and the SLA. As a consequence, the army has been only partially reformed. Effective civilian authority over the security forces remains weak at the local level, and there is still a high level of mutual distrust. Many of the former soldiers who revolted against civilian rule, or who were recruited into the army for political reasons, still remain within its ranks. Many continue to believe in entitlement and in their superiority over the civilian population. Many are deeply suspicious of the current government and the reform process. Others continue to feel bitter about civilians' distrust of the armed forces. Not all of them accept partial responsibility for the war crimes committed during the war, and many are too well established to accept the changes required of them in terms of behaviour, perception, training and strategy. Young recruits, in contrast, many of whom had considerably greater combat experience than their seniors, had to undergo a much more rigorous and competitive recruitment process. Variations in levels of training and differing perceptions of the armed forces' role and responsibilities will continue to disrupt the army's conduct, and they may well lead to conflict both within its own ranks and between the army and the government. These developments may eventually overturn the effects of recent progress in training once the international framework is withdrawn.

The relatively large financial allocations devoted to the reform of the security forces were met with an element of distrust, antagonism and competition from other parts of the GoSL, civil society and the international aid community. Given the country's high level of unemployment and the lack of employment opportunities (outside the military) and overall administrative capacity, the large external appropriations to the armed forces – which were seen as a primary cause of the instability and fighting – were met with envy and dismay. Some civilians and aid workers accused these programmes' funders of training and providing a welfare system for past and future killers.[32] Effectively, the system set up a two-tier society: those who were part of the armed forces or the restructuring programmes (and therefore had opportunities to access money, jobs and training) and those who were not. So far, neither the DDR process nor the British security sector reform programme has sufficiently addressed the problems of those former soldiers who were not integrated into the new armed forces, or of the large group of people dependent on or having been affected by the army (such as child soldiers, families, and women and boys pressed into marriage or prostitution). Up to 2003, many discharged soldiers remained trapped in Freetown. They were unable to return home to their original communities because they had been destroyed; because they were unable to find (or take on) alternative local employment; or because they feared retribution for atrocities committed during the war.

> The British . . . took on the task of creating a new model army, properly trained, equipped and motivated, and also properly paid. But whether the country will be able to afford such an army after the British have left and aid support declines is an open question. It seems almost inevitable that the forces of law and order, commanding cheap modern firepower in an impoverished country rich in readily exploitable mineral resources, will be tempted once again to 'live off the land', if and when government funding becomes tight.[33]

The Security Sector Reform Programme is not an aspect of New Humanitarianism. It has, however, had an important impact, both negative and positive, on the local perception of the overall British engagement and aid operations in general. The British military presence and its work with the Sierra Leonean armed forces were crucial in establishing security and a sense of stability throughout the country. As such, it facilitated access to vulnerable communities and allowed humanitarian emergency assistance programmes to take effect. Indirectly, it may have increased aid agencies' political strength vis-à-vis the GoSL. On the other hand, and especially during the early post-war phase, aid agencies suffered from being implicated by the military forces. Cooperation with the military, and possibly even with the British Government or its field presence (both being parties to the war), may have put aid agencies' workers at risk as they were not perceived as neutral and impartial. Most importantly, in financial and political terms, British support for the restructuring of the security sector was disproportionately larger than any other aspect of its engagement. Many aspects of the overall British intervention would have benefited from a more balanced approach involving greater local ownership.

Governance

DFID is assisting the GoSL in strengthening its individual departments and consolidating democratic authority in a number of ways. First, it pays the salaries of key workers in the social and security services, providing additional security expenditure and logistics, and assisting the GoSL in bridging delays in donor funding disbursement. Secondly, it pays for consultants to be seconded as advisers to government departments and to The National Commission for Social Action (NaCSA). Thirdly, it assists in the restoration and strengthening of legal institutions, in particular in the updating of the legal code, staff training and the rebuilding of the judicial infrastructure. Fourthly, it has supported the creation and management of an Anti-Corruption Commission, with a British Deputy Commissioner and a small team of consultants on secondment. Fifthly, it supports media capacity building and provides a limited amount of equipment for efficient reporting. Finally, it is supporting the re-establishment of local authorities by creating a mechanism and support package to enable Paramount Chiefs to return to their communities (the Paramount Chief Project) and is also assisting in decentralization.

Despite large-scale donor support there has been very limited progress in improving the country's governance, and this has led to increasing donor fatigue. There is fear among the population that things have returned to 'business as usual', with unaccountable, corrupt and undemocratic public offices and an apathetic donor community that is more interested in containment than in achieving real change. According to the International Crisis Group, there has not been significant progress in governance reforms since the elections in May 2002.[34] Nor is there is any systematic plan for decentralization. The DFID-supported Paramount Chief Programme has been fraught with inconsistencies and miscalculations. Elections for Paramount Chiefs and local by-elections took place in 2003/2004, but the system remains tainted by its origin in the colonial politics of 'divide and rule' and the fact that most Paramount Chiefs are government appointees. Areas outside the capital, Freetown, remain essentially isolated: government ministers rarely venture out into rural areas (such visits are sometimes difficult simply for logistical reasons) and local residents have few options to hold their representatives to account.

The British engagement in support of good governance was an important aspect of policy coherence and, most importantly, political leverage over the GoSL. Aid organizations drew on the UK Government's political support when their own negotiations with the GoSL over access and funding issues had broken down.[35]

Justice

The GoSL and the international donor community have set up two mechanisms to promote reconciliation and to bring those responsible for war crimes to justice. The UK Government has supported both, but has not taken on a leadership role to the same extent as in the other programmes.[36] The Truth and Reconciliation Commission (TRC) is intended to encourage post-conflict reconciliation through public displays of disclosure and admission. It also provides a forum for debating issues (regarding the conflict, rights and governance) that citizens deem essential to the national reconciliation process and the rebuilding of Sierra Leone. The Special Court 'seeks to punish those identified as responsible for the brutality of the war . . . and to buttress national security by removing from circulation those who are in a position to destabilise the state'.[37] It focuses on pursuing those bearing the greatest responsibility for war crimes. By mid-2003, neither exercise had received broad support from Sierra Leonean society. This was primarily a reflection of the public's confusion concerning the two institutions' distinct objectives and the level of cooperation between them. It also indicates, however, that both were mainly regarded within the country as exercises in donor politics. This perception was also fostered by their non-transparent staffing procedures and continued wrangling for positions and exchange of personnel. Funding problems have hampered the TRC in particular since its inception. The initial indictments of senior government figures such as the former Minister of Internal Affairs and leader of the CDF, Samuel Hinga Norman, attracted considerable public unrest. It remains to be seen, however, how the GoSL fares in the face of possible prosecutions of other senior members closer to the core of the Sierra Leonean People's Party (SLPP). It will also have to be seen whether these mechanisms will foster reconciliation and reintegration or lead instead to frustration on account of the continued impunity of perpetrators of atrocious violence.

In Chapter 3 we analysed the protracted and complex nature of the war in Sierra Leone, and this chapter has outlined the principal areas of the British intervention in Sierra Leone. We now discuss the state of governance within Sierra Leone, focusing on the role of aid within local politics and the degree of local ownership of the international aid intervention. The analysis that follows will contribute to our overall evaluation of New Humanitarianism's effectiveness in Sierra Leone and its level of coherence and stability.

Maintaining the myth of progress

Sierra Leone has undergone not one, but a series of violent conflicts. Each of these had its own roots in internal political dynamics: the breakdown of public services, the spreading of a regional shadow economy, and regional and international interventions. The complexity of the wars both reflected and exacerbated the problem of governance: the inability to secure and redistribute the resources required to establish and uphold the state's legitimacy, and to build and maintain efficient public administration and provision of social services. In the previous section we discussed the British intervention in Sierra Leone and the particular role of humanitarian emergency assistance. Significantly, most aid was administered outside local government structures. We now analyse the nature of governance in Sierra Leone between 1997 and 2003 in as much as it is relevant to humanitarian aid policies. Until 2004, the GoSL did not have sufficient and sufficiently effective means to set policy priorities or to manage external aid appropriations. This inhibited humanitarian emergency assistance and undermined the transition to development. The inadequacy of governance in Sierra Leone had a direct harmful impact on the implementation of New Humanitarianism and other forms of external intervention.

Governance

Despite the transition to relative peace and stability culminating in the 2002 elections, Sierra Leone remains a 'quasi-state', that is a state 'whose capacity to govern its territory is compromised to a greater or lesser extent by a lack of resources and institutional failure'.[38] While the 2002 elections reconfirmed the formal structures of a democratic system, the stability of this democracy, the effective accountability of democratically elected politicians to the public and the rule of law all remain in doubt. Governance at all levels remains bedevilled by corruption and malpractice. Political and administrative power is centralized in the capital, and largely in the hands of a strong presidency. Both the judiciary and the legislature remain powerless, crippled by endemic corruption. Individual government departments, such as the Ministry of Development (MODEP) or the Finance Ministry, lack the infrastructure (administrative, financial and logistical) they need to set longer-term policy agendas, extend their control over rural areas and effectively execute programmes at the district or community levels.[39]

Although local elections were held in spring 2004, the credibility and effectiveness of local and regional representation is fragile at best. This is not a new development and is only partly a result of the war. Indeed, the population of rural areas has historically regarded the Central Government with a high degree of distrust. Historically, district councils provided the means by which the Central Government exercised control over rural areas, and it was the neglect of such areas that led to the outbreak of war.

In order to boost community rebuilding and capacity building, the GoSL established the National Commission for Social Action (NaCSA) in November 2001. It was originally set up to administer community reintegration projects in response to the partial completion of the demobilization and disarmament processes. It was also intended to complete the remaining tasks of the National Commission for Reconstruction, Resettlement and Rehabilitation (NCRRR). NaCSA was also responsible for overseeing donor-funded projects and helping to assure the transition from relief to development. Its objective was to prevent the 'loss' of donor funding in the gaping national deficit. Working like a social fund, NaCSA funded community projects that built physical and social capital. NaCSA was originally set up as a temporary body. Given its continuing disproportional empowerment, however, it is doubtful whether the government or the donors will ever be able fully to disband NaCSA and return influence to the appropriate departments of the GoSL's civil administration.

In some areas of heightened national and international political interest, NaCSA has assisted the establishment of District Recovery Committees in managing community-based capacity building programmes. These District Recovery Committees have proved rather more efficient than the individual departments of the central government. By working directly with communities in remote parts of the country, NaCSA was meant to support the GoSL's decentralization strategy and rebuild local governance structures. In practice, the individual government departments and NaCSA competed for capacity and responsibility. Information sharing and coordination proved fraught with difficulty, because of the lack of infrastructure (e.g., communication technology) and training, as well as political and organizational competition. In many cases, communities were overwhelmed by the need to administer resources accountably and to manage project implementation effectively. Just as in the cases of similar DFID-led programmes such as CRP, this has led to localized competition and increased corruption. The rural areas remain politically and economically marginalized by the political elite, which is concentrated in the capital. The GoSL is now caught between two seemingly contradicting policy agendas. On the one hand it is decentralizing and empowering the regions; on the other hand, it is extending its capacity to govern throughout the country and building administrative capacity and control.

At the local and district level in particular, traditional forms of leadership such as Chiefs and Paramount Chiefs continue to play dominant roles as political representatives and in the judiciary.[40] During the last 10 years, most Paramount Chiefs have fled to, or been drawn into, the capital and become associated with the national political networks. Their control over, and legitimate representation of, their districts has been weak. While they remain largely under the control of the Central Government, they are in the process of re-establishing themselves regionally. Local militias or defence forces, and the youth councils that were formed during the war, continue to retain some influence in rural areas. In some areas, youth councils had temporarily assumed administrative and/or political responsibility during the war. Some chiefs are now encouraging them to play a role in local politics, although their influence remains limited for the time being. As agents of the recent war and deeply fragmented bodies, the civil militias do not at the moment pose a positive alternative to political representation. Another historic source of local representation and authority that remains relevant (although vague) are the so-called 'Secret Societies' and the belief systems they advocate. Donors and emergency aid organizations have failed to tap into and work with these traditional forms of local leadership.

The underperformance of governmental institutions in Sierra Leone is less damaging in the longer term than the absence of a wider culture of democracy. The political culture is such that agreements and laws are simply temporary arrangements to which the parties will adhere while it is convenient to do so. Personalities, not policies or institutions, lie at the heart of political life. It was charismatic leaders that instigated the coups and rallied mass support throughout the 1990s. It is personal relationships and patronage networks that control personal behaviour and politics. Just as before the war, Sierra Leone displays all the symptoms of a neo-patrimonial state. 'Patrimonialism' is a political system that

> [i]nvolves redistributing national resources as marks of personal favour to followers who respond with loyalty to the leader rather than to the institution the leader represents. Relatively few resources are distributed according to principles of bureaucratic rationality or accountability.[41]

Neo-patrimonial states such as Sierra Leone display elements of modern state and administrative structures. State institutions are weak, however, with only limited formal responsibilities and working practices. They also tend to compete with one another over scarce resources (including budgetary and logistic allocations and trained personnel) and influence. Leaders ensure the loyalty of their subjects through material favouritism, by granting them access to government positions, contracts and licences, or by tolerating corruption and embezzlement. This façade-like official state is buttressed by external aid appropriations and revenues obtained from granting concessions for primary resource extraction. Securing such aid resources was, and still is, critical to the survival of the GoSL. The country remains heavily dependent on external aid to meet the shortfalls in public budgets.

In contrast, the bureaucracies of the modern Western democracies are generally characterized by clear hierarchies and individual responsibility. The private and professional spheres are clearly separate and bureaucratic processes and laws limit the authority of leaders. As a rule, staff are hired and promoted on the basis of competence and receive a fixed and regular income.

Politics and the war have generated pluralistic debate, but the majority of the population is still grappling with economic hardship and political and economic marginalization, and social groups and their political leaders have only partly come to terms with the notion that democracy involves participation in decision-making. Sierra Leoneans are tired of the war, which has not led to any substantial positive change or development apart from the enrichment of a small minority. Far from this, it has cost the country dearly. Nevertheless, it is uncertain whether civil society could resist a political reversal, or whether or when those groups that were instrumental in starting the war and remain marginalized will take up arms again and rally to the call of another charismatic leader. This is especially important, given the levels of disillusion with Western values as a result of frustration with the depth of socio-economic disarray and the flawed nature of the regimes that the West has repeatedly supported.

Implementing aid in a vacuum?

Development aid and developmental emergency assistance lack the legal, institutional and operational tools that are needed to engage effectively in such quasi-states. Aid is 'premised on the assumption that a benign, sovereign government is in place within the recipient country that has the legitimacy and the capacity to distribute aid resources' and set the political agenda.[42] Humanitarian emergency assistance is by nature short-lived. Short-term relief and recovery programmes are designed to provide primary care for people in need. They also supply the hardware that is needed to guarantee people's immediate survival (like drugs and basic shelter) when the structure of public services is either non-existent or incapable of providing adequate protection. Increasingly, developmental humanitarian assistance also provides basic training in, for example, food security and job development. Yet without the existence of stable political and administrative structures that can formulate medium- to long-term policy and guarantee and finance its implementation, such aid is inherently unsustainable. Effective public sector rebuilding and reform requires political priority setting and corresponding mechanisms for resource allocation and policy implementation. Humanitarian emergency organizations can train doctors, but they are not intended to rebuild the public health system. Emergency assistance can work in support of existing public structures, but it cannot easily be retrospectively transformed into a set of public service programmes and structures.

Given the weakness of the GoSL, humanitarian emergency assistance distributed until 2003 was almost entirely independent of governmental control. During the emergency phase of the war, the government just 'rubber-stamped' NGO activities. In the words of one humanitarian emergency assistance organization's country manager in Sierra Leone, 'the GoSL is 100 per cent under-funded and has got no meaningful management plan'. This exacerbated the political vacuum and policy impasse, as international support was being provided in a climate of considerable political uncertainty in which the GoSL was unable to manage external aid efficiently. Until 2004, the country relied on emergency assistance to sustain public services. In some sectors, humanitarian emergency projects inadvertently became the basis of public policy.

As a consequence, most humanitarian and development programmes implemented between 1997 and 2003 were donor driven. The provision of developmental emergency assistance allowed external actors to intervene in the affairs of the Sierra Leonean state without the consent and control of the domestic government and electorate. Whether as a result of scepticism regarding the efficiency and accountability of local decision-making bodies or as a deliberate policy designed to control the GoSL and aid programmes, bilateral donors frequently bypassed the official channels. In doing so they undermined their own efforts to coordinate aid programmes and strengthen national authority. Between 2000 and 2002, this encouraged an influx of international aid agencies, although Sierra Leone never attracted numbers comparable to other complex emergencies such as the Balkans. Even outside Sierra Leone, there has been a general trend since the late 1980s for international intervention to increase at the expense of absolute state sovereignty, and this process has been more noticeable in weak states and/or developing countries. In Sierra Leone there remains an acute power vacuum that no one seems willing or able to fill.

> Predominantly, the GoSL steps back and lets donors get on. This reinforces the lack of a strong political leadership driving the development agenda and therefore the lack of an integrated agenda, ownership and accountability. It remains unclear who is driving the process and it appears essentially unsustainable. This leaves an acute power vacuum, which again allows for corruption.... Right now, things function on a false premise of stability and capacity. This is reinforced by the donors' drive to push the process forward and show progress through symbolic action towards a development aid process. All money is cushioned on a false development structure and is inherently unsustainable.[43]

Working outside state structures and with minimal involvement from the GoSL is a feature of humanitarian aid and, to a large extent, all external engagement in Sierra Leone. As was clearly evident from all our interviews undertaken within Sierra Leone (irrespective of the type of international organization being interviewed), the relationship between the international service providers and the government has been marred by ignorance, distrust, a lack of transparency, hostility, corruption and competition. The staff of most agencies, donors and the United Nations described any cooperation with the government and its bureaucracy as 'intensely frustrating'.[44] This was despite the fact that, given the comparatively lean and easily accessible government bureaucracy, cooperation should in theory be relatively simple. Others mentioned that it 'required bulldozing through, otherwise there was no accountability and nothing happened'.[45] Some agencies mentioned that 'at times it required severe diplomatic pressure from the UK Government to pass things through and guarantee progress'.[46] Implementing agents were noticeably highly critical of, and frustrated with, the GoSL's capacity for effective management and cooperation. Some international humanitarian organizations even regarded it as their 'right' to work independently of an 'inherently corrupt, unaccountable and incapable administrative bureaucracy'.[47] As the provision of humanitarian emergency assistance is deemed a moral action, anything in its path is deemed immoral.[48] Others just dismissed the GoSL altogether, both from planning and management/implementation points of view.[49] By and large, most international NGOs throughout the emergency phase up to 2003 restricted themselves to informing the GoSL of their geographical and contextual area of work, rather than asking for its consent or preferences.[50] Donor preferences, levels of security and access, organizational expertise and perceived humanitarian needs were more important in determining their choice of projects and project areas than government strategy. Cooperation and coordination with the GoSL remain a contentious issue, something that is destined to worsen as the current transition phase deepens. Throughout our field research, the GoSL was unable (or unwilling) to provide an overview of the development and humanitarian funds available in Sierra Leone.

Characteristic of this fraught and sceptical aid relationship with local administrative structures is the habit (and at times the donor condition) of using expatriate personnel rather than local staff to administer donor-funded emergency and development aid projects. Only one UK-sponsored emergency and development aid NGO mentioned that DFID had posited such a condition; indeed several UK-funded projects and organizations are staffed exclusively by local personnel. Organizations funded by USAID or the US State Department, on the other hand, repeatedly mentioned such a donor condition.

Distrust of the GoSL's accountability is certainly not the only reason for the high number of expatriate staff that remain in aid organizations: expatriate salaries also represent essential income for aid organizations. According to some aid workers in Sierra Leone, between 30 and 90 per cent of all aid expenditure commonly flows back into the GDP of foreign countries through procurement, future contracts or staff salaries.

Another example of donor reluctance to trust and invest in local governmental capacity was the creation and maintenance of NaCSA. As an implementing management body, it has no power to set policy priorities and is being overwhelmed by the sheer number of projects for which it is responsible. Nevertheless, the majority of current recovery programmes are administered through NaCSA, international NGOs or other private service providers.[51]

Given its lack of capacity and dependency on external aid appropriations, the GoSL was initially eager to uphold this emergency state. Development aid flows more slowly than emergency assistance contributions and is more commonly subject to compliance with political conditions. However, the national and local administration of external aid appropriations absorbs vital state capacity in terms of personnel, logistics and even funding, none of which the GoSL can spare. Yet, given the relatively strong financial and policymaking influence of humanitarian emergency assistance organizations, the current government has increasingly attempted to regain control of external development aid since it was elected in 2002.

Just as it did before the war, the GoSL needs to have control over aid contributions in order to uphold and control public services, to make up for shortfalls in the state budget and to service its clientele. Since its election, the GoSL has made several futile attempts to regulate external assistance by creating various NGO coordination committees in the Ministry of Development (MoDEP) and NaCSA. Two examples of overlapping and unclear responsibility for NGO coordination are the National Recovery Commission (NRC) and the Development Assistance Coordination Office (DACO). The registration and taxation of international NGOs and MoDEP's attempts to assign geographical areas of responsibility, for example, have been a recurrent cause of conflict and confusion. This was aggravated by inter-departmental miscommunication and competition, in particular between the Finance and Development Ministries and NaCSA. Most personnel interviewed regarded GoSL's attempts at greater coordination and equitable distribution as attempts to control and exploit their efforts: 'It appears as if MODEP doesn't want our presence, but wants our money'. Interviewees also mentioned

that GoSL's requirements sometimes contradicted donor procedures and conditions, thereby putting continued assistance at risk.
A bi-weekly Inter-Agency Meeting provided a forum to coordinate
projects and programmes and to reach a common position regarding
GoSL's attempts to regulate humanitarian assistance. This enabled
agencies to maintain a strong lobby against any GoSL attempts to
increase its control. As the West African region continues to stabilize,
while humanitarian need remains exceptionally high in Liberia, Côte
d'Ivoire and, increasingly, Guinea, several international humanitarian agencies have withdrawn from Sierra Leone altogether or relo-
cated to neighbouring countries.

Joanna Macrae has analysed the way in which the international
policy move towards developmental relief and good governance has
led to a sudden collapse of basic welfare provisions in some states.
Donors increasingly blame states for the ineffective management of
social welfare and aid resources. In response they condition their
engagement on the fulfilment of good governance benchmarks and
decrease overall spending on the humanitarian emergency aid they
provide through NGOs. In doing so they increase the pressure on
already weak governments and may even bring about their collapse.[52]
Such a trend towards stricter donor control and conditionality was
clearly apparent in Sierra Leone in 2004.

Just as the development and relief industry has evolved into a
global network of institutions that increasingly incorporate (and may
even be dominated by) quasi-governmental and privatized or militar-
ized actors, the local governments emerging out of war may similarly
have been transformed into increasingly privatized networks operating beyond the realm of the state. Yet, international aid continues
to expect to work through and depend upon traditional, inclusive
state structures.

Ever since the presidential elections of 2002, the political situation and aid relationships in Sierra Leone have returned to 'business
as usual', while substantial or sustainable change has barely been
forthcoming. The large-scale, donor-driven reform and restructuring
programmes and the influx of international development money are
premised on the faulty assumption that the nation building process
will prove successful. This is based, in turn, on an assumption that

relatively small payments of humanitarian emergency aid and development aid will suffice to rebuild public service administrative structures, change the behaviour of public sector personnel, and breathe life into local economies. No such vision has materialized, and it is not likely to do so in the near future.

The relationships among emergency aid providers, their respective governments, rebel factions and donors after the war have all been determined instead by violence, insecurity, an acute lack of access to all those in need of assistance, and mutual distrust and competition. The political and administrative weakness and contested legitimacy of the GoSL also played important roles, since they further inhibited common agenda setting (or local ownership) and reinforced a culture of secrecy. This threatened to defeat donor reform objectives, and it also threatened sustainability. As a consequence, aid agencies and donors alike were encouraged and compelled to run their aid programmes in Sierra Leone independent of local control and on the basis of limited ownership. Furthermore, these developments encouraged the UK and the UN to support the restoration of previous governance structures – which had been a root cause of the war – rather than to invest in a process of identifying and building new authorities with a greater measure of legitimacy and public support. This is likely to threaten the stability and public legitimacy of the present administration and the peace process.

The nature of the war, Britain's historical position in relation to Sierra Leone and the GoSL's limited capacity to govern effectively have all prejudiced international aid programmes and their implementation. At the national level, public welfare and reconciliation are the responsibility of the state, yet many states, in particular quasi-states, are ill equipped to guarantee the provision of public services or facilitate the end of conflict constructively. For a brief period, international humanitarian emergency assistance can fulfil some of these functions and mitigate the worst effects of human need. Nonetheless, without a long-term political vision that also provides effective public structures and mechanisms, there can be no safeguards against future humanitarian crises. In such a case, a wider humanitarian policy approach to the benefit of conflict prevention will fail to make a lasting impact.

We now conclude this chapter with an assessment of the degree to which British humanitarian engagement in Sierra Leone drew on and contributed to the development of British New Humanitarianism. We also discuss the significance of humanitarian emergency assistance within the overall British intervention. Our aim is to evaluate New Humanitarianism's level of coherence, in terms of both its contents and the breadth of its application. This analysis will contribute to a study of its effectiveness.

Towards a common understanding of New Humanitarianism?

In mid-2003, as the war in Liberia escalated and – following the over-throw of President Charles Taylor – a solution suddenly seemed palpable, British objectives within the region began to shift. According to the desk officers for Sierra Leone at the FCO and DFID, the Mano River Union as a region had now become much more important than Sierra Leone itself.[53] At the same time, the UK became militarily engaged in Iraq, and the government's attention to wars in Africa was correspondingly reduced. UNAMSIL has withdrawn. The comprehensive British peace-building intervention in Sierra Leone was a product of both structural reforms within the British administration and bureaucratic processes. It was also a test case of, and trigger for, policy development.[54] As discussed above, both New Humanitarianism and the British engagement in Sierra Leone developed as DFID asserted itself, both internally and in relation to other government departments. It entered its second, post-conflict or development phase amidst an extensive restructuring of DFID and while Britain was struggling to redefine its global position in the light of the largely unpopular war in Iraq and growing electoral discontent with the Labour Government. The government's efforts in support of public–private partnerships for a wide range of social services and in strengthening the accountability of public services had come under scrutiny. Powerful political players including the Secretary of State for International Development, Clare Short, had resigned. She had been a driving figure in establishing and maintaining Britain's assertive engagement in Sierra Leone. Within Sierra Leone itself, the political and economic situation remained fragile, and sustainable change did not seem to be forthcoming.

The guiding principle of New Humanitarianism in Sierra Leone was that it was expected to address the worst excesses of humanitarian need and also fit into the broader objectives of British foreign policy. As such, it was intended to support the continuing process of peace and restructuring and contribute in the long term to overcoming the root causes of the war. Aid was utilized as an incentive for structural and democratic change. At the policymaking level, British New Humanitarianism had amounted to a vision of a more assertive, morally driven emergency assistance policy, despite its lack of clarity and detail. At the operational level, however, it fell far short of a coherent strategy. With the exception of the suspension of the temporary humanitarian emergency assistance, British policy did not consistently draw on the newly developed principles of New Humanitarianism. Neither was New Humanitarianism supported by the British policy implementation bureaucracy in Sierra Leone. As the most assertively and extensively engaged Western donor, the UK acted almost with impunity in Sierra Leone. It received only hesitant and weak support and political direction from the GoSL. Nonetheless, the UK was unable to bring about effective coordination of donors or humanitarian organizations. The British engagement in Sierra Leone must be understood as a work in progress – or better still as a policy process rather than a policy per se. According to everyone interviewed in the course of this study, the British Government made up rules and procedures as it went along. It did not deliver coherent and clear guidelines, nor did it transparently disseminate British policy objectives or hold implementing agents accountable to the principles of New Humanitarianism. Strategic, headquarters-driven policy guidance remained weak throughout.

The involvement of a large number of departments, and individuals from several of them, in the design and implementation of the British policy in Sierra Leone had important consequences for the programme's cohesion and transparency, and for its application to Sierra Leone. As discussed above, the British intervention in Sierra Leone had been a joint endeavour by several departments of the UK Government, in particular the FCO, DFID and MoD. Individual departments became responsible for implementing aspects of the programme, while DFID took the lead in administering the programme as a whole. A working group at Cabinet level and regular joint meetings were intended to ensure cross-departmental cooperation and exchange of information. Nevertheless, this separation of power, and competing and overlapping sets of responsibilities within

DFID itself, undermined a coherent interpretation of and approach to both the principles of New Humanitarianism and wider policy object-ives within Sierra Leone. 'Individual bureaucrats interpret differently the humanitarian principles laid out by the Secretary of State across the Department, reflecting not so much the different contexts, but rather the emphasis placed on the different elements'.[55] This also allowed for a degree of necessary and welcome flexibility. As a result, British policy on Sierra Leone, and its humanitarian policy in partic-ular, remained vaguely defined and reactive. The vagueness of New Humanitarianism and the British peace-building strategy in Sierra Leone, and the fragmentation of the bureaucratic implementation structure, further weakened coordination. As a result, humanitarian emergency assistance programmes in Sierra Leone were driven by DFID as an administrative umbrella organization. As long as it did not contradict British foreign policy objectives, humanitarian emer-gency assistance policy emerged by default through the process of programme implementation. This may be a necessary aspect of demo-cratic and even locally driven policymaking. Nonetheless, it calls into question the utility of humanitarian emergency assistance as a means of achieving wider political objectives.

As discussed above, the enormous task of providing emergency assistance to a distant clientele on behalf of local taxpayers is made possible by outsourcing it to a specialist bureaucracy. An ideal bureau-cracy has a clearly defined overall goal and is structured in specialist departments with clearly defined powers and the skills to achieve a clearly defined objective. The bureaucratic, administrative and polit-ical compromises that are reached in order to deal with short-term emergencies are incapable of generating broader and longer-term visions. With regard to British emergency assistance in Sierra Leone, the fragmentation of the aid bureaucracy undermined both policy and the clarity of its implementation. Its piecemeal outsourcing to specialist departments and implementing agents prohibited common agenda setting, policy interpretation and policy coordination. This was accentuated by the latent antagonism of some of the actors involved and, in particular, by the reluctance of humanitarian agents to be employed in pursuit of donor foreign policy objectives. Its short-to medium-term scope undermined long-term policy development.

Significantly, emergency assistance programmes were delivered outside formal state structures, largely through NGOs. Mark Duffield

and Joanna Macrae have described this trend as the 'internationaliz-
ation and privatization of public welfare, whereby responsibility for
the financing and provision of basic services has shifted from the
domain of national state structures to that of international NGOs'.[56]
With regard to British-sponsored aid in Sierra Leone, this trend
has solidified and slightly shifted: the provision of public welfare
programmes continues to be internationalized, but it is also being
commercialized and privatized, as international donors, such as DFID,
outsource development and wider relief policy and programmes to
private, profit-driven, companies. Increasingly focused on their own
organizational survival, most aid organizations operating in Sierra
Leone appear complacent, have little interest in influencing donor
policy, and may lack the ability to do so. As a result, despite its
rudimentary political control, British emergency assistance in Sierra
Leone, at least in theory, remains donor-driven.

Despite some success and Sierra Leone's comparatively small size
and total dependence on the UK Government, by 2003 many of the
interviewees involved in the British reconstruction effort in Sierra
Leone spoke of its likely failure. Overstretched on several fronts and
with no clear vision as to the future of humanitarian emergency assistance and peace-building, the UK Government is unlikely to undertake
another such comprehensive endeavour in the near or medium-term
future – despite the assertive rhetoric with which it committed itself
to the peace process in the Democratic Republic of Congo (DRC) and
Sudan in 2004 (which was backed by a serious financial commitment
in the case of Sudan).[57]

An overall perception has taken hold that the UN and the UK
have concentrated on state building within Sierra Leone and allowed
the re-emergence of former governmental and social structures. They
are believed to have addressed the symptoms but not the root
causes of the war, although the use of short-term, palliative mechanisms such as humanitarian emergency assistance has kept the
peace process afloat. At the same time, they have inhibited change,
and have performed poorly in involving marginalized groups and
in supporting mechanisms that will hold governmental officials to
account. Instead, despite the UK Government's vision of ensuring
coherence and comprehensiveness, the international engagement
has been a patchwork, top-down process. It lacked strategic clarity,
transparency and overall control. It also lacked the active support

of either an effective policy implementation bureaucracy or implementing agents. DFID, like other donors, got lost in a 'provision culture'. Our interviews indicated that the UK Government and its personnel in Sierra Leone were deeply conscious of this, but were nonetheless unable to instigate change. In the absence of identifiable alternatives, the UN and UK stormed ahead, resurrecting faulty structures and imposing their own version of statehood. In 2004, the entire country was getting back to business as usual. Despite the absence of physical violence, the states of war and peace in Sierra Leone are worryingly similar: both display a prevalence of 'high unemployment or underemployment, debureaucratized and fragmented systems of public administration, high degrees of autonomy among political actors, dependency on an extensive cross-border shadow trade and non-territorial networking', and similar levels of structural violence.[58] Although even such a negative peace has provided a bit of breathing space and therefore created some new political realities, it is likely that at some stage in the medium-term future some people will use violence in an attempt to change something once again, or at least to increase their personal opportunities. A resumption of hostilities and continued unrest seems likely.

In April 2002, Garth Glentworth argued that DFID had drawn two interesting conclusions from its involvement in Sierra Leone. First, it was not yet able to put together a sufficiently extensive and well coordinated pattern of assistance. Second, the conventional legal and operational limits of donor involvement in assistance had to be reconfigured 'if there [was] not to be cherry picking by aid agencies of what is possible rather than what is needed'.[59] By 2007, with the UK embroiled in a messy and intractable war in the Middle East, the situation had not changed.

In this chapter we have discussed the contents of British relief policy in Sierra Leone, and also explored the role of aid within Sierra Leonean politics and the level of local ownership of external aid programmes. Having analysed the content of the application of New Humanitarianism to Sierra Leone, we will assess the effectiveness of its implementation in Chapter 5. We present a detailed analysis of the administrative process used to implement New Humanitarianism, on the basis of the criteria of successful policy implementation defined above. Our aim in Chapters 4 and 5 has been to evaluate the effectiveness and coherence of New Humanitarianism. We analyse its contents and the implementation process separately in order to determine whether it was the weakness of the policy implementation process or a lack of policy clarity that undermined New Humanitarianism, or a combination of the two.

5
Implementing New Humanitarianism in Sierra Leone

Introduction

In the last three chapters we analysed the policy contents and level of coherence of British New Humanitarianism and its application in Sierra Leone. We now present a case study of the implementation process of British-funded humanitarian emergency assistance programmes and Britain's wider policy engagement in Sierra Leone between 1997 and 2003. This involves an evaluation of selected aspects of the complete project cycle of UK-sponsored emergency assistance projects, which might enable or inhibit the successful implementation of donor-led policy (based on the indicators of successful policy implementation developed in Chapter 1). Our key objective in this chapter is to assess the effectiveness of the policy implementation process of British emergency policy. We will determine whether the administrative process of implementing relief aid undermined coherent interpretation and execution of the policy, irrespective of its overall clarity and appropriateness. We also seek to appraise the implementation of New Humanitarianism in a post-war environment, or indeed the effectiveness of implementing policy change in an emergency environment. We seek neither to analyse the contents nor measure the success of specific emergency assistance interventions, but concentrate rather on the process of policy implementation in order to identify the reasons for the divergence between UK emergency assistance policy at the strategic level and policy output at the field level in Sierra Leone.

Transparency

We have shown above that British policy on humanitarian emergency assistance and Sierra Leone lacked clarity. The donor/implementing agent relationship also suffered from a lack of transparency, poor information sharing and erratic communications. This is by no means unique to Sierra Leone but is characteristic of aid relationships, especially in emergency settings. We begin this chapter by evaluating the policy's transparency and predictability. We therefore discuss (a) agents' comprehension of the British policy in Sierra Leone, (b) the mechanisms and processes of donor/agency communication and cooperation in setting policy parameters and identifying projects, and (c) whether joint agenda setting is a top-down or bottom-up process. We begin by highlighting aspects of the environment that undermine the donor/agent and inter-agency communication process, and by assessing the existing fora of donor/agency cooperation. Our objective in this section is to assess the coherence of British New Humanitarianism and the level of cooperation between the UK Government and the implementing organizations within Sierra Leone.

Agency perception of donor policy and policy impact

Few of the organizations we interviewed professed either to comprehend the British humanitarian and peace-building policy or to have an overview of the British engagement in Sierra Leone. Several stated that there appeared to be no primary British strategy, but several different strategies. All those interviewed had broad, and at times conflicting, views on the reasons for the UK's engagement in Sierra Leone, and on who exactly benefited from it. They repeatedly criticized British humanitarian policy for being dominated by considerations of wider foreign policy, although few organizations were able or willing to explain this argument in greater detail. In fact, most took pains to stress their cordial and successful relationship with DFID staff. The vast majority of implementing organizations also maintained that there had been very little donor interference in British humanitarian emergency programmes at the programme level, notwithstanding donor selectivity in the choice of programmes. The general consensus was that obtaining British funding and political support entailed three main prerequisites. First, programmes should not contradict Britain's wider policy objectives in Sierra Leone, and organizations should maintain cordial partnerships by not being overly critical of donors (or other large emergency organizations). Second, programmes should aid the peace-building and development process. Third, programmes should include rights- and conflict-sensitive components.[1] Despite extensive interviews, however, we were unable to establish whether there was any general agreement on the capacity of humanitarian emergency assistance to take on wider political objectives or the responsibility of its providers to do so. On the contrary, both agencies and donor field representatives seemed more concerned with successfully executing those projects that were already funded than thinking about their wider and longer-term impact.

The majority of those interviewed believed that the British engagement in Sierra Leone had been essential in bringing an end to the violence and in enabling people to get back on their feet. They also felt that it had been important in encouraging other donors to become and remain involved, and, most importantly, in holding the GoSL to account. 'If the United Kingdom pulled out of Sierra Leone, there would be chaos'.[2] 'DFID acts much more as the Government of Sierra Leone than the Government itself . . . It is involved in every aspect of the country'.[3] In spite of this, very few of those interviewed thought the British humanitarian engagement was particularly strong, innovative or even successful. There was an overwhelming consensus that the United Kingdom had played an important role in halting the fighting and establishing the vital aspects of a reconstruction phase, but had then almost abandoned emergency relief and recovery and concentrated exclusively on security sector reform.

> There is great frustration in the NGO community. DFID is dealing with soldiers only, not with communities. Security has to be established first: no question about this. But the UK has been particularly weak up to now on social issues.[4]

Some of those interviewed also voiced regret that the UK had failed to accept its essential responsibility for donor coordination on humanitarian emergency assistance issues – a role it was uniquely equipped to play given its broad engagement in Sierra Leone.

Several agencies argued that the vague British strategic framework (or the UK's failure to explain policy sufficiently to implementing partners) had undermined agencies' agenda setting, and reduced their ability to engage in strategic analysis or draw lessons for future engagement. Attempts to develop standard mechanisms and approaches were regarded as weak or had not filtered down throughout the humanitarian network, or even the British field bureaucracy. All forms of wider strategic agenda setting were clearly viewed as a top-down process with marginal input from the field level. This was confirmed in several interviews with DFID field personnel in Sierra Leone.

Some other humanitarian assistance organizations pointed out that this vagueness in donor agenda setting also allowed implementing organizations a greater degree of leeway to be flexible in their own policymaking. Most believed, however, that donors were able to impose demands on implementing partners and 'hassle them'. Yet they rarely had the means to drive project processes and, therefore, to control implementation and policy setting. Implementing agents argued that field representatives' physical remoteness from donor headquarters ensured that they were more likely to be successful in resisting any such donor attempts to control project contents and implementation. Donor funding was rarely considered to be sufficiently flexible or substantial to enforce the setting of a particular agenda or, conversely, to underpin longer-term or wider approaches.

Most of those organizations we interviewed assumed that their staff who were involved in implementing DFID-funded projects understood donor requirements to the extent that they directly concerned the projects on which they were working. Donor requirements were negotiated in the original project appraisals and written into the contracts, and in theory all contract staff had access to the original funding documentation. Once funding had been agreed, donor conditions regarding specific projects were therefore considered to be relatively transparent, although these did not necessarily include donor strategy at large, or wider political objectives.

Karen Moore, then country director of CARE in Sierra Leone, mentioned that some of the bigger aid agencies like CARE had been asking DFID staff in UK and Sierra Leone for a country strategy paper and clearer guidance on objectives and benchmarks for at least 2 years. At the time of the interview, she hoped that these would soon be available (as had been suggested by the head of DFID in Sierra Leone, Ian Stuart). She expected such a strategy paper to be distributed to partner organizations and other NGOs, 'if DFID does not get bogged down in politics again'. She believed that DFID would share its strategy if it had one, and when approached.[5] This could not be ascertained since then.

Many agencies criticized the donor-driven, early and lengthy transition phase from emergency to development, arguing that Sierra Leone still lacked the most basic social standards. Some assumed that the donors' drive to move from an emergency to a development phase reflected their wish to take over control of aid expenditures and policy within Sierra Leone. They expected DFID and other donors to 'become much more controlling very soon'.[6] Several humanitarian staff accused the UK reintegration programme of being opaque and non-participatory, and that it had set up a 'two-class society and [was] now washing [its] hands of the resulting conflicts'.[7] They claimed that while there was now greater stability and less corruption, neither of these gains would last unless communities were given a voice to hold their politicians to account and public officials were guaranteed adequate, regular incomes. To date, the UK has pursued a top-down approach that focuses on rebuilding the main political and administrative structures on the basis of a Western model of democracy rather than building the capacity and access to decision-making of the electorate. However, several NGOs gave credit to the new DFID-led attempt to get involved in community-based social development and rights programmes. This approach was developed in cooperation with some of the humanitarian emergency organizations present in Sierra Leone.

It was often mentioned that DFID's reputation had been tarnished since the UK Government's involvement with Sandline International and its controversial stand regarding the continuation of humanitarian emergency assistance in 1998. This was aggravated by its apparent inability to hold the GoSL to prior agreements. The assertive and broad British engagement and DFID's politically driven humanitarian approach were seen to undermine humanitarian agencies' neutrality, impartiality and independence as the UK had become a player within the conflict. As a consequence and in order to maintain their neutrality, a few agencies in Sierra Leone had refused British funding, while others that were still sponsored by the British Government reported making a conscious effort to remain independent. They regarded this to be important, in order both to maintain their own legitimacy and to avoid breaking with other organizations that were more critical of their close relationships with the British Government.

Communication and co-ordination

Issues

The implementation process of British New Humanitarianism as applied in Sierra Leone entailed a number of key issues in communication and coordination. These included fragmentation, unstructured communications, information, and contradictory mandates and working practices.

First, many interviewees argued that the British decision-making and implementation structures appeared disjointed, erratic and lacking in transparency. Various staff, both from the aid community and DFID, pointed out that there were clear operational and programmatic differences between the various divisions within DFID. While several praised the professionalism of DFID/CHAD personnel who were involved in the early emergency phase, many criticized the British Government for failing to coordinate across departmental lines to ensure transparency, stability and basic access to decision makers. Several regretted the withdrawal of CHAD from the field. 'Now there is no real programmatic DFID focal point in Sierra Leone ... Right now, DFID implementation in Sierra Leone is ad hoc. With no money, oversight, or linkage.'[8] This fragmented decision-making process was thought to make consultation and cooperation with the UK time-consuming and unstable. This criticism was well summarized by Wael Ibrahim, then the country director of Oxfam in Sierra Leone:

> While the UK administration is meant to be 'joined-up', the reality is that all is under an umbrella organisation, DFID, but internally, DFID is very fragmented with unclear lines of communication, responsibility and control. In Sierra Leone, we deal with about 15 individual DFIDs: CRP, Ian Stuart, WINNAT, but within WINNAT various desks including the desk officer for SL, governance people, security sector reform people, those responsible for social programmes, economic programmes, etc. We find it

hard to identify who is in charge for specific things and where to get reliable information and decisions. Also, there does not appear to be an overarching strategic framework for DFID's engagement in Sierra Leone.

Second, implementing agencies at the field level had to rely mostly on impromptu meetings or personalized contact with British decision-makers to discuss project parameters and strategic objectives. More often than not, their understanding of donor strategies was derived from information given to them on an ad hoc basis, which they could not interpret systematically. The provision of information also differed from one organization to another.

Third, many interviewees stressed that information did not flow rapidly during emergencies, when it was often a critical asset that many organizations were reluctant to share. DFID's limited field presence compelled donor organizations to rely on implementing partners' information and advice. Given the asymmetric donor/implementing agent relationship and the parties' possibly contradictory objectives and working practices, information that was obtained was likely to be distorted or misinterpreted. DFID and implementing agents' personnel repeatedly stressed that information was often simply not filtered through the bureaucratic system. Given implementers' everyday responsibility for the projects' sustainability and overall success, they were more likely to respond to events rather than to unclear or vaguely defined long-term strategic objectives.

Finally, all interviewees demonstrated a frustration either with the general lack of coordination or donors' (and some organizations') continued attempts to enforce it. A quasi-consensus emerged that meaningful coordination beyond the project (or rarely, the sector) level was largely impossible, because of the parties' conflicting mandates and working procedures, and because of the rapid pace of change in the environment in which they worked. When pressed, some organizations conceded that the Office of the Coordination of Humanitarian Affairs (OCHA) sometimes fulfilled an important coordinating function. In Sierra Leone, however, it was considered to have acted almost like a service unit – as a source of information and a mediator only. Given its closeness to UNAMSIL (and therefore to the military), and implementing agents' general disinclination to be controlled, OCHA was thought to face significant distrust and a lack of cooperation.

Communication and cooperation

Several agencies mentioned that there had been frequent consultative meetings during the earlier phases of the conflict (until 1996) between Mukesh Kapila, the then head of CHAD, and NGO partners, both at headquarters level in London and also at times in the field. They believed that Mukesh Kapila had used NGO information, projects and approaches to influence DFID/CHAD's thinking and approach. In addition, in preparing for these donor/agency meetings, several aid agencies (including many large British emergency and development NGOs such as CARE, Oxfam, Save the Children Fund (SCF) and Action Aid) had met informally to coordinate their positions, agree on advocacy strategies and exchange information. It was after these informal discussions that British NGOs claimed that DFID had applied political conditionality to humanitarian emergency assistance to Sierra Leone in 1997/98. Some organizations, like the British Red Cross, had withdrawn from these informal discussions. Since 1998, there has been no formal consultative process, either at the strategic level in Britain or in Sierra Leone. The reasons for the Red Cross's absence in this coordination/advocacy group are contested. Some say that the International Committee of the Red Cross (ICRC) was not welcome due to its close (funding) relationship with DFID and its hesitation to criticize the British Government for political conditionality. Others claimed it had opted out, as this group was considered to be too politically motivated, having acted on the basis of too little substantiated information and with limited competency. They also argued that this group had displayed a picture of competition and disparity in British aid circles, a fact that had influenced DFID's rather negative attitude towards, and impression of, relief agencies.[9]

At the country macro level within Sierra Leone, the UN has attempted – with marginal success – to put into operation a standardized communication process for all the major players. A consultation assembly brings together all ministers, representatives of national and international NGOs and representatives of key UN agencies on a bi-monthly basis, which is co-chaired by the representative of the World Bank, the Deputy Special Representative of the Secretary-General for Governance and Stabilization (at the time by Alan Doss), and the Vice-President of Sierra Leone. According to several organizations interviewed in Freetown, however, the format is not conducive to open discussions of programme details or future developments.[10] Even at the micro level (or the internal agency level), communication and cooperation were not always forthcoming. Different departments (often accountable to superiors who disagree on conflicting mandates, and often regularly overworked, under-staffed and underfinanced) failed to exchange sufficient information or agree on common objectives.

Bi-monthly inter-agency meetings of international NGOs served as a (weak) official forum for consultation and complaints. However, not all organizations were represented or, indeed, appeared to take this forum seriously. In mid-2003, UNAMSIL disengaged from these meetings, in which donor participation had always been sporadic.

Most implementing NGOs interviewed assumed that DFID repres-entatives in Sierra Leone, in particular Ian Stuart, had a significant influence on British strategic decision-making and were familiar with British humanitarian policy. Those that were funded by DFID, that claimed to have a close partnership with the UK, and that had the capacity to engage in political advocacy believed that the DFID field office played an essential role in providing basic informa-tion on British political objectives and humanitarian strategy. Some doubted, however, whether the DFID chief representative in Sierra Leone was aware of the decisions taken in London. One country manager suggested that 'maybe there is no control, transparency and co-ordination of the entire British endeavour full stop'.[11] The head of DFID in Sierra Leone nevertheless provided the implementing organ-izations' most direct contact with DFID. (At least officially, all funding decisions/project proposals had to be approved by Ian Stuart – even though decisions were taken in London.) The vast majority of staff we interviewed valued DFID's field presence and wanted it to expand. They believed that it enabled a greater degree of decision-making to be based on local realities and needs, relative to programmes funded by other donors. They also maintained that it facilitated donor/agency transparency and cooperation, by making the donor organization much more accessible, which, in turn, improved rela-tionships among the local NGOs. Some believed that this direct contact would enable them to exert a greater influence over DFID policy, while others warned that DFID's field offices could monitor project implementation, which might have both facilitating and restraining effects, as the donors were more likely to interfere in everyday project implementation. This was seen to threaten the independence of humanitarian organizations.

Almost all field-level implementing organizations reported that it was only rarely that field-based staff consulted formally with donors, whether at headquarters or field level, since agencies dealt with most strategic or funding-related issues through their regional or international headquarters. Country offices were still able to initiate contact with donor representatives and frequently did so, but this often took place informally. However, field-based staff frequently travelled with DFID officials to project sites for monitoring and evaluation purposes, so there was an ongoing, informal, field-based donor/agent dialogue. Some maintained that these informal, field-based dialogues may well have been influential, given DFID's fragmented decision-making and general lack of strategic policy setting.

Top-down or bottom-up agenda setting

All of those organizations that DFID supported financially claimed that its personnel appeared to listen to its partner organizations' advice – and were therefore much more sympathetic to the concept of partnership than the staff of some other donors. Nevertheless, they also maintained that DFID had been slow to respond and, with some important exceptions, had rarely accepted the analysis of its better-informed partners in developing a humanitarian strategy. Several organizations considered that the new DFID social programme developed in 1993 represented a diversion from the norm. It had been developed on the basis of lobbying from civil society organizations and in partnership with NGOs that were actively engaged in Sierra Leone. A senior, headquarters-based DFID executive claimed that rights-based programmes were another area that had been developed in consultation with partner organizations. They were viewed as examples of a 'bottom-up approach' and a test case for future policy-making.

There seemed to be a general feeling that partner organizations were able to influence donor strategy only to a limited extent at the project level, and most often spontaneously rather than on a formal basis. Donors appeared to be more interested in output indicators, cost recovery and short-term responsibility rather than sustainable impact in terms of meeting needs and supporting longer-term political stability. The relative political weights of the larger, long-established British NGOs such as Oxfam, and their capacity to raise funds independently, were thought to determine the closeness of the donor/agency relationship and to raise advocacy opportunities for such agencies. Wael Ibrahim (Oxfam Sierra Leone) argued that, at least in theory, a major British NGO such as Oxfam should be able to influence the government, and DFID in particular, through public and media campaigns. He was unable, however, to provide a specific example of a case in which Oxfam could be shown to have led DFID to change its position. He suggested that donors might incorporate partner advice into their own programmes without officially acknowledging that they had done so. Two possible examples of this were: (1) NGO complaints regarding the hiring of former RUF combatants into the new Sierra Leonean army without proper background screening; subsequently, a screening mechanism was installed prior to recruitment. (2) Complaints regarding the Poverty Reduction Strategic Programme (PRSP) as being too complicated; subsequently it was agreed to simplify the document and a consultation process with NGOs was started.

Several large NGOs mentioned that neither their own organizations nor DFID (as a donor) would do anything that might substantially threaten their long-term relationship, since both parties were interested in getting and keeping each other involved in programmes in Sierra Leone.

Representatives of several organizations, including the UK's Community Reintegration Programme (CRP), mentioned that they were able to influence DFID's appraisal of the situation on the ground because of their extensive involvement in local programmes. This particularly applied if they had the opportunity to take DFID headquarter representatives to programme sites and were therefore in a position to control the evaluations of their own projects.[12] Given the British commitment to a 10-year Memorandum of Understanding with the GoSL, several organizations suspected that there would be less opportunity to influence the British agenda in the future.

A few organizations were much more critical of the current (as they saw it) 'master and servant' agency/donor relationship. They complained that donors hardly ever acknowledged the partners' contributions and almost never listened to local organizations' assessments and advice. Interestingly, the same organizations welcomed the idea of entering into standing partnership arrangements with donor organizations, which would serve as a basis for guidance, transparency and trust, and medium-term funding relationships. They believed that this would also increase the accountability of implementing agents and donors alike. Their interest in entering into partnership agreements appears to undermine earlier critical statements: their criticism might be more indicative of organizational discontent or the jealousy of others that enjoyed a closer relationship with donor organizations or had an interest in securing maximum funding.

Several humanitarian organizations mentioned their at times relatively close co-operation on community-based projects, in particular regarding rights, conflict-sensitive issues and governance. However, none judged DFID to have been particularly strong on these issues up to now. At the field level, only a few humanitarian organizations undertook policy-focused advocacy with the aim of influencing humanitarian policy implementation or future donor policy making. In particular, large, well-established British NGOs (and one or two US ones) were leading advocacy and government/NGO consultations. They thought they had the means, influence and therefore the responsibility to go beyond implementing projects and influence future policymaking. Some stated that highly public advocacy did not work but threatened to harm relationships with donors and other aid agencies. Quiet diplomacy, on the other hand, had proved much more successful. They reported that DFID maintained a very narrow definition of advocacy, namely 'influencing policy'. As DFID primarily concerned itself with promoting operational activities (and not policy work), it would accept advocacy only if was undertaken in the course of project implementation. This did not really constitute a rule, however, since DFID policy amounted to no more than a collection of individual staff comments. In general, most international emergency NGOs had degenerated into service delivery units.

Conclusion on transparency and coherence

In summary, the results of our research demonstrated that the level of transparency and co-operation with implementing organizations attained during the implementation of British New Humanitarianism in Sierra Leone has been rather limited. Few implementing organizations felt they understood the British country strategy sufficiently, and donor/agent communication was sporadic rather than formal.

Control

We now assess the level of control exercised by DFID as a donor organization over implementing organizations in Sierra Leone, by analysing: (a) the existing mechanisms for the pursuit of common objectives, (b) the process of comparing and identifying projects and project partners, (c) the process of obtaining funding, and (d) the monitoring and evaluation of British-funded programmes and organizational learning.

Promoting New Humanitarianism

We have interpreted humanitarian programmes that support broader political objectives (such as human rights, reconciliation or conflict management, and development or capacity building) as manifestations of New Humanitarianism. We have also found that they support – or are at least consistent with – the wider British political engagement in Sierra Leone. We now assess the level of support they enjoy among implementing agents in Sierra Leone. Our analysis is based on extensive interviews with humanitarian organizations in Sierra Leone and an evaluation of their publications. Most of their staff were remarkably reluctant to discuss these issues, however, so the following must be regarded as a qualitative assessment of staff support rather than a quantitative assessment of country programmes.

The aid community has made considerable efforts to investigate possible links between emergency assistance, conflict management and support for human rights. At least at headquarters level, many organizations have formulated so-called 'conflict-sensitive' or 'rights-based' strategies that are intended to inform country strategies and project implementation. However, despite a general interest in re-conceptualizing and strengthening humanitarian emergency aid policy, such efforts remain confined to individual aid agencies. No network-wide strategy incorporating any of these principles could be identified at the headquarters or local level in Sierra Leone; nor has DFID pushed for one. Our research also identified a surprising lack of awareness of such policy efforts at the tactical level: many field-based staff were either unaware of these concepts, reluctant to give away possibly controversial information, or sceptical about the feasibility of their application. Others appeared generally disinterested or even hostile to broadening relief mandates beyond need (i.e., beyond the provision of basic means for immediate survival), arguing that emergency aid delivery was already complicated enough. In particular, during emergencies, any broadening of the mandate and objectives of humanitarian emergency assistance was thought to put vulnerable populations at risk and threaten to lead to antagonism among stakeholders and local leaders. They also doubted whether a consensus could be established concerning the objectives of any such broader mandate.

Despite this overall reluctance, many of the agencies that have been supported by DFID have pursued strategies involving rights and capacity building initiatives. Some have done so predominantly at the headquarters level or purely rhetorically, but most have also implemented wider programmes at the community level in some selected areas of operation. The latter include CARE, Action Aid, Oxfam, Christian Aid and the Sierra Leonean Red Cross Society (in cooperation with the British Red Cross).

Conflict sensitivity and peace-building

In its three White Papers on development (1997, 2000 and 2006) and within its principles of humanitarian emergency assistance, the UK Labour Government – and DFID in particular – have committed themselves to an approach that takes account of the wider impact of humanitarian emergency assistance, in particular its effect on, and role in, violent conflict.[13] DFID has also committed itself to coherent and coordinated policymaking, in conjunction with other departments and implementing partners. We have assumed that humanitarian emergency assistance need not actively support wider political objectives, but will certainly not contradict them. DFID has published several policy papers on humanitarian emergency assistance and conflict, including a manual on conflict impact assessment. This belief underpinned our assumptions that DFID would strive to promote a conflict-sensitive or rights-based approach to humanitarian emergency assistance, and also encourage or even insist on the application of its guidelines on conflict impact assessment. However, we were unable to substantiate these hypotheses, either at the strategic or the local level, either within the DFID bureaucracy itself or at the NGO level. On the contrary, we have already shown in Chapter 2 that there was no consensus on the impact of humanitarian emergency assistance on conflict and its role in support of conflict prevention at the level of policy formulation. DFID staff across the board neither supported nor promoted the criteria for a conflict impact assessment as identified by CHAD or a conflict-sensitive approach to humanitarian emergency assistance. In Sierra Leone, a conflict-sensitive approach to humanitarian emergency assistance was certainly far from ubiquitous. None of the DFID-supported humanitarian agencies appeared to be aware of DFID's manual on conflict impact assessment, and none had been approached on this matter by the donor organization.

Some agencies, at least at headquarters level, had undertaken independent efforts to integrate conflict indicators into project appraisal and evaluation. However, such an understanding of emergency assistance mandates had filtered down to few of the organizations' field staff that we interviewed in the Sierra Leone. Not only were agencies apparently reluctant to share information regarding their guidelines on conflict-sensitive approaches, but some staff were not even aware that any such internal or international strategy papers or endeavours existed. Some organizations that were actively engaged in Sierra Leone intended to address the root causes of conflict and analyse reasons for communal strife within their work, but had not formulated universal programme standards to that end. Others, in particular the more development-oriented agencies, had listed conflict prevention as one of their strategic crosscutting goals. However, not all of these organizations were able or willing to show evidence of such programmes. Several mentioned a belief that their presence and work were a 'bridge for peace' in themselves. Since their work entailed peace-building objectives 'by default', there was no need for a specific approach to include conflict sensitivity. Through their work, these organizations claimed to have provided a forum for the exchange of needs and experiences, as well as advocacy against war. They also cautioned that not all staff members were equally trained to address issues concerning conflict or rights.

Several organizations voiced strong concerns about the mixing of humanitarian emergency assistance with peace-building or conflict prevention objectives. They warned against the vagueness of the

British peace-building agenda (and its likely short-term commitment) and the possible harmful effects of extending relief mandates. As an example, several cited the Sierra Leonean ICRC's position of working on all sides of the conflict. At the height of the war, this had caused concern in GoSL circles and eventually led to the ICRC's temporary expulsion. According to ICRC staff, at the height of the conflict in Sierra Leone, 'there was clearly a white and black conception of the conflict, and neutrality was misunderstood and misinterpreted'.[14] It is conceivable in the context of humanitarian emergency assistance that entailed conflict resolution objectives that any greater involvement in the war might have caused considerable unrest. Mindful of attacks on aid agencies in Iraq, such as the attack on the Red Cross and Red Crescent, and many organizations' subsequent withdrawal, some organizations are currently in the process of reviewing their policies on neutrality and impartiality.[15]

Most organizations appeared sceptical about the aid community's ability to identify a common, network-wide agenda. Some also mentioned they thought few donors would be prepared to fund programmes beyond limited emergency objectives. A few expressed strong doubt whether any donor organization would integrate humanitarian emergency assistance into wider peace-building strategies or set conditions to that effect. They argued that such work often depended on the availability of donor-independent private funding.

One country director mentioned that his organization had abandoned any further engagement in peace-building and conflict prevention in Sierra Leone, once it became clear that an incomplete understanding of the conflict and the complexity of conflict prevention had led it to make significant operational mistakes during the genocide in Rwanda. However, he did not suggest that there was no need for conflict sensitivity in planning an appropriate engagement within conflict-ridden environments. Another organization argued that it was essential to support training on conflict issues for the staff of local NGOs. It was important to develop early warning mechanisms, to enable them to identify the locations of conflict and means of alerting those responsible for taking preventive action. However, despite a real need for conflict-focused projects, only limited donor funds and limited agency capacity were available for such projects.

At the community level, today there is a much stronger will to talk about issues and to express the desire for change, as long as either doesn't threaten stability. No one seems to want to return to war. This creates an opportunity to work towards political and societal change, not just to provide the basic facilities or training. Therefore Sierra Leone is in a critical transition phase . . . it has yet to be clear whether donors are prepared to maximize on progress to date and to sit it out.[16]

Without a strong donor commitment to conflict-sensitive humanitarian emergency assistance, the prospects for the incorporation of issues of conflict and rights into humanitarian emergency assistance policy remain bleak. This applies all the more strongly if the current trend for increased funding of private (profit-driven) service providers continues in the field of emergency assistance. Experience in Sierra Leone showed that profit-driven companies shied away from undertaking efforts that went beyond their immediate contracts and those that required additional expenditure and time (see also Chapter 5).

Do No Harm

Thinking and programmes based on the doctrine of Do No Harm were not widely pursued across the majority of aid organizations engaged in Sierra Leone. Most aid personnel interviewed were reluctant to discuss the potential broader and/or negative side effects of their organizations' emergency assistance programmes. Only some of them were interested in working more with Do No Harm indicators, and few had hardly received any formal training in this field. Few could see how to incorporate this approach effectively into their everyday work. However, almost all of the organizations interviewed felt compelled to achieve and prove accountability to both their donors and their stakeholders. To some extent, ensuring accountability required them to undertake ongoing project impact (and conflict impact) assessments. However, most organizations' responses to questions concerning their projects' impact consisted of quantitative data on outputs, such as number of workshops held, patients treated, sacks of rice dispersed, and so on. These criteria were part of programme contracts established with donors. Few of the field staff interviewed

thought it necessary to evaluate the broader effects of their aid intervention on a society's condition and future (political) development
or indeed a populations' survival. All of those that were able and
willing to discuss their work's impact and conflict impact assessment
methodologies complained of a lack of financial capacity to undertake conflict impact assessment in a meaningful way.

Rights-based programming

A rights-based approach to humanitarian emergency assistance
assumes that the protection of human rights (including political
rights) is a priority of humanitarian emergency operations. In some
of its publications and public statements on humanitarian emergency assistance, DFID has adopted the rhetoric of such a rights-
based approach. But a high level of confusion, misunderstanding and
disagreement remained in the humanitarian emergency community
about the meaning of the term and its impact on operations. Some
organizations, including the United Nations Department of Political Affairs (DPA), have sought minimum rights-based criteria for the
delivery of humanitarian emergency assistance. DPA writes that the
objective of a rights-based approach is to 'provide the human rights
framework necessary to find long-term solutions to the root causes of
conflict and to . . . facilitate the successful transition between peacekeeping operations and humanitarian emergency assistance to long-
term peace-building and sustainable development'.[17] According to
this definition, human rights are understood as the crucial binding
element between humanitarian emergency assistance, development
and security.

In Sierra Leone, rights issues were widely regarded as an instrument to ensure the local ownership of emergency and development
programmes and a means of linking relief and development. In
some cases, addressing rights issues was also seen as a means of
supporting community capacity building and conflict prevention.
The limited success of community reintegration and community
capacity building programmes had pushed rights-based and social
programmes to the fore, as reflected in DFID's investment in a
new civil society programme.[18] Several humanitarian organizations
engaged in Sierra Leone (though not the majority) undertook integrated programmes that addressed human rights in the framework of,
for example, food security programmes. Their objective was to use

the opportunity of food delivery to educate the population about their legal rights and thereby empower them to hold their political leaders accountable. Before implementing projects in Sierra Leone, for example, Action Aid undertook so-called 'participatory review processes' to get feedback from the community regarding their needs, expectations and capacity (or lack thereof). The objective was to train people to make demands, analyse their situation and work as a community, rather than as individuals.

Speaking out against rights abuses and suspending aid programmes in protest against such abuses are further examples of addressing rights issues by means of humanitarian emergency assistance. MSF-Holland, for example, speaks out and withdraws if necessary in cases of grave violations of humanitarian law, as opposed to mere incidents of human rights abuse.[19] All agencies had general policies on how to deal with such abuse. Nevertheless, the results of our interviews indicated that the interpretation of mandates on how to respond to the abuse of human rights or humanitarian principles was often left to individual staff. One country manager reported that it was more important to 'stay and do our job'. Most stated they preferred to pass on information on human rights abuses to human rights groups rather than take action themselves, or advocate a broadening of their organizations' mandates. Several maintained that it was important to act only on the basis of information they had obtained themselves during the course of their work, and they did not have the capacity to investigate the allegations that came to their attention. They warned that it was not appropriate to rely on information on rights abuses provided by local partners, since this was often tainted by rumours, fears and personal prejudices.

Most of the humanitarian personnel we interviewed did not feel competent to get involved in rights issues. Overall, rights-based principles certainly did not form the basis of a strategy that was widely pursued in Sierra Leone. It appeared, however, that such principles were becoming adopted more widely, and that donors were becoming more interested in funding socially or community-oriented programmes. One DFID executive in London stated that that rights-based programmes were considered 'a plus', but not a prerequisite for entering into a funding relationship with organizations engaged in Sierra Leone. He also mentioned that DFID had only just begun to get engaged in that line of work.[20]

Impact of a wider approach to humanitarian assistance

We were unable to obtain sufficient and sufficiently meaningful data to undertake an assessment of the impact of humanitarian emergency assistance. This would have required a comprehensive and resource-consuming evaluation of aid programmes, and the full cooperation of the humanitarian organizations involved in Sierra Leone. This lay beyond the means of a single study and was not an objective of our analysis, although we were able to draw four preliminary conclusions.

First, at the height of the violence, those humanitarian organizations that remained in Sierra Leone, including the Red Cross, found it difficult to maintain their neutrality and impartiality, or the perception thereof. The concept of impartiality was actually frequently misunderstood: organizations working in all parts of the war zones were often judged to be operating in support of specific factions. This caused hostility and eventually led to the suspension of some humanitarian aid projects. At this stage of the war, any greater involvement in support of peace-building or human rights was likely to complicate or threaten humanitarian access and aid delivery.

Secondly, the operations of humanitarian emergency relief organizations in Sierra Leone were frequently hampered by a lack of information. This caused (and was caused by) poor coordination and pooling of resources, which reduced its efficacy. In the absence of greatly strengthened coordination mechanisms and coordinated and cross-cutting mandates, humanitarian projects can have little leverage to initiate significant political change.

Thirdly, headquarters and field representatives differed significantly in their interpretations of conflict- and rights-sensitive theories of emergency assistance. However, many field staff, while critical of the language of New Humanitarianism and Do No Harm, were actively (and often passionately) engaged in wider humanitarian and development projects. Their direct interaction with local communities encouraged their involvement in political affairs.

Finally, the failure of DFID's Community Reintegration Project to address community empowerment and capacity building on a significant and sustainable basis led to criticism within the broader humanitarian community and to some extent within DFID itself. This led to our assumption that DFID favoured the promotion of rights- or conflict-sensitive programmes, and was prepared to invest in them. We could not substantiate this assumption, however, on the basis of the findings of our research undertaken in Sierra Leone.

None of these hypotheses suggests that a conflict- or rights-sensitive humanitarian approach in Sierra Leone was counterproductive or futile. On the contrary, wider humanitarian projects appear to have benefited from greater awareness of the political environment and issues of conflict and rights. Those humanitarian emergency projects that went beyond the immediate delivery of emergency aid, by addressing issues of human rights, peace-building and community capacity building, had involved greater proportions of the local population. They were also thought to be more sustainable and more effective then many other programmes.

Choice of projects, project areas and partner

The rationale for and process of selecting projects and programmes demonstrate the level of symmetry within donor/agency relations and the parties' common objectives. Consequently, they also affect and reflect the strength and ease of policy implementation, under the assumption that projects constitute the practical output of policy. Table 5.1 provides an analysis of DFID and implementing NGOs' indicators for project selection. It also shows implementing partners' perceptions of DFID's criteria for project selection and discusses the significance of the data. The analysis that follows was drawn from a large number of interviews with policymakers and practitioners undertaken in Sierra Leone during 2002–2003. The majority of personnel interviewed supported the following indicators; others that were mentioned by only a few interviewees were dropped from this list. Nonetheless, the list should not be regarded as exclusive or complete. Programming decisions depend on circumstances, organizational or political necessities, and personalities. Neither did all organizations necessarily list all of the following indicators.

Bearing in mind the indicators of successful policy implementation defined previously, this analysis leads to the following observations.

Table 5.1 Indicators of project identification

DFID indicators re. project selection	NGO indicators re. project selection	NGO perception of DFID indicators re. project selection	Analysis
Security	Security	DFID perceived as very worried about security, more so than some other donors	A minority of agencies mentioned that security was an indicator very much secondary to need
Programme focus fits DFID's strategic objectives	Programme lies within donor's main strategic objectives or in area where donor funding seems available	In keeping with donor's main strategic objectives	The large majority of interviewees stated that their organizations made an effort to understand donor strategic objectives and would attempt to work on like-minded projects. Many stated that they would be compelled to accept geographical and contextual direction from donors
			Several blamed other NGOs for 'running after the money'
			Most suggested that donor goals were based on political objectives rather than local need and implied that this was objectionable
		Within institutional strategic objectives	Some interviewees implied that NGOs were too tied up in organizational ethics and too reluctant to cooperate with all actors including the military

Need and number of people benefiting from intervention	Need and number of people benefiting from intervention (possibly based on community assessment)	Repeatedly NGOs pointed out that only independent or private funding (and the availability of core funds) enabled organizations to work solely on the basis of assessed needs and internal objectives
		While almost all agencies reported perceived need as a primary factor in the decision to undertake projects, many were unable to explain needs assessment strategies. Prior and post assessment including impact assessment were rarely standardized
		Some agencies mentioned OCHA, UNAMSIL or GoSL assessments as a basis for project allocation
Accessibility of area including quality of local infrastructure (or need to improve accessibility)	Access	Donors and implementing partners blamed one another for shop fronting (i.e., not moving out of safe areas into newly liberated ones) but focusing on strategically valuable or more comfortable regions. It was not possible to substantiate these claims. Nevertheless, a clustering of agencies and projects in selected areas was perceptible

Table 5.1 (Continued)

DFID indicators re. project selection	NGO indicators re. project selection	NGO perception of DFID indicators re. project selection	Analysis
Likelihood (or even guarantee) of success	Likelihood of success		This indicates risk-averse organizational behaviour
Visibility	Visibility	Visibility, high output and visible peace dividend as quickly as possible	This substantiates claims that both donor interest and/or media interest have a significant effect on the choice of projects and project areas
Level, duration and success of previous funding			
Availability of information	Availability of information		Given the often volatile and obscure implementation environment, the lack of information introduced an element of chance and possibly partiality into the selection of projects and project areas
Cost recovery and comparative cheapness		Cost recovery and comparative cheapness, but high output	Both the reality and the perception of a need for low-cost projects with high output caused over-ambitiousness and under-funding of projects. They also introduced a likelihood of failure to reach project benchmarks. In order to overcome negative results, these encouraged an element of simplification or deception in project appraisals

Interesting approach that supports strategic objectives (e.g. a rights-based approach, community capacity building, etc.)	Reactive	DFID as a donor organization gave the impression of being reactive yet interested in terms of rights-based or conflict-sensitive emergency approaches. Instead of being based on standard guidelines, such an interest appeared to depend on personal rather than institutional concern
Longer-term projects/funding	Short-term responsibility	There appears to be a contradiction that cannot easily be overcome between DFID's perceived interest in longer-term funding relationships and its short-term emergency responsibilities
Preference for funding aspects of larger programmes funded by other donors rather than total funding of specific projects		Increases the burden of lengthy and complicated application processes on implementing agents
		At the same time, guards against sudden project collapse upon a donor's withdrawal. Partial funding also leverages supplementary contributions
	Personal interest	It was repeatedly suggested that the rather fragmented operational environment driven by DFID as an umbrella organization that lacks strategic control means that strategies are determined by broader national foreign policy objectives and

Table 5.1 (Continued)

DFID indicators re. project selection	NGO indicators re. project selection	NGO perception of DFID indicators re. project selection	Analysis
			personal interest. Strategies were also often perceived to be manipulated by the GoSL. Several country managers stated they believed their good reputation with high-ranking UK Government personnel and the relevant personnel's personal interest in a specific approach enabled them to receive and maintain funding
	Area in which no other project is running or large donor is active (minority indicator)		
	Ability to work independently from donor or GoSL pressure		

DFID indicators re. partner selection

Large, well-known multilateral organizations or NGOs with which it maintains framework agreements		Assumed and perceived preference for large British bilateral organisations or private companies	Cause of emergence of NGO oligarchies
			Perception of upsurge of private (including military) companies in the implementation of developmental emergency assistance. Experience

History of partnership and perception of accountability. Completed partnership agreement		Completed partnership agreement	of technicalization of relief to the detriment of integrated, community-based and sustainable programmes that go beyond the immediate delivery of aid
			Simplifies application and implementation processes. Increases stability and to some extent long-term planning as it introduces an amount of guaranteed and possibly non-earmarked funding
			Depending on symmetry of relationship, this may introduce a degree of control and donor agenda setting
		Nationality	This contributes to the establishment of multiple national offices in lead donor countries, thus adding to the fragmentation and competitiveness of the international aid network
Expertise and perception that organization controls the resources required to undertake and implement the project successfully	Expertise	Expertise	It was repeatedly suggested by interviewees (in particular governmental ones) that many NGOs were too slow and lacked the necessary broad expertise, ability to pre-finance and essential logistics. This raises questions regarding the privatization and militarization of emergency aid and, more generally, emergency preparedness

- First, there appeared to be a high degree of antagonism and mutual mistrust between DFID (and donor organizations in general) and field-based implementing NGOs, despite the NGOs' considerable positive feedback and general support for and interest in DFID.
- Secondly, there seemed to be a conviction that donor and agency indicators of project selection were essentially different, although this may not be correct.
- Thirdly, our interviews suggested that implementing agencies believed that they needed to mould themselves and their operations in accordance with donor objectives and demands, but did not have sufficient knowledge to do so.
- Fourthly, projects appeared to be selected on the basis of chance, circumstance and personalities just as much as strategy.
- Fifthly, the identification of projects that are in the interests of both donors and implementing organizations and on the basis of need required a high degree of transparency with regard to their political and organizational objectives and requirements, which is not always forthcoming.
- Sixthly, the headquarters and field offices of implementing agencies pursued widely differing objectives, were subject to divergent needs, and reported to different superiors – and both lacked information.
- Seventhly, the majority of implementing agents stated that they had received mixed and sometimes contradictory messages concerning priorities from different DFID personnel/offices. There did not seem to be any consensus or clear lines of communication within DFID, and the various desks were not always informed of each other's work.
- Eighthly, given the breadth and vagueness of indicators, a high degree of flexibility remained concerning the contents of policy. At the same time, there appeared to be a lack of agreement on common political and strategic principles to guide project development and direction.
- Ninthly, humanitarian need and local necessity were only two indicators among several. This suggests an asymmetry of aid relationships, a vulnerability of the target group and a lack of ownership.
- Finally, the selection of projects and programmes, in summary, appears to represent a set of compromises among divergent interests.

Process of funding submissions

The process of project appraisal and funding applications demonstrates a great deal about internal and external lines of communication, transparency and the parties' awareness of essential (project) objectives. Most of all, it demonstrates implementing organizations' and donors' capacity to initiate programmes and, therefore, to control programme selection. DFID has worked with a wide variety of agencies to implement humanitarian and development programmes in Sierra Leone. Funding for external implementing agencies was either multilateral block funding or, more frequently, earmarked bilateral funding.

'Multilateral funding' is block funding for a multinational organization, such as the European Union or the OCHA. It is not tied to specific projects or programmes and can be used by implementing agents at their own discretion. 'Bilateral funding' is funding for national or international humanitarian organizations that is reserved for specific programmes, projects or locations.

Increasingly, DFID grants bilateral humanitarian relief funding to selected, larger international humanitarian implementing partner organizations.[21] In such cases, funds are earmarked for specific programmes or projects (or specific parts of projects, such as funds for water and sanitation facilities within a specific refugee camp in Freetown), some of which form part of a UN Consolidated Inter-Agency Appeal (CAP). CAPs are agreed upon by UN agencies involved in humanitarian assistance in consultation with non-UN international humanitarian organizations and humanitarian NGOs. The Consolidated Appeals Process summarizes country- or region-wide humanitarian needs and lists funding proposals. 'Bilateral Development Aid' consists of transfers from one government to another. It is generally assumed that bilateral funding enables donors to exert a greater degree of control over spending.

The graphic in Figure 5.1 displays an analysis of the most common funding relationships and project appraisal processes.

In funding relationship 3, a field manager in an implementing organization, sometimes working jointly with the local community, develops a project proposal and sends it to his/her regional line manager, who passes it on to the organization's country director. After an internal consultation and negotiation process, the

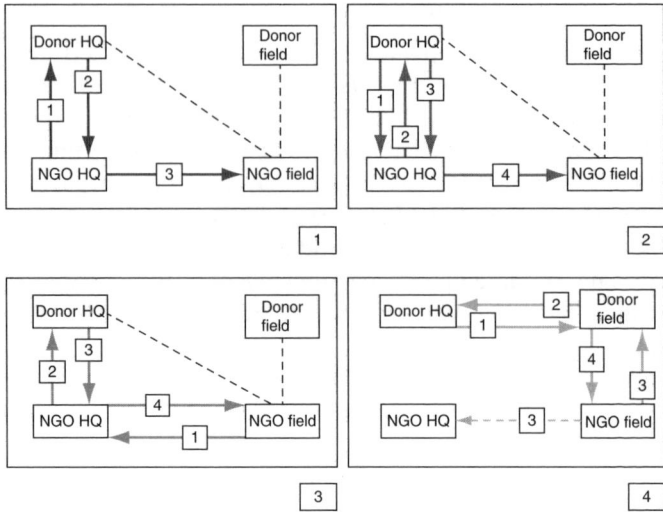

Figure 5.1   Donor – agent funding relationship and sequence of initiation

completed proposal is submitted to the organization's international headquarters (possibly via the regional headquarters). In most cases, the international headquarters must approve funding requests before potential donors are addressed, as projects need to comply with the organization's strategic objectives. By and large, the international headquarters itself then approaches possible donors, especially if the potential funding sources are based in Europe or overseas.

In funding relationship 4, where regional or local funding is being sought, the country office may approach donors directly.

Funding relationship 1 illustrates the more common case, where the staff of the organization's international headquarters seeks to identify strategic objectives and areas of engagement. On this basis, they draft a project proposal and submit it for funding to international donors. Such proposals are sometimes discussed with in-country teams, although such teams are generally not deployed until a funding commitment has been received, since most organizations cannot pre-finance such operations. After a donor/agency consultation process, donors allocate funding to agency headquarters on the basis of clear terms of reference for the project. These are then shared with in-country field offices, and the agency's international headquarters allocates funding to the field. In particular, larger implementing agencies that maintain partnership agreements with DFID were allocated bulk funding that was often not earmarked to specific country programmes. In such cases, projects were identified and funds dispersed at the national headquarters level on the basis of medium-term strategic objectives and need.

In funding relationship 2, a donor headquarters (or, more rarely, a donor country office) either writes a proposal and invites applications (or asks partner organizations directly to develop a project) or publishes a tender. According to interviews conducted with DFID personnel in Sierra Leone, this process was very rare. DFID Sierra Leone (prior to oversight over the DFID's Sierra Leone programme being devolved to the DFID in country office) retained very limited funding for such projects, which included a temporary small grant scheme and a limited infrastructure recovery programme. CHAD operational field consultants also held limited funds, which could be used at the discretion of field personnel (up to a certain limit) and could be dispersed quickly and informally in the field.

DFID London outsourced the British CRP to a private contractor, Agrisystems, which had operational control of large sums of project funds. It was therefore responsible for contracting other agencies and/or NGOs to implement projects in Sierra Leone. Agrisystems managed this process from its operational headquarters in Freetown. CRP was widely regarded as another wing of DFID, and it therefore gave the impression that DFID published tenders and gave out contracts at the local level.

In all cases, the international donor headquarters (DFID London) determined funding conditions and output requirements. Depending on the nature of the donor/agency relationship, such contracts were open to negotiation to a greater or lesser extent. The greater the degree of private funding, the greater was the implementing organization's independence from donor conditions. Funding negotiations were rarely committed to paper before the completion of a project's terms of reference.

DFID made decisions on programmes, projects and funding relationships. DFID was also implementing these decisions, but it did not set the strategic policy framework independently. It was compelled instead to coordinate its actions and make compromises with other departments of the British Government. Strategic political objectives were necessarily watered down, and at no point was DFID able to act unilaterally.

All project appraisal processes lack institutionalized direct communication mechanisms between donor headquarters or policymakers and field-level implementation offices. This does not imply that field offices never communicate directly with donor headquarter personnel. In fact, direct donor/agency communications are not uncommon. They are, however, not institutionalized and often not transparent. Given the high turnover of staff, such contacts are rarely sustainable or reliable. This at once reduces the transparency and awareness of donors' strategic political objectives and field requirements, as well as increasing project independence once funding has been received.

Most agency country directors interviewed stressed that all those involved in a project or programme had been consulted throughout its design, negotiation and implementation phase, and were therefore aware of agency and donor objectives. This appears highly unlikely, given the long-term and remote location of the appraisal and negotiation process and, at times, the rather different levels of education and communication skills of those involved in project implementation.

In most cases, funding is granted for periods of 6–12 months, so it is not sufficiently flexible or substantial to enable long- or medium-term strategic planning to take place. Several DFID personnel stressed that between 1998 and 2001, the UK focused on providing humanitarian emergency assistance, without placing any further conditions on their contents or area of implementation. However, DFID was highly selective in its choice of implementing partners, with a bias towards multinational organizations (for which it would usually still earmark its funding) or well-established NGOs with which CHAD already had bilateral framework agreements. This standardization of the choice of implementing partners was moderated, however, by multinational organizations' ability to outsource aspects of their programmes on a bilateral basis to NGOs.

Programme evaluation, monitoring and organizational learning

The withholding or suspension of funding is a donor's only effective instrument in controlling, albeit not directing, programme implementation. In order to do this once funding has been granted, donors must rely on the mechanisms of programme evaluation and monitoring. Programme evaluations and impact assessments also form the basis of most programming decisions. In essence, they guide the scope and approach of New Humanitarianism. The processes whereby programmes will be evaluated and monitored are determined within programme contracts and display wide variation (depending, e.g., on the type of organization, the scope of the programme and the country of implementation). We now provide an analysis of DFID/implementing agents' most common approach to the monitoring and evaluation of programmes in Sierra Leone.

Mechanisms of prior project and needs assessment

Pre-mission needs assessments form an essential aspect of project appraisal. Most implementing agents undertook assessments of some sort before designing their projects and applying for funding. However, interviews with their staff in Sierra Leone (and analysis of their appraisal documents) indicated that many organizations tended to promote and pursue those projects for which they knew they could secure funding or which fell within primary donors' strategic goals, and which at least vaguely formed part of their own organizations' strategic objectives.

As discussed above, the United Kingdom tends to finance NGO proposals that support specific British political interests, or that are generally consistent with DFID objectives. DFID also tends to support well-established partner organizations. To date, DFID has neither published nor promoted a specific pre-(or post-)mission appraisal and assessment strategy. CHAD's conflict-sensitive approach has not, as yet, been standardized across programmes; nor is conflict-sensitive impact assessment a condition for obtaining programme funding.

Contrary to agents' public rhetoric, procedures for strategic conflict and impact analysis as preparation and contingency planning have not been standardized. Our research indicated there had been only limited direct pre-mission needs or impact assessments, apart from those undertaken by the GoSL, multilateral organizations (like

OCHA) or donor consultations. This applied especially in tense emergency environments. In particular, with regard to the emergency and the early transition phase, most organizations interviewed professed a distinct distrust towards (and lack of consideration for) GoSL needs assessments or programme plans.

None professed to undertake pre-programme impact assessments, that means none attempted to assess the likely impact of their intervention prior to deployment. Many argued that pre-mission appraisals and needs and impacts assessment often faltered because of a lack of funding or time. Almost all organizations needed to receive their headquarters' approval before beginning a project, and almost all had to apply for funding once programmes or projects had been identified. This process could require considerable time, and the situation on the ground often threatened to change fundamentally in the mean time, which in turn required new needs and impacted assessment appraisals. A small minority of organizations mentioned they could begin programmes after a needs assessment but before receiving their headquarters' approval, provided they had adequate local security guarantees. Most external emergency programmes in Sierra Leone, therefore, were chosen on the basis of their effectiveness, sufficient security, and a cost-benefit analysis (or in other words, their costs needed to be as low as possible).[22]

Project monitoring and evaluation

Simon Arthy (on secondment from DFID to NaCSA) argued that

> DFID is the most socially aware donor I have come across. They constantly ask for input and evaluation and whether this is the right way to go. DFID constantly sends consultants from London to assess our work and to consider where to go next in terms of policy development. They are always trying to learn lessons.[23]

Several emergency agencies supported this statement and mentioned that DFID's London headquarters frequently sent consultants to monitor and evaluate projects. These evaluation teams tended to be small and short term; their assessments were therefore often based on data provided by the implementing agencies themselves. Nevertheless, over the last few years DFID has made an effort to increase its in-house capacity to monitor and evaluate programmes. This was done mostly by enlarging its pool of affiliated consultants and hence strengthening its operational capacity.

In almost all cases, programme evaluation rested on agents' self-evaluation. Many of the organizations interviewed included some form of evaluation as part of their projects' terms of reference, and some had standardized these procedures across all sectors. However, many stated that donors were hesitant to finance mission evaluations and impact assessments. Most agencies mentioned that evaluations were undertaken in-house through local (and at times headquarters-based) evaluation teams. Few of them focused distinctly on programme impact assessment. Action Aid and Oxfam reported that they undertook programme evaluations in Sierra Leone on the basis of local workshops and assessments, as a standardized approach for project appraisal and implementation, with the aim of increasing local ownership and project sustainability. This, however, was an exception. Such evaluations and impact assessments were rarely standardized, and even more rarely filtered into local, regional or international databases that would facilitate and encourage the learning of lessons or the development of early warning mechanisms that could be used by other agencies. In the words of one aid worker in Sierra Leone: 'lessons learned are a joke, so far. We have got neither the time nor the money to undertake the necessary assessment. If evaluations are undertaken, they are often donor driven and financed'.[24]

Most importantly, evaluations were frequently based on prior project outlines, or terms of reference. These assessed overall change according to quantifiable contractual indicators, such as medical statistics. Such an approach to programme evaluation entailed a danger of over-emphasizing the importance of quantitative indicators (such as lives saved), while paying insufficient attention to those important parts of the comprehensive impact assessment that lie beyond the project's limited outlines. Furthermore, such quantitative evaluations based on a project's success or failure risked disregarding the project's overall value or relevance. All our interviews displayed a clear focus on comparing inputs and outputs, rather than local change. A programme's success was, therefore, assessed in terms of fulfilment of contract indicators rather than any real and substantial change in the circumstances of a vulnerable population. As a result, programme success could easily be 'guaranteed' to a donor. As one aid worker put it: 'generally DFID cares less than other donors who implements what projects and how, as long as audit figures are OK and accountability can be assumed'.[25]

According to Wael Ibrahim, for example, Oxfam analysed who the main beneficiaries of the intervention were, and whose interests were harmed by it, as an essential part of its impact assessments. It also regularly assessed its programmes' impact on conflict. These assessments formed part of Oxfam's strategic accountability as they involved analysis of the alternative strategies that might have been pursued. Oxfam staff mentioned that it had a clear interest in moving towards 'best practices' and re-informing strategies. This, however, was also an exception. Most agencies interviewed professed they had not standardized impact assessments; and such evaluations were often not undertaken at all.[26] Interviews also showed that there was a high degree of misunderstanding or disagreement regarding the contents of and rationale for impact assessment evaluations. As one aid worker put it: 'impact assessment is a sexy trend, but what else?'.[27]

Mechanisms of donor evaluation and monitoring

All interviewees reported that DFID required frequent project evaluations. Many also mentioned that DFID had displayed an interest in assisting organizations in reporting on and evaluating projects. DFID's reporting requirements were considered to be extensive but more straightforward and flexible than those of other donors. DFID did not require implementing agents to assess their programmes' impact on the ongoing peace process. According to the head of DFID in Sierra Leone, Ian Stuart, at times DFID paid external contractors to assess funded work's impact on the peace process, but such evaluations did not usually form part of the project contracts with implementing organizations.[28] Most agencies interviewed argued that donors, which included but were not limited to DFID, regularly visited projects in Sierra Leone, and that donor oversight was tight. However, most also argued that donors rarely had a clear understanding of project content and processes. Several pointed out that such monitoring provided an opportunity to introduce donors to local realities and project successes. They were also thought a liability and burden, since it hindered ongoing work and sometimes led to donor interference.[29]

None of those interviewed was aware of DFID-specific evaluation or guidelines. Most professed to have vague memoranda of understanding (MoU) with donor organizations on every project. All of these contracts entailed clear output indicators that the organization had meet for audit purposes. Each agency had to account for those objectives and report frequently on the programme's status.

DFID reporting guidelines were thought to have become much stricter and demanding once the emergency phase had passed, irrespective of the clear continuing need for emergency interventions. Some organizations mentioned that it was 'very hard to justify funding now'. Most donors, including the UK Government, tended to be too late to intervene in humanitarian emergencies and too eager to exit (most often within 2 or 3 years).[30] Given the lack of clarity regarding the grey area between emergency and development, agencies and donors alike appeared confused with regard to the applicable rules, regulations and emphasis of process.[31]

Several interviewees argued that it was much easier to work with DFID than with some other donors.[32] The majority of those interviewed believed that DFID was as flexible and lenient as other donor organizations, despite its demand for complex reporting. During the emergency, it was thought to have been comparatively easy to alter a project's focus once funding had been agreed, provided the implementing organization made a formal request and justified its decision.[33] Some organizations complained that standards did not apply equally to all organizations funded through the British Government, and that DFID itself did not comply with its own guidelines. All criticized DFID for rarely giving meaningful feedback on project evaluations and negative funding requests.

Most interviewees also argued that the British policy formulation and evaluation processes appeared poorly integrated. In particular, the fact that most evaluations were based on organizations' self-evaluations limited the ability to aggregate comparable data that could have informed future policymaking and project implementation. This allowed implementing organizations greater independence, but it also enabled them to avoid programme impact assessment and reduced donor control. A DFID consultant mentioned:

> It is completely unclear how many international civilian advisors there are within the GoSL. There are very confused reporting

lines to London, in particular as the responsible line managers constantly change. I report to DFID in London on a monthly basis, but I never receive any feedback. I send a copy of my report to Ian Stuart. There is no central strategic control or formalized meetings with everybody, even though about every two weeks there is some sort of DFID meeting. I have also got ad hoc meetings on and off whenever required. Despite this loose control, I work off very clear DFID guidelines, yet am forced to overstep these all the time as about 80 per cent of our work is pure troubleshooting.[34]

This view was supported by a bilateral humanitarian organization's country director, who argued that DFID had employed a large number of people as individuals, but not as teams with a specific purpose. The result was fragmented operations driven by DFID as an umbrella organization but with limited control. Some interviewees mentioned a belief that donors in the field were often ignorant of policy developments and more concerned about ticking off quantitative output indicators than making an assessment of the real impact and progress of a programme.[35] Some also mentioned that accountability and evaluation only made a difference if they were based on local information and an understanding of local requirements. In their opinion, donors were often too far removed and obliged to meet goals too different from those of implementing agents, to have an adequate understanding of local conditions and requirements.

Organizational learning by implementing agents[36]

The vast majority of all non-governmental humanitarian organizations interviewed in Sierra Leone criticized both their own organizations' and their partners' lack of organizational learning mechanisms. Most attributed this to a lack of analysis and contingency planning, and the high turnover of staff, all of which forced organizations to begin from scratch for each emergency.[37] This had a negative effect on strategic policy formulation, the upholding of partnerships and cost efficiency. Strategic policy formulation was also affected by an organizational failure to plan for the longer term, because of short-term funding and the inability to maintain stand-by regional logistics capacities. Given their total dependence on project funding, many organizations acknowledged that a general loss of institutional memory occurred with each completed project. Given the resultant need to identify partner organizations, train staff and build capacity once more with each new project, these organizations incurred significantly high start-up costs. Some NGOs reported that they had attempted to retain their local staff in order to ensure stability and sustainability beyond funding periods, but this often proved difficult. With the onset of the development phase in Sierra Leone and the resultant bilateral (government-to-government) aid relationship, international organizations were obliged to end their so-called 'incentive schemes' (top-up payments to the salaries of locally engaged staff). This frequently resulted in the loss of trained local staff (in particular as the GoSL continued to face a real shortfall in public funds). Some organizations invited their field personnel to attend annual strategic reviews, at which the staff themselves set future strategic objectives. Most often, however, field staff appeared to have little involvement in strategic agenda setting, although they maintained a relatively high degree of input on project objectives. Because of the remoteness of most areas of engagement, they remained fairly independent and far removed from headquarters control. This allowed agency field offices to essentially shape local policy, limited only by the availability of resources.

Conclusion on control

In summary, we have uncovered a wide-ranging absence of donor control over field-based policy implementation. Also, we were unable to establish common mechanisms of a wider humanitarian emergency strategy or donor mechanisms of effective programme evaluation. Our research has furthermore demonstrated a high degree of flexibility and, at the local level, agent independence. However, such independence was severely restricted by a general absence of long-term funding and strategic planning.

Nevertheless, DFID had the ability to place conditions on funding agencies and programmes, some of which may have been politically motivated. It is difficult to differentiate between political conditionality and perceived operational necessity (as for example in the case where several governments and ECHO selectively withdrew the funding of agencies working within the Taliban-controlled Afghanistan). With regard to humanitarian operations in Sierra Leone, some humanitarian NGOs report that DFID has used the lack of staff security as an argument to force DFID-funded organizations to work in specific areas only, to suspend operations or to withdraw altogether.[38] Allegedly, such security risks were exaggerated, applied inconsistently or used only when it was politically convenient. This could indicate either donor control or conditionality of humanitarian emergency assistance.

Conclusion

In this chapter we have evaluated selected aspects of UK-sponsored emergency assistance projects in Sierra Leone that enabled or inhibited the successful implementation of donor policy. We concluded that policy implementation fell short of most of the minimum standards of successful policy implementation we defined in Chapter 1. New Humanitarianism was not explicitly communicated to implementing agents; nor did humanitarian emergency organizations make a consistent effort to coordinate their efforts on the basis of common objectives. On the contrary, the fragmentation and diversity of the aid environment and a pervasive lack of information undermined effective common agenda setting. Both were aggravated by the vagueness of British New Humanitarianism and by the breadth and complexity of the British intervention in Sierra Leone. Greater policy clarity and more assertive publication of donor objectives would have mitigated some of these inconsistencies. However, without much more effective rules of implementation, agreed division of responsibility and more rigorous donor monitoring of field programmes, it remains highly unlikely that New Humanitarianism could have functioned effectively in Sierra Leone.

In order to avoid unnecessary repetition, we leave an assessment of the effectiveness of the implementation process of British emergency assistance policy to the final chapter. Chapter 5 also appraises the likelihood of a successful implementation of British New Humanitarianism in a post-war environment within Sierra Leone.

6
Shifting Sands: British New Humanitarianism

We have analysed the contents and rationale of British New Humanitarianism and its implementation in Sierra Leone in order to investigate the policy's coherence and efficacy. To that end, we have explored the development of UK humanitarian emergency assistance policy since 1997 to include broader concerns for human rights and peace-building, assessed the new policy's development into a country strategy and set of programmes for Sierra Leone, and finally assessed the efficiency of the British bureaucracy in implementing policy change. We have identified the strengths and weaknesses of the implementation process in order to isolate those aspects that must be addressed in order to raise policy efficiency and effectiveness.

Our analysis was underpinned by two key hypotheses. First, senior policymakers within the Cabinet Office and DFID had sought to introduce concerns for human rights and peace-building into humanitarian emergency assistance. Secondly, the process of policy implementation and the disjointedness of the implementation environment had prevented policy change and were not conducive to the delivery of policy goals. We found support for both hypotheses, but New Humanitarianism had been promoted less assertively at the local level than the strategic policy guidelines had led us to expect. British humanitarian relief policy as implemented in Sierra Leone changed less than we originally anticipated, and less than the Government's rhetoric had suggested. These results highlight a tension between the rhetoric at headquarters level and policy execution in Sierra Leone. Despite this, we have reached significant conclusions on the coherence of New Humanitarianism and the effectiveness of policy implementation.

At the policy formulation level, key personnel assumed that humanitarian emergency assistance had the capacity to address wider political objectives and could be integrated into peace-building strategies. In order to improve the efficacy of policy, they developed British New Humanitarianism and advocated the concept of a relief-to-development continuum. New Humanitarianism was neither consistently implemented nor consistently promoted in Sierra Leone, however, where it proved far less compatible with, and complimentary to, the broader peace-building strategy than originally anticipated. Also, its implementation could not easily be controlled. Neither at the headquarters level nor in the field was this disconnect between strategy at the senior policymaking level and the country strategy as implemented in Sierra Leone ever acknowledged or addressed. At a rhetorical level, British senior policymakers within DFID continued to argue for the integration of emergency assistance within the overall British peace-building strategy in Sierra Leone, but this was not mirrored by their actions. On the contrary, field workers broadly disregarded New Humanitarianism and were allowed to do so. Both the lack of clear policy guidelines and the ineffectiveness of the policy implementation process undermined a coherent interpretation of New Humanitarianism and its application in Sierra Leone.

Even if the British Government had developed and disseminated a clear and effective humanitarian policy, our results indicate that inconsistencies within the policy implementation structure would probably still have weakened its coherent application in Sierra Leone. At the headquarters level, New Humanitarianism was neither explained nor forcefully pursued. External shocks (i.e., shifts in foreign policy objectives because of international developments or changes within the policy coalition) and UK foreign policy (i.e., the intervention in Iraq) significantly impacted on humanitarian assistance policy and the UK's engagement in Sierra Leone. The focus of British humanitarian policy shifted towards support for reform of the global humanitarian system.

In this chapter we draw out our key results regarding the effectiveness of the implementation process of New Humanitarianism and its impact on policy coherence (both at the strategic level and in Sierra Leone). We then discuss significant changes in the operational environment (more specifically the increasing privatization and militarization of British emergency assistance) and the Government's efforts to draw lessons from its previous engagement in, and overall commitment to, humanitarian assistance. We conclude by identifying overall recommendations that may contribute towards the improvement of British humanitarian emergency assistance.

Conclusions on the implementation process of UK policy

In this section we summarize our principal findings on the process of policy implementation, in terms of the key criteria of successful policy implementation as identified in Chapter 1. In order to avoid repetition, the analysis here is kept brief. Conclusions that were previously drawn in other sections are not repeated here.

Policy implementation
Clear and consistent policy objectives
Chapter 2 analysed the contents of the British New Humanitarianism in some detail and concluded that the principles of engagement remained too vague to provide the basis of a common, network-wide approach. Furthermore, the British Government had provided no guidelines on how to deal with possible contradictions in foreign policy. Nor did the majority of those employed in the DFID administration support a rights- or conflict-sensitive approach to humanitarian emergency assistance. On the contrary, such an approach was initially a top-down process, driven by a minority of key decision-makers. Chapters 4 and 5 showed that this lack of policy agreement and coordination was exacerbated in the field, given the linkages between emergency assistance, development and security programmes (which demanded quite a different focus and *modus operandi*). The results of many interviews with governmental and non-governmental personnel in Sierra Leone indicated that the UK Government had made up the rules as it went along. Consequently, policy interpretation depended on the beliefs of key personnel, and the behaviour of the personnel engaged in policy implementation was unlikely to be coherent. This inconsistent interpretation of principles led to contradictory communications between DFID's field staff and partner organizations, and did not facilitate a common

understanding of Britain's objectives in Sierra Leone with regard to the role of emergency assistance. Given the policy's vulnerability to external shocks, neither DFID nor its implementing organizations were able to define long-term strategies.

Similarly, as in any area of engagement, the international aid community pursued a wide variety of objectives and mandates. Even more than donor organizations, non-governmental humanitarian organizations proved reluctant or unable to define clear operational strategies beyond the setting of general priorities. This was mainly because relief organizations (1) usually react spontaneously to need rather than engaging in longer-term prior strategic planning; (2) have few resources with which to undertake strategic planning; and (3) at the field level tend to believe that strategic policy planning is neither the focus of, nor even relevant to, their work but rather the responsibility of far-removed headquarters.[1] This was emphasized by several field workers interviewed in Sierra Leone, who complained about shortages of information, time and the resources that would enable them to analyse regional conditions and need effectively, or to engage in longer-term programme planning.

Credibility and empirical and theoretical reasoning

From the outset, New Humanitarianism was based on a set of disputed assumptions, as the British Government cherry-picked from the international debates on 'new wars', 'Do No Harm' and 'humanitarian principles', as discussed in detail in Chapters 2 and 3. The theoretical underpinnings of the broader aspects of DFID's humanitarian emergency assistance policy were not adequately relayed to its implementing agents and did not gain their support. Given the remoteness of many areas of engagement, donor programming and decision-making were often based on limited information of local conditions, despite DFID's own representation in the field. DFID relied heavily on information provided by humanitarian organizations and other British actors present in Sierra Leone, including, for example, the military. Interviews in London and Freetown showed inconsistencies between headquarters' and field staff's interpretations of policy objectives, which were possibly exacerbated by their divergent access to policy debates and their accountability to different clienteles. Senior policy decision-makers were accountable to ministers and the electorate; field staff were accountable to UK bureaucrats and Sierra Leoneans, that is, the local stakeholders.

The UK Government's image in Sierra Leone has taken considerable flak, despite its extraordinary and generous engagement. The UK's credibility had been damaged following its involvement with Sandline in breaking the UN arms embargo and DFID's lack of transparency in donor/agency relations. Furthermore, some humanitarian organizations in Sierra Leone stressed that the UK's military involvement in Sierra Leone implied that any cooperation with British Government departments compromised their own neutrality. All of these arguments highlight a lack of donor credibility, but this could not be substantiated in the course of the interviews undertaken within Sierra Leone. Despite criticism, the majority of those interviewed expressed their interest in and overall respect for British personnel and the British engagement in Sierra Leone.

Transparency, predictability and long-term policy stability

In the absence of any clear principles on humanitarian emergency assistance and rules of implementation, our interviews pointed towards a lack of transparent decisions regarding both programmes and partners, which was naturally exacerbated by the British engagement's vulnerability to external shock, as discussed in the last section. The absence of formalized channels of communication and frequent staff rotation contributed further to incomprehensible policy and programme decisions and a lack of policy predictability. At the operational level in particular, relationships between organizations were heavily influenced by personal contacts. This overall lack of information and the volatile and rushed emergency environment encouraged the spreading of rumours and decision-making on the basis of anecdotes. More transparent policy formulation and decision-making by donors, or more open dialogue with implementing organizations (at both strategic and local levels), would have gone a long way towards preventing this.

An overall lack of transparency and policy predictability, together with the need to ensure programme and organizational survival, led to 'shopping bag' behaviour on the part of humanitarian organizations. As a result, instead of basing their programme proposals on in-house principles and prior needs assessments, organizations were tempted to second-guess donor priorities and jump onto the donor funding bandwagon.

The volatility of the local environment and the scarcity of resources (both within Sierra Leone and in terms of available donor funding for emergency programmes) undermined the long-term planning and sustainability of programmes. It also inhibited the aggregation of comparable data, the drawing of lessons, and reform. Furthermore, a move from relief to development (as demanded by DFID and other donors) required the presence of a functioning state. Neither the future political development of Sierra Leone nor donor engagement was predictable. Without predictable donor behaviour and aid flows, aid conditionality was even less likely to function successfully. Not only does (humanitarian) aid conditionality incur high costs, but it also has a very limited impact on political change. The latter is especially relevant in so-called 'poor performing countries', that is, those that do not comply with the UK Government's governance standards. Furthermore, it is particularly relevant in the case of Sierra Leone because of the limited ownership of reform endeavours and, most importantly, a lack of donor reliability and predictability.

Rules of implementation and support by a committed and well-qualified bureaucracy and implementing agents

DFID's early enthusiasm for rights-based humanitarianism and conflict management rhetoric was clearly driven by a minority within the department's leadership. Despite the tendency of the British development bureaucracy to favour longer-term, developmental approaches, the speed and contents of bureaucratic adaptation did not match the potentially significant policy innovation of New Humanitarianism. On the contrary, the British implementation bureaucracy showed itself reluctant to take forward a politically informed New Humanitarianism, both strategically in Britain and operationally in Sierra Leone.

The involvement of a large number of divisions and individuals from several departments in the design and implementation of the British policy in Sierra Leone had important consequences for the programme's cohesion and transparency. While this separation of powers and the competing and overlapping responsibilities and objectives within the British administration allowed for a degree of necessary and welcome flexibility, they also undermined the coherent interpretation of, and approach to, the principles of New Humanitarianism in Sierra Leone. The fragmentation of the aid bureaucracy and interdepartmental confrontation, suspicion and rivalry undermined the clarity of both policy and implementation. Its piecemeal outsourcing to specialized departments and implementing agents prevented common agenda setting, policy interpretation and coordination. This was accentuated by the latent antagonism of some of the actors involved.

Most importantly, humanitarian organizations made only minimal investment in setting priorities on the basis of a common agenda. They were cautious about becoming a tool for donor foreign policy objectives, in part because donors and humanitarian organizations were accountable to different clients. More fundamentally, humanitarian non-governmental actors received their legitimacy from acting on behalf of their clients, the recipients of aid, independently of governmental direction. As a result, active donor engagement in decision-making in programmes was regarded as detrimental and interpreted as a sign of micromanagement.

Given the multitude of actors involved in its design, implementation and evaluation, DFID's policymaking and implementation suffered from unclear lines of responsibility and lack of control. They were further undermined by the distance of those responsible for DFID's humanitarian emergency policy from the implementation area and the difficulty of assigning responsibility for programmes' success or failure. The failure to ensure the assertive dissemination of donor objectives or uphold transparent lines of communication proved detrimental to the consolidation of New Humanitarianism.

Control

Overall, DFID had little capacity to drive or control programme implementation. This was exacerbated by frequent staff rotation a lack of institutional memory and a fast-moving policy environment. In addition, DFID arguably had little interest in becoming involved in (or taking responsibility for) project execution. Such an endeavour would have been beyond its capacity. Furthermore, both the donor organization and its implementing partners were interested in, and depended upon, programmes' execution and success (whether real or perceived), which further weakened the potential strict application of control mechanisms.

As a donor organization, DFID controlled the contents and implementation of programmes through the power of the purse. Contracts with implementing partner organizations usually outlined the programmes' contents and areas of operations. Such contracts also specified mandatory reporting and evaluation conditions. However, once funding had been granted, DFID had little capacity to influence each programme's direction or the details of project implementation, other than through continued programme monitoring or the suspension of funding. In terms of resources (personnel and time), DFID had little in-house capacity to monitor programmes in remote areas of operation and on a recurrent basis. To some extent, this was improved with the increased appointment of staff and the delegation of DFID's authority to its field offices. DFID was unlikely to have grounds for the suspension of funding other than in exceptional cases of non-performance. More importantly, both DFID and implementing organizations relied on the successful release of funds and positive programme evaluations, and both had an interest in long-term, successful partnerships. This further reduced the likelihood of the suspension or withdrawal of funding. In Sierra Leone, DFID did not make good use of the available control mechanisms, but it did demand extensive reports on programme implementation and generally expected project impact assessments. (These were mostly based, however, on quantitative indicators of project output rather than a comprehensive impact assessment.)

Ownership and proportionality of impact

Given the extreme lack of local resources, Sierra Leone and its government were vulnerable. Furthermore, although it had been democratically elected, the GoSL's legitimacy remained contested both domestically and, to a lesser extent, internationally. It depended on the backing of the international donor community and the provision of security through international peacekeepers and the British 'force on the horizon'. As such, the GoSL was pliable to donor demands, but this did not make it controllable. On the contrary, at the time of writing, the GoSL lacks the capacity to control its own members, to set an effective policy agenda, or to organize the efficient provision of public services. Just as much as its primary donors, in particular the British Government, it depends on continued stability and the eventual success of the peace and reconstruction process. Having invested disproportionately in the restoration of peace and democracy in Sierra Leone, the UK Government has tied itself to the success of its intervention and the fate of the Kabbah administration. The British Government has long been searching for a more effective way to hold the GoSL accountable and for an exit strategy from Sierra Leone. Furthermore, there was no consensus within the British Government as to the future direction of policy. Parts of the British administration found it more important to make further investment in Sierra Leone and its government in order to uphold the overall peace process, while others placed greater emphasis on the need to hold the GoSL to its commitments regarding democratic decision-making and reform.

More importantly, while the UK may have had some means of controlling the political administration in Sierra Leone, it had little leverage over those forces that may still seek to exploit or stall the peace process. The available mechanisms of control and conditionality do little to determine the behaviour of the perpetrators of human rights abuses or those that benefit from instability and illicit extraction. This further puts into question the merits of using aid conditionality in order to change the behaviour of rogue forces. The impact of suspending relief programmes would fall disproportionately on the victims of abuse and the stakeholders of relief aid.

Given the extreme level of vulnerability, ownership of relief and reconstruction programmes has been limited. This was despite the attempts of many aid organizations to undertake needs assessment missions and programme appraisals with stakeholder involvement. Only in the long term will it be possible to assess the wider impact of rights- and conflict-sensitive programmes. It remains doubtful, however, whether such a time frame will be available, given the likelihood of an earlier withdrawal of the donor community.

Co-ordination and coherence

In the above sections we have seen that there was only limited coordination in the execution of humanitarian emergency programmes in Sierra Leone, which was in part the result of *a priori* vague and possibly even contradictory political guidelines. For the most part this was due to highly fragmented and competitive policymaking and policy implementation environments, and the presence of a multitude of mandates. Given the nature of the international relief network and the complexity of many areas of operation, this will not change, so the utility of conditional wider relief as an instrument to achieve political change is therefore fundamentally reduced. That said, this is not to deny a potential positive impact at the project level. Also, it must be noted that

> there is evidence that UK stakeholders are coordinating their activities more effectively than was the case prior to 2001 before the [Conflict Prevention] Pools were set up. As one official put it, 'we now have scrutiny of each other's activities and have input into them that would not have happened pre-Pools'. Both in the field and in Whitehall there is regular formal and informal coordination and information sharing.[2]

Monitoring, evaluation and accountability

Humanitarian emergency operations and policymaking are both hampered by a lack of solid information. This absence of information relates to local environments, evaluations of existing relief interventions and policy objectives. An overall information asymmetry between all actors involved in the process, in particular between headquarters level and the field, limits not only coordination and coherence but also future agenda setting. Both donors and relief organizations in Sierra Leone invested resources in programme monitoring, evaluation and impact assessment. All were aware of a need to improve such assessments and record programme data on an ongoing basis. Nevertheless, too few resources (in terms of time, money and personnel) were made available for meaningful and sufficiently wide-ranging evaluations to be undertaken. This was due in part to the volatility and rushed nature of emergency programme areas and the immediate and extreme needs of vulnerable populations, but it may also have reflected a general lack of will among donors and agencies alike to 'waste' valuable resources on quasi-administrative exercises. To some extent, it was also caused by the reluctance of donors and humanitarian organizations alike to give away information that they deemed to be highly valuable. Last but not least, engagement in complex emergencies causes high levels of insecurity and personal stress, and it requires considerable imagination, commitment and personal sacrifice. All of this further limits aid workers' ability to accept criticism and policy change, especially if driven by a remote donor.

Flexibility

Relief aid programmes in Sierra Leone were constricted by either a lack of access to vulnerable populations or a lack of resources. To some extent they were limited by donor selection of programmes and partner organizations, or by donor priority setting. On the whole, aid agencies operating in Sierra Leone were free to operate independently.

DFID increasingly focuses on strengthening its reporting and evaluation requirements (although data from the field contradict this finding to some extent). The department is itself under increasing pressure from other parts of the government to account for resources spent on aid operations. It remains to be seen whether the department will make an effort to go beyond limited project evaluations on the basis of short-term quantitative output indicators, or whether it will be given the means to invest in longer-term programme impact assessment. It also remains to be seen whether such an undertaking will increase the perception of a donor/agency 'master and servant' relationship, or whether the department can undertake meaningful evaluations in partnership with the aid community.

Conclusions on the British New Humanitarianism

In 1997–99, the British Government assumed at the strategic, policymaking level that humanitarian emergency aid had a role within the pursuit of wider political objectives, including development, management of violent conflict and support for human rights. To that end, DFID drafted the 1998 principles of New Humanitarianism and top-level bureaucrats developed an assertive rights-based and conflict-sensitive rhetoric. New Humanitarianism incorporated objectives beyond the immediate mandate to save lives that had long characterized traditional or principled humanitarian emergency assistance and was more informed by – and supportive of – conflict prevention and development. In theory, instead of responding to need alone, British aid was also meant to 'identify and address root causes of conflicts and integrate humanitarian emergency assistance into approaches to bring about lasting peace'.[3]

Regardless of this, British New Humanitarianism never amounted to a clear and rigorously supported humanitarian aid policy. While a vision of this New Humanitarianism existed on the strategic level, it failed to generate sufficient support from the policymaking and implementation bureaucracies to translate general policy guidelines into clear country strategies for humanitarian emergency assistance. The policy's general vagueness had important consequences for the implementation of humanitarian emergency operations and for DFID's relationship with implementing partner organizations. Ambiguity allowed for flexibility in implementation; but it also precluded coherence and coordination, two essential aspects the British Government had set out to improve. What is more, the British Government did not assist aid organizations in maximizing their impact on behalf of a coordinated peace-building strategy.

Once power structures within DFID and between British Government departments had shifted, and as Britain became increasingly engaged on other military fronts, such as in the Middle East, senior executives within DFID and the Cabinet Office scaled down their rhetoric. New Humanitarianism was then replaced by a less public, more selective, improvised and bilateral approach to the implementation of humanitarian emergency assistance policy. Instead of further strengthening its key policy priorities and disseminating them widely to implementing organizations, DFID concentrated on strengthening its managerial oversight of the delivery of humanitarian emergency relief. Furthermore, the department increased its control over policy implementation by being more selective in its choice of implementing partner organizations and by 'privatizing' large aspects of it.

Overall, New Humanitarianism lacked an agreed framework understood by the majority of organizations involved in its implementation, a clear and coordinated goal and, as a consequence, leverage. This includes leverage over potential spoilers of the peace process in Sierra Leone and those parts of the British policy implementation network that oppose the broadening of humanitarian mandates. DFID did not promote an ongoing, active, impartial and critical network-wide dialogue with non-governmental humanitarian relief organizations on the future of humanitarian aid. Instead, like other large donors, it tacitly promoted an agenda that encouraged the privatization and militarization of relief aid. At the international level, its primary focus shifted towards a reform of the humanitarian emergency relief system.

UK New Humanitarianism and Sierra Leone

British New Humanitarianism also fell far short of a clear and coherent strategy at the operational level in Sierra Leone. Contrary to the British rhetoric of humanitarian emergency aid strategy and our original assumptions, we were unable to distinguish any clear or coordinated wider emergency aid strategy and policy on Sierra Leone. At no point was it implemented in Sierra Leone beyond some localized areas of engagement. Nor did the UK consistently apply political conditionality to humanitarian emergency assistance programmes. Britain's *de facto* humanitarian emergency assistance policy in Sierra Leone differed significantly from that spelled out in the Government's published guiding principles, and the principles of successful policy implementation. It remained reactive and improvised, and commanded little leverage over stakeholder behaviour. It also lacked stability and predictability. At no point did the British Government, its field office in Sierra Leone and the broad aid implementation network achieve agreement on policy objectives and co-ordinate their implementation.

British engagement in Sierra Leone has to be understood as a work in progress. As one senior British staff member put it: 'DFID has been making up rules while going along with little prior planning and assessment'. Initially the overall British engagement in Sierra Leone benefited from a high-level political commitment (since both the Secretary of State for International Development and the Prime Minister were personally involved in decision-making) and inter-ministerial coordination. Yet, both inter-ministerial and inter-departmental coordination became increasingly difficult during the policy's implementation.

The guiding principle of humanitarian emergency assistance in Sierra Leone was that it was expected to fit in with overall British foreign policy objectives. As such, it was to support the ongoing peace and restructuring process and contribute in the long term to overcoming the root causes of the war. Aid was utilized to keep the peace process afloat and as an incentive for structural and democratic change. In other respects humanitarian programmes in Sierra Leone were no different from those adopted under the traditional humanitarian approach. The UK showed interest in aid agencies' addressing of conflict and human rights, but it neither identified clear, strategic objectives for the delivery of emergency assistance in their support nor encouraged coherent, country-wide implementation of New Humanitarianism in Sierra Leone.

In Chapter 5, we reached four main conclusions. First, British-funded aid agencies operating in Sierra Leone cherry-picked those programmes they believed to provide responses to local needs, that were in key donors' interests, and which they thought they would be able to complete. Second, humanitarian relief was integrated within peace-building objectives to the extent that it became merged (both deliberately and inadvertently) with programmes of developmental reintegration and community empowerment, and the humanitarian programmes were designed not to conflict with British foreign policy objectives. Humanitarian programmes were not consistently adapted, however, to include conditionality requirements. Third, the UK was unlikely to run a comparably comprehensive programme in Africa in the near future. Finally, the British Government was intending to strengthen its efforts to outsource humanitarian programmes in complex political emergencies to private (profit-driven) or security companies.

Given the current vulnerability of the Sierra Leonean state and the scarcity of resources, the country was a relatively easy target for assertive donor agenda setting. As the most extensively engaged Western donor, the UK acted almost with impunity in Sierra Leone. Without stronger support and political agenda setting from a functioning Sierra Leonean Government and greater donor coordination, the British intervention (in particular the aid intervention) threatens to remain unsustainable. The British intervention in Sierra Leone stopped the large-scale violence and set the ground for a political solution. The immediate influx of large amounts of relief aid sustained the ceasefire and laid the foundation for a peace process. The death or disappearance of key figures within the leadership of the RUF and rogue units of the Sierra Leonean army (in particular Fodoy Sankoh, Sam Bokarie and Johnny Paul Koroma) and the uprooting of President Charles Taylor in Liberia all brought a new political reality to Sierra Leone and curtailed the opportunities for rebellion. At the time of writing, however, none of this has yet led to sustainable change independent of the aid community. The British intervention did not sufficiently address the root causes of the conflict; rather it contained it for the time being. Humanitarian emergency assistance and development aid in their present form became functional aspects of the former patronage network and shadow economy.

The impact of the implementation process on policy content

From the outset this study suggested that a policy's strength is directly related to the extent to which it has been bureaucratized. Our evidence suggests that a policy's *efficiency* is directly related to the extent to which it has been bureaucratized, although this need not imply that such a policy is also *effective*. British humanitarian aid policies have acquired a high level of bureaucratization and consequently compartmentalization, which has resulted in a highly technical approach to humanitarian relief aid. British New Humanitarianism was crucially undermined by the reluctance of the British aid bureaucracy to support its implementation and invest in stronger conflict- and rights-sensitive agenda setting.

Our evidence shows that the implementation environment had a crucial effect on the contents and impact of British humanitarian emergency assistance in Sierra Leone, and conflict environments in general. Four key facts led us to this conclusion. First, when DFID was faced with internal and external criticism (and when it began to lose some of the turf wars against other departments) it dropped its assertive, conflict-focused humanitarian rhetoric, leaving an ambiguous policy vacuum.

Secondly, the rhetoric and contents of New Humanitarianism and British-supported emergency aid programmes in Sierra Leone differed significantly. Humanitarian policy and programmes remained 'personalized': especially in terms of implementation, their contents and interpretation depended more on the priorities and personal belief systems of key implementing personnel than on strategy.

Thirdly, the fragmented nature of the international humanitarian system and inherent contradictions of both the mandates and the working processes of the numerous implementing agents prevented common agenda setting and closer coordination. From the outset this undermined the effective implementation of New Humanitarianism and reduced leverage.

Fourthly, given the absence of formalized mechanisms of communication, the process of negotiation among competing interests depended on informal contacts between individuals. So did the process by which competing strategies were translated into operations, which lacked transparency and stability. Most importantly, many humanitarian aid organizations lacked the institutional memory to draw lessons from their engagement, which would have been useful for future agenda setting and donor/agency coordination. In the absence of any coherent, long-term international political strategy and its coherent and coordinated implementation, New Humanitarianism as defined by the British Government had little leverage over local and international policy environments and behaviour.

Changes in the operational environment: The 'privatization' and militarization of humanitarian assistance

Despite the negative evidence presented here and elsewhere, emergency assistance has now become a political and even a military instrument for broader political objectives, as has been, or can be, seen in Sierra Leone, Kosovo, Sudan and Iraq. It is employed on an inconsistent and reactive basis in selected areas of engagement. Increasingly, international humanitarian relief NGOs are being employed, and market themselves, as public service contractors. They enter contractual relationships with donor organizations on the basis of either one-off or standing partnership agreements that include detailed implementation guidelines and measurable output benchmarks. Humanitarian relief organizations are increasingly forced to work where they are told or where donors are prepared to invest money. This undermines their independence, impartiality and neutrality and decreases investment in cross-sectoral, rights-based or conflict-sensitive work. At the same time, in Sierra Leone and Iraq there are increasing indications that the British Government is outsourcing programmes to private (profit-driven) or security companies. There are also indications that military forces are being used to deliver humanitarian emergency assistance, especially in volatile areas of engagement or so-called 'countries at risk of instability'. The repercussions of this merging of broader security objectives with humanitarian emergency assistance, and of emergency aid personnel with military units, are not yet foreseeable.

However, the merging of emergency aid and security policy has already had an important impact on relations between donors and humanitarian agencies. The privatization and militarization of humanitarian aid and the development of public private partnerships are an expression of ongoing and possibly irreversible changes in the nature of humanitarian emergency operations. These are taking place despite a growing unease in national and international political circles with regard to the increasing employment of private security companies to implement the policies of the British Government (and other influential governments). [4] This raises important questions about the future sustainability and effectiveness of humanitarian aid.

The international intervention in Kosovo was one of the first examples of this increasing use of private security contractors and military humanitarianism. The trend continued in East Timor, Afghanistan and now Iraq. Private (and security) service providers now fulfil an ever-greater role in governmental development strategy. DFID is not the only international donor that works with such contractors: the European Union and in particular the United States have made extensive use of the technical, logistical and manpower support of private contractors and private security companies. This trend mirrors the widespread political tendency to privatize social and public services. There are no clear political mechanisms for controlling such private companies or private military (security) companies.

The growing use of military forces in the implementation of aid programmes and the embedding of humanitarian programmes within military operations have led to a violent backlash from local groups against aid organizations in some areas of engagement. This is due in part to the increased difficulty of distinguishing clearly between civilian and military personnel and aid agencies' loss of neutrality. There has also been a worsening of the difficulties of organizational cooperation and common agenda setting. Military and civilian humanitarian organizations work in pursuit of different objectives (winning the war or organizing the peace) and on the basis of very different working processes, organizational structures and processes. The structure of military forces is much more hierarchical than that of aid agencies. Military forces operate secretively, while relief agencies take pains to ensure local ownership and transparency.

In Iraq, this interaction between humanitarian aid workers and the military has led to major political and operational quandaries, especially given that the military 'intervention is seen as illegitimate by significant segments of the population'.[5] It has also caused a chasm between some donors and large parts of the international humanitarian aid network. Given that Western donors fund most aid organizations, the latter are increasingly perceived as instruments of Western hegemony.

The UK Government's selective employment of large British and international humanitarian NGOs and private security companies in Sierra Leone and Iraq, and possibly its secondment of staff to the GoSL, are indicators of a general international trend for governments to engage with the inner workings of foreign governments.[6]

Relief organizations are currently undergoing a momentous evaluation of their rationale, justification and role within international peace operations and development. They are facing a choice between either accepting co-option into the evolving and increasingly merged international security and aid system, or maintaining their independence but also potential loss of influence. If the political trends that are identifiable today solidify, refusing co-option in the short term may lead to a reduction of their overall funding base and loss of access to vulnerable populations in more volatile areas of engagement.[7]

DFID: A learning organization?

Despite the criticism of DFID's structures and political processes presented above, it must also be stressed that DFID has shown itself to be interested in and willing to learn from its engagement and from the general improvement in the effectiveness and efficiency of its policy. DFID has engaged in a long-term restructuring of in-house aid departments and strengthened its contractual guidelines and mechanisms for enhanced programme evaluation. The UK has also established several new mechanisms and units, both within DFID and at the Cabinet Office, which are designed to enhance policy effectiveness and public service delivery. These include: DFID's 'Aid Effectiveness Group', 'Service Delivery Group' and 'Working in Difficult Environment Group' (all within the Policy Department established in 2003), Whitehall's 'Post Conflict Reconstruction Unit' (PCRU), and the Cabinet Office's 'Countries at Risk of Instability' (CRI) unit (within the Prime Minister's Strategy Unit). In mid-2004, DFID was also in the process of re-conceptualizing aid conditionality, and it has been a strong supporter since then of international efforts to reform the humanitarian system. The Government should be complimented for its generous and innovative support.

The establishment of all of these units or mechanisms demonstrates the UK Government's awareness of the shortcomings within policy implementation and cross-departmental coordination. It is also an indication of its increased focus on managerial oversight and its continued striving to develop generic models of engagement. Most of all, it displays the administration's willingness to learn and its strong efforts towards increasing its understanding of complex environments and engagement therein. None of these units was set up specifically in order to improve humanitarian emergency assistance policy and practice. Nor have they addressed the role of emergency relief in any detail to date. Nonetheless, all of them have indirectly affected emergency policy or are likely to do so in the future.

Born out of the quandary of the Iraq war and the subsequent violence-ridden and shambolic reconstruction phase (and to some extent out of the crisis in Sierra Leone), the inter-ministerial Post Conflict Reconstruction Unit (PCRU) and the Countries at Risk of Instability (CRI) unit are intended to increase the UK's understanding of conflict and of working therein.

The PCRU is intended to fill the gaps (and draw on the linkages) between humanitarian emergency assistance, peace-building and development aid. Its rationale and objectives express a somewhat novel conception of the relief-to-development continuum. The unit recognizes not only the limits of emergency assistance in addressing peace-building and long-term reconstruction, but also its contextual and operational distinctness from development aid. Furthermore, it recognizes that military forces lack the capacity and willingness to undertake post-conflict reconstruction and capacity building. The unit is meant to advise the British administration in coordinating the immediate post-conflict phase with regard to reconstruction and capacity building. It was set up to bridge the gap between the provision of humanitarian emergency assistance and more developmental types of assistance (prior to the transition to bilateral, state-to-state development assistance). It is also intended to strengthen Whitehall's ability to accumulate and process information on complex environments, and translate government policy into operational plans and processes. In the long term, the PCRU is also meant to provide an international personnel pool for post-conflict reconstruction operations. It remains to be seen whether the unit will be granted the full support of UK Government departments and whether its remits will be extended beyond areas of large-scale military engagement.

Conclusions by the 'Working in Difficult Environments' and 'Countries at Risk of Instability' units display a changing governmental attitude towards complex emergencies. They also demonstrate a realization of the much more limited capacity of humanitarian emergency assistance to further development and stability, a clear awareness of the common failure of donor coordination, and a drastic lack of quality information and assessment. In 2004, comments by senior DFID personnel showed that the UK hoped to assume a principal position in fostering donor coordination and good donorship in the future, and that it will strengthen its commitment to delegating authority to regional DFID field offices.[8] This is now being implemented in the ongoing humanitarian reform process, which is focusing on improving predictability, sustainability and coordination.

Since its first election victory in 1997, the Labour Government has linked the allocations of public spending to the performance of ministerial departments. As mentioned earlier in this chapter, 'successful delivery of effective and efficient programmes... [is] rewarded with financial resources in future spending rounds'.[9] After New Labour's re-election in 2001, 'the reform and delivery of public services became the defining theme of the second Blair administration'.[10] The Government committed itself to so-called 'evidence-based' or 'performance-based' policymaking and evaluation.

Overall, a narrow, output-focused and rather technical policy approach to humanitarian assistance and public accountability has negative and restrictive repercussions for the humanitarian emergency system. Nevertheless, if new resources are made available to improve and standardize effective programme evaluation, if field personnel become further integrated within the policymaking process, and if targets are linked more closely to stakeholder needs, the British Government's agenda towards policy reform might well generate positive change.

It remains to be seen whether the new DFID and CHAD structures, and the increasing reliance on field-based DFID representation, will show positive results. It also remains to be seen to what degree and how quickly newly established units within DFID and the Cabinet Office will be able to influence policymaking, and how encompassing their remit will be. Early indications show both unwillingness and a lack of capacity within the bureaucracy to engage with and support the newly established units. Most of all, despite DFID's willingness and ability to learn, doing so (and instigating policy change) could engender the strong opposition from other sectors of government and from the private (security) service providers discussed above. Both have a strong organizational motivation to oppose a reversal of policy. As has been shown, DFID has few mechanisms to drive sustained policy change in opposition to large sectors of the policy (implementation) establishment. Given the high-level ministerial interest, it is to be hoped that the present level of British support (in both financial and political terms) and appointment of a senior British diplomat to the post of UN Emergency Relief Coordinator in 2007 will be indicative of Britain's continued strong and broad support for the reform of the international humanitarian system.

In conclusion, in order to increase the efficacy of New Humanitarianism, the government must refine the policy's objectives, in terms of both strategic principles and country strategies. As an aspect of this, it must clearly differentiate between military and humanitarian objectives. In order to increase transparency and enable coordination, these objectives should be disseminated widely and assertively, both internally and externally. It is hoped that this will strengthen the support of the implementation bureaucracy and the humanitarian community at large.

We have highlighted shortcomings within the implementation process of British humanitarian emergency assistance. In order to overcome these, the government must agree rules on implementation, responsibility for action, and individual, departmental and organizational accountability for humanitarian relief. Clear lines of responsibility and personal accountability would greatly increase the effectiveness and reliability of policy implementation.

Similarly, the government will wish to maintain an active and critical dialogue with the national and international aid communities in order to increase transparency and common agenda setting. In order to increase control and quality of impact, it will also want to undertake an ongoing evaluation of emergency programmes' longer-term impacts. This must include a conflict impact assessment. Any meaningful impact assessment will require additional funds, and standardization of such assessments is an essential aspect of all funding relationships.

The quality and sustainability of programmes would benefit from improved and standardized collection, monitoring and analysis of regional inter-agency humanitarian data, on the part of both donor and aid organizations. In terms of coherence and longer-term planning, it would also benefit from monitoring humanitarian emergency and development aid flows to Sierra Leone and other countries in the region. Information on evaluations and lessons learned must remain available for all actors concerned beyond the duration of programmes.

Lastly, efficient humanitarian emergency assistance (in particular as an aspect of a peace-building process) requires coordination of key donors on common objectives. Even more importantly, it demands rapid, sustainable and predictable funding. In particular, in cases like Sierra Leone, in which the United Kingdom assumed a lead nation position, the British Government is in a position to coordinate and maintain effective consultation forums. Most of all, effective humanitarian engagement in complex emergencies and political change will both require a longer-term and coherent political commitment to areas of operation. This commitment must go beyond the provision of assistance during the emergency and the immediate post-conflict phase.

None of these recommendations is altogether new. Nevertheless, if they were to be implemented, they would go a long way towards improving the efficacy of the international relief system and increasing the impact of strategic agenda setting by donors.

Notes

1 The Politics of New Humanitarianism

1. Mark Duffield, 'Humanitarian Conditionality: Origins, Consequences and Implications of the Pursuit of Development in Conflict', in: Geoff Loane and Tanja Schümer (eds), *The Wider Impact of Humanitarian Assistance. The Case of Sudan and the Implications for European Union Policy*, Aktuelle Materialien zur Internationalen Politik 60,6 (Baden-Baden: Nomos, 1999), 97–130, 100.
2. Michael Clarke and Steve Smith (eds), *Foreign Policy Implementation* (Winchester Mass.: Allen & Unwin, 1985), 173.
3. Hugo Slim, 'A Call to Alms: Humanitarian Action and the Art of War', *Humanitarian Dialogue Opinion* (Geneva: The Centre for Humanitarian Dialogue, 2004), 1–18, 4.
4. Mark Bradbury, 'Behind the Rhetoric of the Relief-to-Development Continuum', paper prepared for the NGOs in Complex Emergencies Project (London: September 1997), 11.
5. See for example: Hugo Slim, 'International Humanitarianism's Engagement with Civil War in the 1990's: A Glance at Evolving Practice and Theory', *Journal of Humanitarian Assistance* (19 December 1997), http://www.jha.spa.cam.ac.uk/a/a565.htm, posted on 1 March 1998.
6. For a discussion of the negative side effects of humanitarian emergency assistance, see: Mary B. Anderson, *Do No Harm. How Aid Can Support Peace – or War* (Boulder, London: Lynne Rienner, 1999); Geoff Loane and Tanja Schümer (eds), *The Wider Impact of Humanitarian Assistance*; Geoff Loane and Celine Moyroud, *Tracing Unintended Consequences of Humanitarian Assistance: The Case of Sudan. Field Study and Recommendations for the European Community Humanitarian Office*. Aktuelle Materialien zur Internationalen Politik 60/9 (Baden-Baden: Nomos, 2000).
7. David Bryer and Edmund Cairns, 'For Better? For Worse? Humanitarian Aid in Conflict', *Development in Practice* 7, 4 (1997), 363–74, 363.
8. Mikael Barfod, 'Humanitarian Aid and Conditionality: ECHO's Experience and Prospects Under the Common Foreign and Security Policy', in Nicholas Leader and Joanna Macrae (eds), 'Terms of Engagement: Conditions and Conditionality in Humanitarian Action', Report of a Conference Organized by the Overseas Development Institute and the Centre for Humanitarian Dialogue in Geneva, 3–4 May 2000, *HPG Report* 6 (London: Overseas Development Institute, 2000), 37–43, 38.
9. See: Peter Uvin, *The Influence of Aid in Situations of Violent Conflict: A Synthesis and a Commentary on the Lessons Learned from Case Studies on the Limits and Scope for the Use of Development Assistance Incentives and*

Disincentives for Influencing Conflict Situations, 'Informal Task Force on Conflict, Peace and Development Co-operation' (Paris: Development Assistance Committee, September 1999), 9; Austen Davis, 'Thoughts on Conditions and Conditionalities', in: Nicholas Leader and Joanna Macrae (eds), 'Terms of Engagement: Conditions and Conditionality in Humanitarian Action', Report of a conference organized by the Overseas Development Institute and the Centre for Humanitarian Dialogue in Geneva, 3–4 May 2000, *HPG Report* 6 (London: Overseas Development Institute, 2000), 27–32.

10. International Development Committee, *Fifth Special Report, Government Response to the Fifth Report from the Committee*, House of Commons, Session 1998 (London: DFID, 1999); International Development Committee, *Sixth Report, Conflict Prevention and Post-Conflict Reconstruction, Vol. I, Report and Proceedings of the Committee*, The House of Commons, 20 July 1999, Session 1998/99 (London: DFID, 1999).

11. See for example: Mark Walkup, *Policy and Behavior in Humanitarian Organizations: The Institutional Origins of Operational Dysfunction*, PhD Dissertation, University of Florida (1997); Richard W. Waterman and Kenneth J. Meier, 'Principal – Agent Models: An Expansion?', *Journal of Public Administration Research and Theory* 8, 2 (April 1998), 173–203; Tony Waters, *Bureaucratizing the Good Samaritan: The Limitations of Humanitarian Relief Operations* (Boulder/Col. and Oxford: Westview, 2001).

12. Morton H. Halperin, *Bureaucratic Politics & Foreign Policy* (Washington, DC: Brookings Institution, 1974), 313.

13. Refer to Mark Walkup, *Policy and Behavior in Humanitarian Organizations*. Also see: Irving L. Janis, *Groupthink: Psychological Studies of Policy Decisions and Fiascoes*, 2nd ed. (Boston: Houghton Mifflin Company, 1972).

14. Ibid., 3. Also see: Richard W. Waterman and Kenneth J. Meier, 'Principal–Agent Models', 2.

15. Michael Clarke and Steve Smith (eds), *Foreign Policy Implementation*, 175.

16. Alexander Cooley and James Ron, 'The NGO Scramble: Organizational Insecurity and the Political Economy of Transnational Action', *International Security* 27, 1 (Summer 2002), 5–39, 13.

17. Alexander Cooley and James Ron, 'The NGO Scramble', 15–16.

18. See: Ian Smillie, 'Relief and Development: The Struggle for Synergy', *Occasional Paper* 33 (Providence: Humanitarianism and War Project, 2000), 35–51.

19. Ibid., 14f.

20. See: Alexander Cooley and James Ron, 'The NGO Scramble', 1 (Summer 2002), 5–39, 15; and Tony Waters, *Bureaucratizing the Good Samaritan*, 42.

21. Richard W. Waterman and Kenneth J. Meier, 'Principal–Agent Models', 176. Also see: Mark Walkup, *Policy and Behavior in Humanitarian Organizations*, 189.

22. See: Joanna Macrae *et al.*, 'Uncertain Power: The Changing Role of Official Donors in Humanitarian Action', *HPG Report* 12 (London: Overseas Development Institute, December 2002), 20.

23. Ann M. Fitz-Geralds and F. A. Walthall, 'An Integrated Approach to Complex Emergencies: The Kosovo Experience', *Journal of Humanitarian Assistance*, http://www.jha.ac./articles/a071.htm, 16 August 2001, 7.
24. Overseas Development Institute, '*The Changing Role*', 2. Also see: Mark Duffield, *Global Governance and the New Wars: The Merging of Development and Security* (London and New York: Zed Books, 2001), 258f.
25. Joanna Spear, *Carter and Arms Sales. Implementing the Carter Administration's Arms Transfer Restraint Policy* (Houndmills, London and New York: Macmillan Press and St. Martin's Press, 1995), 11.
26. Alexander Cooley and James Ron, 'The NGO Scramble', 12.

2 DFID and New Humanitarianism

1. See in particular the writings of: Mark Duffield, 'Aid Policy and Post-Modern Conflict: A Critical Review', *Occasional Paper* 19 (Birmingham: University of Birmingham, 1998); David Keen, *The Benefits of Famine: A Political Economy of Famine and Relief in South-Western Sudan 1983–1989* (Princeton, New Jersey: Princeton University Press, 1994); Mary B. Anderson, *Do No Harm*; Paul Collier *et al.*, 'Redesigning Conditionality', *World Development* 25, 9 (1997), 1399–408.
2. Robin Cook, 'Ethical Foreign Policy' (London: Foreign and Commonwealth Office, 12 May 1997). Also see: Robin Cook, 'Foreign Policy and National Interest', Royal Institute of International Affairs, Chatham House (London: FCO, 28 January 2000); Robin Cook, 'Human Rights – A Priority of Britain's Foreign Policy', Foreign Office (London: FCO, 28 March 2001); Robin Cook, 'Human Rights Into a New Century' (London: FCO, 17 July 1997).
3. Tony Blair, 'Address to the Chicago Economic Club', 22 April 1999, http://www.pbs.org/newshour/bb/international/jan-june99/blair_doctrine4-23.html, 15 January 2003.
4. Tony Blair, 'Address to the Chicago Economic Club'.
5. Joanna Macrae and Nicholas Leader, 'Shifting Sands: The Search for "Coherence" Between Political and Humanitarian Responses to Complex Emergencies', *HPG Report* 8 (London: Overseas Development Institute, August 2000), 23.
6. Department for International Development (DFID), *Eliminating World Poverty: A Challenge for the 21st Century. White Paper on International Development* (London: DFID, November 1997).
7. Ibid.
8. Clare Short, 'Conflict Prevention, Conflict Resolution and Post-Conflict Peace-building – From Rhetoric to Reality', Speech by the Secretary of State, Clare Short, at International Alert (London: International Alert, 2 November 1999); George Foulkes, 'UK Policy on Conflict and Humanitarian Assistance', Speech of the Parliamentary Under-Secretary of State, George Foulkes, at the Overseas Development Institute (London: ODI, 12 March 1998). Also see: Camilla Brueckner, 'Towards a Human Rights

Approach to European Commission Humanitarian Aid?', *Echo Discussion Paper* (Brussels: European Union, 1999); Jonathan Moore (ed.), *Hard Choices*; OSCE Development Assistance Committee (DAC), *Conflict, Peace and Development Co-Operation on the Threshold of the 21st Century* (Organisation for Economic Co-Operation and Development: Paris, 1997); European Commission, *Linking Relief, Rehabilitation and Development – An Assessment* (EU: Brussels, 23 April 2001); David Keen, *Benefits of Famine*; John Prendergast, *Frontline Diplomacy: Humanitarian Aid and Conflict in Africa* (Boulder/Col.: Lynne Reinner, 1996).

9. Adele Harmer, 'The Road to Good Donorship: The UK's Humanitarian Assistance', *Humanitarian Exchange* 24 (July 2003), 33–36, 34.

10. See: Mark Hoffman, *DFID Policy on Humanitarian Assistance: A Case of Politics as Usual?* (London: LSE, 1999), 4. Also refer to: Department for International Development (DFID), *Eliminating World Poverty*, 19.

11. Department for International Development (DFID), *Conflict Reduction and Humanitarian Assistance* (London: DFID, 1999), 93–5.

12. Overseas Development Institute, 'The New International Development Act: The Case for Definition of Humanitarian Assistance', notes for a presentation to a meeting of DFID officials/members of the International Development Committee (London: Overseas Development Institute, 27 January 1999), 5.

13. Clare Short, Secretary of State for International Development, 'Principles for a New Humanitarianism', Conference on 'Principled Aid in an Unprincipled World' (London: Church House, April 1998), 2.

14. George Foulkes, 'International Development: Beyond the White Paper', 2–3.

15. Department for International Development (DFID), *Guidelines on Humanitarian Assistance* (London: DFID, May 1997).

16. Department for International Development (DFID), *Code of Conduct for Humanitarian Operations* (London: DFID, 1999), 4.

17. British troops had been involved in the training and restructuring of the Sierra Leonean army; which had been included in the peace agreement.

18. Tony Waters, *Bureaucratizing the Good Samaritan*, 47–50.

19. John Vereker, Permanent Secretary, Department for International Development, 'Can Poverty be Eliminated Through Development Co-Operation?', address to the North South Roundtable, 28 June 1998, http://www.DFID.gov.uk/public/news/sp28june.html, 15 May 2002; Clare Short, Secretary of State for International Development, 'Principles for a New Humanitarianism'. Also see: Clare Short, 'From Rhetoric to Reality'.

20. See for example: Department for International Development (DFID), *Realising Human Rights for Poor People. Strategies for Achieving the International Development Targets* (London: DFID, October 2000), 7.

21. Refer, for example, to exchanges between Clare Short and Action Aid in 1997/98 and discussion in the International Development Committee over suspension of aid operations in Sierra Leone: International

Development Committee, , *Government Response to the Sixth Report from the Committee, Session 1998/99: Conflict Prevention and Post-Conflict Reconstruction* (London: House of Commons, 1999). Refer in particular the minutes of evidence on Sierra Leone and the annexed memoranda by Action Aid and Clare Short on DFID humanitarian policy in Sierra Leone; International Development Committee, *Government Response to the Sixth Report from the Committee, Session 1998/99: Conflict Prevention and Post-Conflict Reconstruction* (London: House of Commons, 1999).

22. Department for International Development (DFID), *Conflict Reduction*, 93; also refer to: Department for International Development (DFID), *Code of Conduct*, 2.

23. Department for International Development (DFID), *Code of Conduct*, 4.

24. Department for International Development (DFID), *The Causes of Conflict in Africa*, consultation document (London: DFID, March 2001), 15.

25. Overseas Development Institute, The New International Development Act, 5.

26. Mary B. Anderson, *Do No Harm*. Mary Anderson's work was first published in 2005.

27. For an in-depth analysis of the concept of the merging of relief, development and security see: Mark Duffield, 'Humanitarian Conditionality: Origins, Consequences and Implications'; Joanna Macrae *et al.*, *Conflict, the Continuum and Chronic Emergencies: A Critical Analysis of the Scope for Linking Relief, Rehabilitation and Development Planning in Sudan*, paper prepared for the Department for International Development (London: Overseas Development Institute, 19 December 1996).

28. Department for International Development (DFID), *Code of Conduct*, 5.

29. Joanna Macrae, *Aiding Recovery? The Crisis of Aid in Chronic Political Emergencies* (London and New York: Zed Books, 2001), 75.

30. International Development Committee, *Sixth Report*; Hoffman, *DFID Policy*, 7; United Nations Department of Humanitarian Affairs (UNDHA), *Sierra Leone Humanitarian Situation Report* (*SLHSR*) (New York: United Nations, 24–30 June 1997).

31. Overseas Development Institute, 'The New International Development Act', 10.

32. Graham T. Allison and Morton H. Halperin, 'Bureaucratic Politics: A Paradigm', 42.

33. Randolph Kent, *Anatomy of Disaster Relief: The International Network in Action* (London and New York: Pinter, 1987), 68f.

34. Discussion with Mark Hoffman.

35. Department for International Development (DFID), *About the Public Service Agreement and Service Delivery Agreement* (London: DFID, 2002), http://www.DFID.gov.uk/AboutThisWebsite/files/AboutPubServ.htm, 24 January 2003.

36. National Audit Office, *Overseas Development Administration: Emergency Relief. Report by the Comptroller and Auditor General, Parliamentary Session 2001–2002* (HC 739) (London: The Stationary Office, 2002), 5.

37. National Audit Office, *Overseas Development Administration*, 5f.
38. Confidential interview with senior FCO staff summer 2004.
39. See: Randolph Kent, *Anatomy of Disaster Relief*, 119–22.
40. Alexandra Galperin, 'Discourses of Disasters, Discourses of Relief and DFID's Humanitarian Policy. A Diagnostic Snapshot of the Crisis of Relief as a Legitimate and Universal Instrument in Contemporary Conflict, *DESTIN Working Paper Series* April 2002 (London: London School of Economics and Political Science, 2002), 28–31.

3   Agents of War and the Causes of Violent Conflict

1. Regarding patrimonialism refer to: Paul Richards, *Fighting for the Rain Forest: War, Youth & Resources in Sierra Leone*, African Issues, 4th edn (Oxford/Portsmouth: James Currey and Heinemann, 2002), 34–5.
2. Confidential interview with a senior commander in the Republic of Sierra Leone Armed Forces, Civil Military Co-operation/International Military Advisory Team (IMATT) in May 2003.
3. Confidential discussion with British IMATT officer, London, 2004.
4. David Keen, *The Best of Enemies: Conflict and Collusion in Sierra Leone* (Oxford: James Currey, 2004) (Palgrave Macmillan, 2006), 291. This argument was supported in several confidential interviews with senior UN and UK officials in Sierra Leone in May 2003.
5. Confidential interview with British soldier, Freetown, June 2003.
6. DFID, *Code of Conduct*, 2.
7. Department for International Development, *Conflict Reduction and Humanitarian Assistance* (London: DFID, http://www.62.189.42.51/DFIDstage/AboutDFID/files/conflict_main.htm#The%20humanitarian%20response, 6 January 2004, 91. Also see: Department for International Development (DFID), *Conflict Reduction Through British Co-operation. A Briefing for Agencies Seeking Support for Conflict Reduction Activities* (London: DFID, June 1997).
8. Department for International Development (DFID), *The Causes of Conflict in Africa* (London: DFID, March 2001), 13.
9. Ibid., 8–9.
10. Clare Short, 'Conflict Prevention', 1.
11. Also see: Department for International Development (DFID), *Conflict Reduction*, 91.
12. Ibid., 2.
13. Refer to: David Keen, 'Incentives and Disincentives for Violence', in: Mats Berdal and David M. Malone (eds), *Greed and Grievance: Economic Agendas in Civil Wars* (Boulder, London: Lynne Rienner, 2000), 19–42; William Reno, 'Shadow States and the Political Economy of Civil War', in: Mats Berdal and David M. Malone (eds), *Greed and Grievance: Economic Agendas in Civil Wars* (Boulder, London: Lynne Rienner, 2000), 43–68; Mark Duffield, *Global Governance*.

14. Drawn from: Paul Richards, *Fighting for the Rain Forest*, 19–25; William Reno, *Corruption and State Politics in Sierra Leone* (Cambridge: Cambridge University Press, 1995); William Reno, 'Resources and the Future of Violent Conflict in Sierra Leone', BISA Conference London December 2002; David Keen, *The Best of Enemies*; David Keen, 'Since I am a Dog, Beware My Fangs: Beyond a 'Rational Violence' Framework in the Sierra Leonean War', *Crisis States Programme Working Papers* 14 (August 2002).
15. Also see: Paul Richards, *Fighting for the Rain Forest*, 51.
16. Department for International Development (DFID) (Alice Jay, Paul Richards and Tennyson Williams), *Sierra Leone: A Framework for DFID Support to Civil Society* (London: DFID, 2003) (unpublished report).
17. David Keen, *The Best of Enemies*, 318.
18. Paul Collier, 'Doing Well out of War: An Economic Perspective', in: Mats Berdal and David M. Malone (eds), *Greed and Grievance: Economic Agendas in Civil Wars* (Boulder/London and other: Lynne Rienner, International Development Research Centre, 2000), 96, 106f.
19. David Keen, 'Since I am a Dog', 3.
20. Steven Archibald and Paul Richards, 'Converts to Human Rights? Popular Debate About War and Justice in Rural Central Sierra Leone', in: *Africa* 3, 72 (22 June 2002) (Edinburgh: Edinburgh University Press, 2002), 14.
21. See: House of Commons, Sir Thomas Legg and Sir Robin Ibbs, *Report of the Sierra Leone Arms Investigation* (London: House of Commons, 27 July 1998); John Kampfner, *Blair's Wars*, 66; Select Committee on Foreign Affairs, Second Report, Summary of Conclusions and Recommendations, http://www.parliament.the-stationery-office.co.uk/pa/cm199899/cmselect/cmfaff/116/11613.htm, 5 April 2003.
22. Confidential interview with a member of the British Foreign Office, London, 2003.
23. David Keen, 'Beyond a "Rational Violence" Framework: Psychological Causes of Civil War Violence', *Crisis States Programme/DESTIN Briefing Paper* 7 (May 2003); David Keen, 'Greedy Elites, Dwindling Resources, Alienated Youths: The Anatomy of Protracted Violence in Sierra Leone', *Internationale Politik und Gesellschaft* 2 (2003), 67–94.
24. Toby Porter, *The Interaction Between Political and Humanitarian Action in Sierra Leone, 1995 to 2002* (Geneva: Centre for Humanitarian Dialogue, March 2003), 18.

4 Pax Britannica: New Humanitarianism in Sierra Leone

1. See for example: Foreign and Commonwealth Office (FCO) and Department for International Assistance (DFID), *Sierra Leone Medium-Term Strategy Action Plan*; Foreign and Commonwealth Office (FCO) and Department for International Assistance (DFID), *Africa Conflict Prevention Pool*.
2. Toby Porter, *The Interaction Between Political and Humanitarian Action*, 72.

3. According to John Davison from Christian Aid, in October 2003 'the government diverted aid to fund reconstruction Iraq... totaling £544 million' over a 3-year period. That is almost five times more than the money allocated to Sierra Leone. BBC News, 'Poor Paying for War on Terror', http://www.news.bbc.co.uk/go/pr/fr/-/2/hi/uk_news/3696683.stm, 20 May 2004.
4. See: Randolph Kent, *Anatomy of Disaster Relief*, 12.
5. Interview with Paul Jenkins, ICRC UK, West & Central Africa Desk Officer, London, 4 May 2003, and interview with Tim Shorten, Department for International Development (DFID), Desk Officer Sierra Leone, Africa Department, London, 25 April 2003.
6. Official figures show that in 2000 the UK exported ammunition to Sierra Leone up to a total of $10,000. For the complete period between 1997 and 2004 these figures are considered to be substantially higher. See: Graduate Institute of International Studies (GIIS), *Small Arms Survey 2004 – Rights at Risk* (Geneva: Oxford University Press, 2004), 128–9.
7. Compare to: Toby Porter, *The Interaction Between Political and Humanitarian*, 70f.
8. In a confidential interview DFID personnel confirmed that Mukesh Kapila had publicly agreed that humanitarian emergency assistance was suspended for a brief period in 1997 as it undermined broader British political objectives. Yet he also stressed that Mukesh Kapila's comment had been misinterpreted as there existed very practical reasons for such a suspension. Confidential interview with DFID personnel 2003.
9. Alexandra Galperin, 'Discourses of Disasters', 22.
10. See: David Keen, *The Best of Enemies*, 160ff.
11. Toby Porter, *The Interaction Between Political and Humanitarian*, 19–20.
12. International Development Committee, *Fifth Report*, Departmental Report 20 July 1999, House of Commons, Session 1998–99 (London: DFID, 1999); International Development Committee, *Fifth Special Report*; International Development Committee, *Sixth Report*.
13. Toby Porter, *The Interaction Between Political and Humanitarian Action*, 28.
14. Ibid., 12.
15. Department for International Development (DFID) and the Government of Sierra Leone, *Sierra Leone: A Long-Term Partnership for Development* (Freetown: Government of Sierra Leone, February 2003), 3.
16. Department for International Development (DFID) and the Government of Sierra Leone, *Sierra Leone: A Long-Term Partnership for Development* (Freetown: Government of Sierra Leone, February 2003).
17. Interview with Ian Stuart, 29 May 200; and interview with Alan Jones, Foreign and Commonwealth Office, British High Commissioner, Freetown, 15 May 2003.
18. Confidential interview with DFID personnel, 2003.
19. Adele Harmer, 'The Road to Good Donorship', 35.
20. Mark Hoffman, *DFID Policy on Humanitarian Assistance*, 5.
21. Alexandra Galperin, 'Discourses of Disasters', 29.
22. Foreign and Commonwealth Office/Department for International Assistance (DFID), *Africa Conflict Prevention Pool*, 7.

23. Interview with Karen Moore, Care, Country Director, Freetown, 8 May 2003.
24. Confidential interview with DFID personnel in Sierra Leone, 2003.
25. Confidential interview with CRP field personnel in Sierra Leone, June 2003.
26. Confidential interview, Freetown, 14 May 2003.
27. Confidential interview with DFID personnel, London, 2003.
28. IMATT, the former British Military Advisory Training Team, included some non-British personnel.
29. Department for International Development (DFID), *Understanding and Supporting Security Sector Reform* (London: Department for International Development, 2002). Also see: Department for International Development (DFID)/Foreign and Commonwealth Office (FCO)/Ministry of Defence (MoD), *Security Sector Reform*, 3.
30. Clare Short, Secretary of State for International Development, 'Security Sector Reform and the Elimination of Poverty', 1.
31. Refer to: OECD Development Assistance Committee (DAC), 'Security Issues and Development Co-Operation: A Conceptual Framework for Enhancing Policy Coherence', *The DAC Journal* 2, 3 (2001), 33–68; N. Ball, 'Transforming Security Sectors: The IMF and World Bank Approaches', *Journal of Conflict, Security and Development* 1, 1 (2001), 45–66.
32. Interview with Charles Achodo, NCDDR (formerly GTZ), Reintegration Advisor, 23 May 2003 and 27 May 2003.
33. Paul Richards, 'The Political Economy of Internal Conflict in Sierra Leone', *Working Paper* 21 (Clingendael: Clingendael Conflict Research Unit, August 2003), 32.
34. International Crisis Group (ICG), 'Sierra Leone: The State of Security and Governance'.
35. Interview with Karen Moore, 8 May 2003.
36. The UK has so far contributed £6.6 million to the court's total yet under-funded 3-year budget of $57 million. Apart from some start-up funding, no further financial support for the TRC is anticipated.
37. Conflict, Security and Development Group (CSDG), *A Review of Peace Operations: A Case for Change* (London: King's College, 2003).
38. Joanna Macrae, *Aiding Recovery?*, 4.
39. Interview with Simon Arthy, National Commission for Social Action (NACSA), Recovery and Reintegration Advisor (seconded by DFID) Free-town, 14 May 2003.
40. In Sierra Leone, each province is split into several districts and chiefdoms. Each chiefdom is headed by a Paramount Chief who presides over several chiefs, section chiefs and village-headmen. Traditionally, the Paramount Chiefs have played an important role as adjudicators and heads of the Chiefdom Courts. In 1993–94, the Governance Reform Secretariat of the GoSL has overseen the reform of the system of provincial governance. DFID is one of its greatest supporters. Elections for Paramount Chiefs took place in 2004.
41. Paul Richards, *Fighting for the Rain Forest*, 34–5.
42. Joanna Macrae, *Aiding Recovery?* 4.

43. Interview with international aid agency in Sierra Leone.
44. Interview with Colonel Mike J. Dent, Republic of Sierra Leone Armed Forces, Civil Military Co-operation/International Military Advisory Team (IMATT) (CBE FIMgt, Commander Joint Support Sierra Leone Army and Deputy Commander International Military Assistance and Training Team), Freetown, 28 May 2002.
45. Interview with Tony Conley.
46. Interview with Patrick Hammer, Community Reintegration Programme (CRP), Programme Manager, 20 May 2003.
47. Confidential interview with NGO country manager in Freetown, May 2003.
48. Tony Waters, *Bureaucratizing the Good Samaritan*, 67.
49. Interview with Christophe de Meerschalk, GTZ-International Services, Freetown, 30 May 2002.
50. Various confidential interviews with NGO personnel in Freetown, May/June 2003. Some agencies pointed out their frustration with the 'destructive behaviour' of others in sidelining the government and therefore inhibiting national capacity building.
51. Interview with Simon Arthy. The official objective eventually is to disband NACSA and to pass responsibility to line ministries.
52. Joanna Macrae, *Aiding Recovery?* 103.
53. Interview with Tim Shorten; interview with Caron Roehsler, Foreign and Commonwealth Office, Desk Officer for Sierra Leone, Africa Department, London, 24 April 2003.
54. Confidential interview with senior executive, Department for International Development (DFID), 2003.
55. Overseas Development Institute, 'The New International Development Act', 8.
56. Joanna Macrae, *Aiding Recovery?* 18; Mark Duffield, 'The Privatization of Public Welfare, Actual Adjustment and the Replacement of the State in Africa', paper presented at the conference on 'International Privatization: Strategies and Practices', St. Andrews College, 12–14 September 1991.
57. Comments by David Batt, Deputy Director Africa Division, Department of International Development (DFID), 'DFID and FCO Meeting with NGOs to Discuss the Democratic Republic of Congo', 16 June 2004.
58. Mark Duffield, *Global Governance*, 88.
59. Garth Glentworth, *Post-Conflict Reconstruction: Key Issues* (London: Department for International Development, April 2002), 72. Quoted after Toby Porter, *The Interaction Between Political and Humanitarian Action*.

5 Implementing New Humanitarianism in Sierra Leone

1. Conversely, several organizations mentioned that DFID had only informally shown itself to be supportive of rights and accountability programmes.

2. Interview with Lieutenant Colonel Richard Thwaites, Republic of Sierra Leone Armed Forces, Civil Military Co-operation/International Military Advisory Team (IMATT), 27 May 2002.
3. Interview with Christophe De Maerschalck, 30 May 2002.
4. Confidential interview with a country director of a DFID supported humanitarian emergency assistance organization in Freetown, 2002.
5. Interview with Karen Moore, 8 May 2003.
6. Confidential interview with a country director of a DFID supported humanitarian emergency assistance organization in Freetown, 2002.
7. Confidential interview with senior aid workers of several NGOs in Freetown, May/June 2003.
8. Confidential interview with DFID consultant in Freetown, Sierra Leone contracted by CHAD.
9. Confidential interviews with aid agencies in London, 2003.
10. Interview with Karen Moore, 28 May 2002 and 8 May 2003; Interview with Colin Waugh.
11. Confidential interview Freetown, Sierra Leone May 2003.
12. Interview with Patrick Hammer, Agrisystem, CRP Community Reintegration Programme (CRP), Programme Manager, Freetown/Sierra Leone, 20 May 2003.
13. Department for International Development (DFID), *Eliminating World Poverty: A Challenge for the 21st Century* (London: DFID, 1997); Department for International Development (DFID), *Eliminating World Poverty: Making Globalisation Work for the Poor* (London: DFID, 2000); Department for International Development (DFID), *Eliminating World Poverty: Making Governance Work for the Poor* (London: DFID, 2006).
14. Robert, MSF-Belgium, Head of Mission, 21 May 2003.
15. Confidential interview with ICRC-UK staff, London, 2003.
16. Confidential interview with a humanitarian aid organization's country director of a DFID supported aid organization in Sierra Leone May 2003.
17. United Nations Department of Political Affairs, 'Human Rights and Conflicts', in: *Human Rights Today: A United Nations Priority* (New York: United Nations, 1998), http://www.un.org/rights/HRToday/hrconfl.htm, 10 May 2004.
18. Department for International Development (DFID), *Sierra Leone: A Framework for DFID Support.*
19. Interview with Rebecca Golden, MSF-Holland, Head of Mission, 30 May 2002.
20. Confidential interview with DFID personnel in London, 2003.
21. Interview with Ian Stuart, First Secretary for Aid and Development, DFID SL, UK High Commission, in Freetown, Sierra Leone, 22 May 2002.
22. Interview with Karen Moore, 8 May 2003.
23. Interview with Simon Arthy.
24. Confidential interview with regional manager of humanitarian aid organization in Freetown, 2003.

25. Confidential interview with humanitarian aid organization, Freetown, 2003.
26. Confidential interview with humanitarian aid organizations and private contractors, Freetown, 2003.
27. Confidential interview with humanitarian aid organization, Freetown, 2003.
28. Interview with Ian Stuart, 29 May 2003.
29. Confidential interview with a multilateral humanitarian emergency organization, Freetown 2003.
30. Jonathan Marshall, Strategy Unit, Cabinet Office, Government of the United Kingdom, lecture at the Peaceworkers UK Annual General Meeting (21 May 2004).
31. Confidential interview with large bilateral humanitarian emergency organization, Sierra Leone, 2003.
32. Confidential interview with large bilateral humanitarian organization, Sierra Leone, 2003.
33. Interviews with Tanja Zulevic, International Medical Corps (IMC), Country Manager, Freetown, 8 May 2003; interview with Christian Smida, GTZ-International Services, Freetown, 1 May 2003.
34. Confidential interview with DFID consultant, Sierra Leone, 2003.
35. Confidential interview with humanitarian emergency organization, Sierra Leone, 2003.
36. Please note that the concluding chapter seven includes an analysis of DFID's capacity for organizational learning. It is therefore not subject of this sub-section.
37. A range of confidential interviews with humanitarian aid organizations in Sierra Leone in 2002 and 2003.
38. Action Aid, 'Inter-Agency meeting'.

6 Shifting Sands: British New Humanitarianism

1. Randolph Kent, 'Humanitarian Futures: Practical Policy Perspectives', *HPN Network Paper* 46 (April 2004), 5.
2. Department for International Development (DFID), *Evaluation of the Conflict Prevention Pools: Sierra Leone*, Evaluation Report 647 (London: DFID, March 2004).
3. Overseas Development Institute, The New International Development Act, 5.
4. Antony Barnett, Solomon Hughes and Jason Burke, 'Mercenaries in "Coup Plot" Guarded UK Officials in Iraq', *The Observer* (6 June 2004), 12.
5. Antonio Donini, Larry Minear and Peter Walker, 'Iraq and the Crisis of Humanitarian Action', *HNP Practice and Policy Notes* 26 (March 2004), 37–40, 37.
6. Mark Duffield, 'Governing the Borderlands: Decoding the Power of Aid', paper presented at an ODI seminar on 'Politics and Humanitarian Aid:

Debates, Dilemmas and Dissension' (Commonwealth Institute, London, 1 February 2001).

7. Antonio Donini, Larry Minear and Peter Walker, 'Iraq and the Crisis of Humanitarian Action', *HPN Practice and Policy Note* 26 (March 2004), 37–40, 39.

8. David Batt, 'DFID and FCO Meeting with NGOs'.

9. Philip Davies, 'Policy Evaluation in the United Kingdom', paper presented at the KDI International Policy Evaluation Forum, Seoul, Korea 19–21 May 2004 (London: Cabinet Office/Government Chief Social Researcher's Office), URL: http://www.policyhub.gov.uk/docs/policy_evaluation_uk.pdf, 15 June 2004, 15.

10. Ibid., 14.

Selected Bibliography

Primary and secondary material

Action Aid, 'Inter-Agency Meeting on DFID's Humanitarian Policies and Related Advocacy' (London, 19 October 1998).

Mark Adams and Mark Bradbury, *Conflict and Development: Organisational Adaption in Conflict Situations* (Oxford: Oxfam Publications, 1995).

Graham T. Allison and Morton H. Halperin, 'Bureaucratic Politics: A Paradigm and Some Policy Implications', *World Politics* 24, Issue Supplement: Theory and Policy in International Relations (Spring 1972), 40–79.

Mary B. Anderson, *Do No Harm. How Aid Can Support Peace – or War* (Boulder and London: Lynne Rienner, 1999).

Steven Archibald and Paul Richards, 'Converts to Human Rights? Popular Debate About War and Justice in Rural Central Sierra Leone', *Africa* 3, 72 (22 June 2002) (Edinburgh: Edinburgh University Press, 2002).

N. Ball, 'Transforming Security Sectors: The IMF and World Bank Approaches', *Journal of Conflict, Security and Development* 1, 1 (2001), 45–66.

Yusuf Bangura, 'Understanding the Political and Cultural Dynamics of the Sierra Leone War: A Critique of Paul Richards's Fighting for the Rain Forest' (*sic*), *Africa Development* 23, 3/4 (1997), 117–48.

Mikael Barfod, 'Humanitarian Aid and Conditionality: ECHO's Experience and Prospects Under the Common Foreign and Security Policy', in: Nicholas Leader and Joanna Macrae (eds), 'Terms of Engagement: Conditions and Conditionality in Humanitarian Action', Report of a Conference Organized by the Overseas Development Institute and the Centre for Humanitarian Dialogue in Geneva, 3–4 May 2000, *HPG Report* 6 (London: Overseas Development Institute, 2000), 37–43.

Antony Barnett, Solomon Hughes and Jason Burke, 'Mercenaries in "Coup Plot" Guarded UK Officials in Iraq', *The Observer* (6 June 2004).

David Batt, Deputy Director Africa Division, Department of International Development (DFID), 'DFID and FCO Meeting with NGOs to Discuss the Democratic Republic of Congo', 16 June 2004.

BBC News, 'Poor Paying for War on Terror', http://www.news.bbc.co.uk/go/pr/fr/-/2/hi/uk_news/3696683.stm, 20 May 2004.

Tony Blair, 'Address to the Chicago Economic Club', 22 April 1999, http://www.pbs.org/newshour/bb/international/jan-june99/blair_doctrine4-23.html, 15 January 2003.

James K. Boyce, 'Investing in Peace: Aid and Conditionality after Civil Wars', *Adelphi Paper* 351 (London: The International Institute for Strategic Studies, 2002).

Mark Bradbury, 'Behind the Rhetoric of the Relief-to-Development Continuum', Paper prepared for the NGOs in Complex Emergencies Project (London: CARE September 1997).

Camilla Brueckner, 'Towards a Human Rights Approach to European Commission Humanitarian Aid?', *Echo Discussion Paper* (Brussels: European Union, 1999).

David Bryer and Edmund Cairns, 'For Better? For Worse? Humanitarian Aid in Conflict', *Development in Practice* 7, 7 (1997), 363–74.

George Bush, 'You Are Either With Us or Against Us' (CNN: Washington, 6 November 2001), http://www.cnn.com/2001/US/11/06/gen.attac.on.terror. html, 30 June 2002.

Michael Clarke and Steve Smith (eds), *Foreign Policy Implementation* (Winchester, Mass.: Allen & Unwin, 1985).

Paul Collier, 'Doing Well out of War: An Economic Perspective', in: Mats Berdal and David M. Malone (eds), *Greed and Grievance: Economic Agendas in Civil Wars* (Boulder and London and other: Lynne Rienner, International Development Research Centre, 2000).

Paul Collier *et al.*, 'Redesigning Conditionality', *World Development* 25, 9 (1997), 1399–408.

Conflict, Security and Development Group (CSDG), *A Review of Peace Operations: A Case for Change* (London: King's College, 2003).

Robin Cook, *Ethical Foreign Policy* (London: FCO, 12 May 1997).

——, *Foreign Policy and National Interest*, Royal Institute of International Affairs, Chatham House (London: FCO, 28 January 2000).

——, *Human Rights – A Priority of Britain's Foreign Policy*, Foreign Office (London: FCO, 28 March 2001).

——, *Human Rights into a New Century* (London: FCO, 17 July 1997).

——, Statement in Response to the Sierra Leone: Foreign Affairs Committee Report (9 February 1999), http://www.fco.gov.uk/servlet/Front?pagename= OpenMarket/Xcelerate/ShowPage&c=Page&cid=1007029391638&a= KArticle&aid=1013618395777, 26 May 2002.

Alexander Cooley and James Ron, 'The NGO Scramble: Organizational Insecurity and the Political Economy of Transnational Action', *International Security* 27, 1 (Summer 2002), 5–39.

Philip Davies, 'Policy Evaluation in the United Kingdom', paper presented at the KDI International Policy Evaluation Forum, Seoul, Korea 19–21 May 2004 (London: Cabinet Office/Government Chief Social Researcher's Office, May 2004), http://www.policyhub.gov.uk/docs/policy_evaluation_uk.pdf, 15 June 2004.

Austen Davis, 'Thoughts on Conditions and Conditionalities', in: Nicholas Leader and Joanna Macrae (eds), 'Terms of Engagement: Conditions and Conditionality in Humanitarian Action', Report of a Conference Organized by the Overseas Development Institute and the Centre for Humanitarian Dialogue in Geneva, 3–4 May 2000, *HPG Report* 6 (London: Overseas Development Institute, 2000), 27–32.

Department for International Development (DFID), *About the Public Service Agreement and Service Delivery Agreement* (London: DFID, 2002), http://www.DFID.gov.uk/AboutThisWebsite/files/AboutPubServ.htm, 24 January 2003.

——, *The Causes of Conflict in Africa*, consultation document (London: DFID, March 2001).

——, *Code of Conduct for Humanitarian Operations* (London: DFID, 1999).

——, *Conflict Reduction and Humanitarian Assistance* (London: DFID, 1999).

——, *Eliminating World Poverty: A Challenge for the 21st Century. White Paper on International Development* (London: DFID, November 1997).

——, *Eliminating World Poverty: Making Globalisation Work for the Poor. White Paper on International Development* (London: DFID, December 2000).

——, *Evaluation of the Conflict Prevention Pools: Sierra Leone*, Evaluation Report 647 (London: DFID, March 2004).

——, *Guidelines on Humanitarian Assistance* (London: DFID, May 1997).

——, *Realising Human Rights for Poor People. Strategies for Achieving the International Development Targets* (London: DFID, October 2000).

——, *Understanding and Supporting Security Sector Reform* (London: DFID, 2002).

Department for International Development (DFID) (Alice Jay, Paul Richards and Tennyson Williams), *Sierra Leone: A Framework for DFID Support to Civil Society* (London: DFID, 2003).

Department for International Development (DFID) and Foreign and Commonwealth Office (FCO)/Ministry of Defence (MoD), *Security Sector Reform Policy Brief* (London: DFID, 2003).

Department for International Development (DFID) and the Government of Sierra Leone, *Sierra Leone: A Long-Term Partnership for Development* (Freetown: Government of Sierra Leone, February 2003).

Antonio Donini, Larry Minear and Peter Walker, 'Iraq and the Crisis of Humanitarian Action', *HNP Practice and Policy Notes* 26 (March 2004), 37–40.

Mark Duffield, 'Aid Policy and Post-Modern Conflict: A Critical Review', *Occasional Paper* 19 (Birmingham: University of Birmingham, 1998).

——, *Global Governance and the New Wars: The Merging of Development and Security* (London and New York: Zed Books, 2001).

——, 'Governing the Borderlands: Decoding the Power of Aid', paper presented at an ODI seminar on 'Politics and Humanitarian Aid: Debates, Dilemmas and Dissension' (London: Commonwealth Institute, 1 February 2001).

——, 'Humanitarian Conditionality: Origins, Consequences and Implications of the Pursuit of Development in Conflict', in: Geoff Loane and Tanja Schümer (eds), *The Wider Impact of Humanitarian Assistance. The Case of Sudan and the Implications for European Union Policy*, Aktuelle Materialien zur Internationalen Politik 60/6 (Baden-Baden: Nomos, 1999), 97–130.

——, 'The Privatization of Public Welfare, Actual Adjustment and the Replacement of the State in Africa', paper presented at the conference on 'International Privatization: Strategies and Practices', St. Andrews College, 12–14 September 1991.

European Commission, *Linking Relief, Rehabilitation and Development – An Assessment* (Brussels: European Commission, 23 April 2001).

Ann M. Fitz-Geralds and F. A. Walthall, 'An Integrated Approach to Complex Emergencies: The Kosovo Experience', *Journal of Humanitarian Assistance* (document posted 16 August 2001), http://www.jha.ac/articles/a071.htm, 25 July 2002

Foreign and Commonwealth Office (FCO) and Department for International Assistance (DFID), *Africa Conflict Prevention Pool – Conflict Prevention Strategy 2002/03 Review* (London: FCO/DFID, 2003).

Foreign and Commonwealth Office (FCO) and Department for International Assistance (DFID), *Sierra Leone Medium-Term Strategy Action Plan* (London: FCO/DFID, 2003).

George Foulkes (MP, Parliamentary Under-Secretary of State, DFID), 'International Development: Beyond the White Paper. UK Policy on Conflict and Humanitarian Assistance: Questions for a New Humanitarianism', Talk given at the Overseas Development Institute (ODI), 12 March 1998.

Alexandra Galperin, 'Discourses of Disasters, Discourses of Relief and DFID's Humanitarian Policy. A Diagnostic Snapshot of the Crisis of Relief as a Legitimate and Universal Instrument in Contemporary Conflict', *DESTIN Working Paper Series* April 2002 (London: London School of Economics and Political Science, 2002).

Garth Glentworth, *Post-Conflict Reconstruction: Key Issues* (London: DFID, April 2002).

Government of Sierra Leone, *National Recovery Strategy: Sierra Leone 2002–2003* (Freetown: Government of Sierra Leone, 2002).

Graduate Institute of International Studies (GIIS), *Small Arms Survey 2004 – Rights at Risk* (Geneva: Oxford University Press, 2004).

Morton H. Halperin, *Bureaucratic Politics & Foreign Policy* (Washington DC: Brookings Institution, 1974).

Adele Harmer, 'The Road to Good Donorship: The UK's Humanitarian Assistance', *Humanitarian Exchange* 24 (July 2003), 33–6.

Mark Hoffman, *DFID Policy on Humanitarian Assistance: A Case of Politics as Usual?* (London: London School of Economics and Political Science, 1999).

House of Commons, Sir Thomas Legg and Sir Robin Ibbs, *Report of the Sierra Leone Arms Investigation* (London: House of Commons, 27 July 1998), http://www.fco.gov.uk/servlet/Front?pagename=OpenMarket/Xcelerate/ShowPage&c=Page&cid=1007029391629&a=KArticle&aid=1013618393894, 3 July 2003.

——, Foreign Affairs Committee, *Second Report* (London: House of Commons, 3 February 1999), http://www.parliament.the-stationery-office.co.uk/pa/cm199899/cmselect/cmfaff/116/11602.htm, 5 April 2003.

International Crisis Group (ICG), 'Sierra Leone After Elections: Politics as Usual?', *Africa Report* 49 (Freetown, Brussels: International Crisis Group, 12 June 2002).

——, 'Sierra Leone: Managing Uncertainty', *Africa Report* 35 (Freetown, Brussels: International Crisis Group, 24 October 2001).

——, 'Sierra Leone: The State of Security and Governance', *Africa Report* 67 (Freetown, Brussels: International Crisis Group, 2 September 2003), http://www.reliefweb.int/w/rwb.nsf/0/f6e3e4585edf18e485256d95006f823a?OpenDocument, 18 January 2004.

——, 'Sierra Leone: Time for a New Military and Political Strategy', *Africa Report* 28 (Freetown, Brussels: International Crisis Group, 11 April 2001).

International Development Committee, *Fifth Report*, Departmental Report 20 July 1999, House of Commons, Session 1998–99 (London: DFID, 1999).

——, *Fifth Special Report,Government Response to the Fifth Report from the Committee*, House of Commons, Session 1998 (London: DFID, 1999).

——, *Sixth Report,Conflict Prevention and Post-Conflict Reconstruction,Vol. I,Report and Proceedings of the Committee*, House of Commons, 20 July 1999, Session 1998/99 (London: DFID, 1999).

Irving L. Janis, *Groupthink: Psychological Studies of Policy Decisions and Fiascoes*, 2nd edn (Boston: Houghton Mifflin Company, 1972).

John Kampfner, *Blair's Wars* (London: Free Press, 2003).

David Keen, *The Benefits of Famine: A Political Economy of Famine and Relief in South-Western Sudan 1983–1989* (Princeton and New Jersey: Princeton University Press, 1994).

——, *The Best of Enemies: Conflict and Collusion in Sierra Leone* (Oxford: James Currey, 2004) (Palgrave Macmillan, 2006).

——, 'Beyond a "Rational Violence" Framework: Psychological Causes of Civil War Violence', *Crisis States Programme/DESTIN Briefing Paper* 7 (May 2003).

——, 'The Economic Functions of Violence in Civil Wars', *Adelphi Papers* 320 (Oxford: Oxford University Press, 1998).

——, 'Greedy Elites, Dwindling Resources, Alienated Youths: The Anatomy of Protracted Violence in Sierra Leone', *Internationale Politik und Gesellschaft* 2 (2003), 67–94.

——, 'Incentives and Disincentives for Violence', in: Mats Berdal and David M. Malone, *Greed and Grievance: Economic Agendas in Civil Wars* (Boulder and London: Lynne Rienner, 2000).

——, 'Since I am a Dog, Beware My Fangs: Beyond a "Rational Violence" Framework in the Sierra Leonean War', *Crisis States Programme Working Papers* 14 (August 2002).

Randolph C. Kent, *Anatomy of Disaster Relief: The International Network in Action* (London and New York: Pinter, 1987).

——, 'Humanitarian Futures: Practical Policy Perspectives', *HPN Network Paper* 46 (April 2004).

Nicholas Leader, 'The Politics of Principle: The Principles of Humanitarian Action in Practice', *HPG Report* 2 (London: ODI, 2000).

——, 'Proliferating Principles: Or How to Sup With the Devil Without Getting Eaten', *Disasters* 22, 4 (1998), 288–308.

Nicholas Leader and Joanna Macrae, 'Terms of Engagement: Conditions and Conditionality in Humanitarian Action', Report of a conference organized by the Overseas Development Institute (ODI) and the Centre for Humanitarian Dialogue in Geneva, 3–4 May 2000, *HPG Report* 6 (London: ODI, 2000).

Geoff Loane and Celine Moyroud (eds), *Tracing Unintended Consequences of Humanitarian Assistance: The Case of Sudan. Field Study and Recommendations for the European Community Humanitarian Office*, Aktuelle Materialien zur Internationalen Politik 60/9 (Baden-Baden: Nomos, 2000).

Geoff Loane and Tanja Schümer (eds), *The Wider Impact of Humanitarian Assistance. The Case of Sudan and the Implications for European Union Policy*, Aktuelle Materialien zur Internationalen Politik 60/6 (Baden-Baden: Nomos, 1999).

Joanna Macrae, *Aiding Recovery? The Crisis of Aid in Chronic Political Emergencies* (London and New York: Zed Books, 2001).

Joanna Macrae *et al.*, *Conflict, the Continuum and Chronic Emergencies: A Critical Analysis of the Scope for Linking Relief, Rehabilitation and Development Planning in Sudan*, paper prepared for the Department for International Development (London: ODI, 19 December 1996).

Joanna Macrae *et al.*, 'Uncertain Power: The Changing Role of Official Donors in Humanitarian Action', *HPG Report* 12 (London: ODI, December 2002).

Joanna Macrae and Nicholas Leader, 'Shifting Sands: The Search for "Coherence" Between Political and Humanitarian Responses to Complex Emergencies', *HPG Report* 8 (London: ODI, August 2000).

Jonathan Marshall, 'Strategy Unit, Cabinet Office, Government of the United Kingdom', lecture at the Peaceworkers UK Annual General Meeting (21 May 2004).

Jonathan Moore (ed.), *Hard Choices: Moral Dilemmas in Humanitarian Intervention* (Geneva and Lanham: Rowman & Littlefield Publishers, 1998).

National Audit Office, *Overseas Development Administration: Emergency Relief. Report by the Comptroller and Auditor General, Parliamentary Session 2001–2002* (HC 739) (London: The Stationary Office, 2002).

OSCE Development Assistance Committee (DAC), *Conflict, Peace and Development Co-Operation on the Threshold of the 21st Century* (Paris: OECD, 1997).

——, *The DAC Guidelines: Helping Prevent Violent Conflict* (Paris: OECD, 2001), http://www.oecd.org/document/45/0,2340,en_2649_33721_1886125_1_1_1_1,00.html, 12 March 2004.

——, 'Security Issues and Development Co-Operation: A Conceptual Framework for Enhancing Policy Coherence', *The DAC Journal* 2, 3 (2001), 33–68.

Overseas Development Institute (ODI), 'The New International Development Act: The Case for Definition of Humanitarian Assistance', notes for a presentation to a meeting of DFID officials/members of the International Development Committee (London: ODI, 27 January 1999).

——, 'The Changing Role of Official Donors in Humanitarian Action: A Review of Trends and Issues', *HGP Briefing* 5 (London: Overseas Development Institute, December 2002).

Toby Porter, *The Interaction Between Political and Humanitarian Action in Sierra Leone, 1995 to 2002* (Geneva: Centre for Humanitarian Dialogue, March 2003).

John Prendergast, *Frontline Diplomacy: Humanitarian Aid and Conflict in Africa* (Boulder/Col.: Lynne Reinner, 1996).

William Reno, *Corruption and State Politics in Sierra Leone* (Cambridge: Cambridge University Press, 1995).

——, 'Resources and the Future of Violent Conflict in Sierra Leone', BISA Conference (London: December 2002).

——, 'Shadow States and the Political Economy of Civil War', in: Mats Berdal and David M. Malone, *Greed and Grievance: Economic Agendas in Civil Wars* (Boulder and London: Lynne Rienner, 2000), 43–68.

Paul Richards, *Fighting for the Rain Forest: War, Youth & Resources in Sierra Leone*, African Issues, 4th edn (Oxford and Portsmouth: James Currey and Heinemann, 2002).

——, 'The Political Economy of Internal Conflict in Sierra Leone', *Working Paper* 21 (Clingendael: Clingendael Conflict Research Unit, August 2003).

Adam Roberts, 'Humanitarian Action in War: Aid, Protection and Impartiality in a Policy Vacuum', *Adelphi Paper* 305 (1996).

Select Committee on Foreign Affairs, Second Report, Summary of Conclusions and Recommendations, http://www.parliament.the-stationery-office.co.uk/pa/cm199899/cmselect/cmfaff/116/11613.htm, 5 April 2003.

Clare Short, 'From Rhetoric to Reality: It is Time To Translate Fine Words Into Action' (London: DFID, 1999), http://www.DFID.gov.uk/public/news/pr2nov99.html, 15 May 2002.

——, 'Principles for a New Humanitarianism', Conference on 'Principled Aid in an Unprincipled World' (London: Church House, April 1998).

——, Secretary of State for International Development, 'Conflict Prevention, Conflict Resolution and Post-Conflict Peace-Building – From Rhetoric to Reality', International Alert (2 November 1999).

Hugo Slim, 'Relief Agencies and Moral Standing in War: Principles of Humanity, Neutrality, Impartiality and Solidarity', *Development in Practice* 7, 4 (1997), 342–52.

——, 'A Call to Alms: Humanitarian Action and the Art of War', *Humanitarian Dialogue Opinion* (Geneva: The Centre for Humanitarian Dialogue, 2004), 1–18.

——, 'Military Humanitarianism and the New Peacekeeping: An Agenda for Peace?', *Journal of Humanitarian Assistance*, http://www.jha.ac/articles/a003.htm (document posted: 3 June 2000), 15 June 2003.

Ian Smillie, 'Relief and Development: The Struggle for Synergy', *Occasional Paper* 33 (Providence: Humanitarianism and War Project, 2000).

Joanna Spear, *Carter and Arms Sales. Implementing the Carter Administration's Arms Transfer Restraint Policy* (Houndmills, London and New York: Macmillan Press and St. Martin's Press, 1995).

Olav Stokke (ed.), *Aid and Political Conditionality* (London: Frank Cass, 1995).

United Nations Department of Humanitarian Affairs (UNDHA), *Sierra Leone Humanitarian Situation Report (SLHSR)* (New York: United Nations, 24–30 June 1997).

United Nations Department of Political Affairs, 'Human Rights and Conflicts', in: *Human Rights Today: A United Nations Priority* (New York: United Nations, 1998), http://www.un.org/rights/HRToday/hrconfl.htm, 10 May 2004.

United Nations Development Programme (UNDP), *Human Development Report 2003* (Geneva: UNDP, 2003).

United Nations Office for the Co-ordination of Humanitarian Assistance (OCHA), 'Do as I Say, Not as I Do: The Limits of Political Conditionality', *The European Journal of Development Research* 5, 1 (1993), 63–84.

——, *The Influence of Aid in Situations of Violent Conflict: A Synthesis and a Commentary on the Lessons Learned from Case Studies on the Limits and Scope for the Use of Development Assistance Incentives and Disincentives for Influencing*

Conflict Situations, Informal Task Force on Conflict, Peace and Development Co-Operation (Paris: Development Assistance Committee, 1999).

——, *United Nations Consolidated Inter-Agency Appeal for Sierra Leone 2002* (New York: OCHA, 26 November 2001).

——, *United Nations Inter-Agency Appeal for Relief & Recovery for Sierra Leone 2003* (New York: OCHA, November 2002).

Peter Uvin, *The Influence of Aid in Situations of Violent Conflict: A Synthesis and a Commentary on the Lessons Learned from Case Studies on the Limits and Scope for the Use of Development Assistance Incentives and Disincentives for Influencing Conflict Situations*, Informal Task Force on Conflict, Peace and Development Co-Operation (Paris: Development Assistance Committee, 1999).

Koenraad Van Brabant, *Organisational and Institutional Learning in the Humanitarian Sector: Opening the Dialogue*, A Discussion Paper for the Active Learning Network on Acccountability and Performance in Humanitarian Assistance (London: ODI, 1997).

John Vereker, Permanent Secretary, Department for International Development, 'Can Poverty be Eliminated Through Development Co-Operation?', address to the North South Roundtable, 28 June 1998 http://www.DFID.gov.uk/public/news/sp28june.html, 15 May 2002.

Mark Walkup, *Policy and Behavior in Humanitarian Organizations: The Institutional Origins of Operational Dysfunction*, PhD Dissertation, University of Florida (1997).

Richard W. Waterman and Kenneth J. Meier, 'Principal–Agent Models: An Expansion?', *Journal of Public Administration Research and Theory* 8, 2 (April 1998), 173–203.

Tony Waters, *Bureaucratizing the Good Samaritan: The Limitations of Humanitarian Relief Operations* (Boulder, Col. and Oxford: Westview, 2001).

Patrick Wintour and Charlotte Denny, 'Overruled: Short Loses In Aid Row', *The Guardian* (20 December 2001), http://www.guardian.co.uk/gardian-politics/story/0,3605,622012,00.html, 16 May 2002.

Interviews

Please note that several personnel of both DFID and humanitarian NGOs who were interviewed in the course of this study asked not to be personally named. Therefore they are not included in the following list. Within the text their statements are referred to as 'confidential interview'. So are those statements that were judged possibly too controversial or where permission to publish could not be ascertained. For details please refer to the references.

Governmental/Donor

Department for International Development (DFID), Sierra Leone/London (2002/03/05).
Emergency Response Team (ERT)/Crown Agents, Sierra Leone (March 2002).

Foreign and Commonwealth Office (FCO), Sierra Leone/London (March 2002/03).
NaCSA (National Commission for Social Action), Sierra Leone (2002).
NCDDR (National Committee for Disarmament, Demobilisation and Reintegration), Sierra Leone (2003).
Republic of Sierra Leone Armed Forces, Civil Military Co-operation/ International Military Advisory and Training Team (IMATT), Sierra Leone (2002/03).

Multilateral Organization

European Community Humanitarian Office (ECHO), Sierra Leone (2003).
International Organization for Migration (IOM), Sierra Leone (2002).
Office for the Co-ordination of Humanitarian Affairs (OCHA), Sierra Leone (2002/03).
United Nations Mission in Sierra Leone (UNAMSIL), Sierra Leone (2002/03).
World Food Programme (WFP), Sierra Leone (2003).

Humanitarian Non-Governmental Organization (Sierra Leone and London)

Action Aid (2002).
Action Contra la Faim (ACF) (2003).
Agrisystem (Community Reintegration Programme (CRP)) (2003).
American Refugee Council (ARC) (2003).
CARE (2002/03).
Catholic Relief Service (CRS) (2002/03).
Children's Aid Direct (CAD) (2002).
Christian Aid (2002).
Concern (2002).
CORD- Sierra Leone (2002).
GOAL (2003).
GTZ-International Services (2002/03).
Federation of the Red Cross Movement (2003).
International Committee of the Red Cross (ICRC), Great Britain (2003).
International Medical Corps (IMC) (2003).
Marie Stopes Society (2003).
Merlin (2003).
MSF-Belgium (2003).
MSF-France (2002).
MSF-Holland (2002/03).
Norwegian Refugee Council (NRC) (2003).
Oxfam (2002/03).
PAE (2003).
Save the Children Fund (SCF) (2002/03).

The United Methodist Committee on Relief (UMCOR) (2003).
World Vision International (2003).

Academic

Institute for Public Policy Research (IPPR) (2002).
London School of Economics (LSE) (2004).

Index

Note: Page numbers in **bold** refer to figures and tables